LITERATURE, PHILOSOPHY AND THE IMAGINATION

Indiana University Press | *Bloomington*
London

LITERATURE

PHILOSOPHY

& the Imagination

ALBERT WILLIAM LEVI

SECOND PRINTING 1969

This book has been published with the assistance
of a grant from the Ford Foundation

WOODCUT ON TITLE PAGE BY RUDY POZZATTI

Copyright © 1962 by Indiana University Press
Library of Congress catalog card number: 62–16163
Manufactured in the United States of America

Seit ich sie sah, empfand ich, dass ich lebte,
Und in der Tage truebem Einerlei
War sie allein mir Wesen und Gestalt.

THERE is another faculty, whose seat is the intermediate cavity among the cavities of the brain; it is called the active Imagination. At the place where it resides, there is a channel in the shape of an arch, as it were tracing a long vault. The part of the brain that lies here resembles a worm; hence in Arabic it is called *dūda* (worm). Sometimes it shortens, sometimes it lengthens, as a worm does when it contracts and stretches out. The active Imagination has the right to inspect the treasury of forms and the treasury of significances. . . .

AVICENNA

From Henry Corbin, *Avicenna and the Visionary Recital*, Bollingen Series LXVI, (Pantheon Books), New York, 1961. Reprinted by permission of Bollingen Foundation, New York.

Preface

THIS book began in my mind four years ago in a seminar on *The Critique of Pure Reason* when I asked: "What does Kant mean when he says that 'fortune' and 'fate' are *usurpatory* concepts?" It narrowed into focus as I wrote the last section of Chapter II of my *Philosophy and the Modern World* ("Science and Illusion"). And its theory finally sprang into place in the spring of 1960 during a graduate seminar in comparative aesthetics in which we read the *Poetics, The Critique of Judgment,* and *Art as Experience.* Since then I have only had to mix into the crucible reactions to those novelists, favorite contemporary poets, and tragic dramatists (whom I never could distinguish from metaphysicians) who have been my constant daytime companions and bed-table neighbors. The rest has been a scholar's uneventful wrestle to impose form upon sympathetic materials.

My impression is that I have talked less than usual to others about the topics here contained. No part has been previously published. As a guest lecturer in the course in "Masterpieces of Literature" at Washington University, I have tried out a few of the ideas in Chapter V and Chapter VIII. And a preliminary version of the end of Chapter VII entitled "Three Suicides" was read to the Language and Literature Club at Washington and given as a guest lecture to the Philosophy Club at the University of Kansas.

Once again (on principle) I have tried not to be technical. I hope I may interest philosophers who love literature and literary people who are charmed by philosophy. Most of all I should like to be read by nonprofessionals to whom, nevertheless, both literature and philosophy are a taste of honey and a loaf of wheaten bread.

To the publishers of the various works quoted, specific acknowledgment will be made in the Notes. Miss Alice Hole-
man of Washington University has once again been a faithful
and responsible typist.

Since this book was first written has occurred the event registered on its dedication page. Personal feelings are perhaps
tedious in a public place, but a preface is the opportunity for
acknowledgments. I could not let this book go to press without testimony about what it owes to Tita, my wife—how, in
fact, on the solid support of her love and good humor has
rested all that I have thought and written in the last ten years.

ALBERT WILLIAM LEVI

St. Louis
March 1, 1962

Contents

LITERATURE, PHILOSOPHY AND THE IMAGINATION

One / Introduction

1 THE AIM of this book is to provide a philosophical account (and to this extent, per-
haps, a philosophical justification) of the humanities. In this
respect—and in absolutely no other—it may be compared with
Kant's *Critique of Pure Reason*, which, in the eighteenth century, aimed to provide just such a justification for Newtonian
science. I agree with Kant that the human *Understanding*
is the "faculty of the mind" upon which natural science is
founded, and my own modest addition is that the *Imagination*
is that human faculty from whose active functioning the humanities stem.

Kant's justification of seventeenth-century science took
plane geometry and mathematical physics for granted. In effect
he said: "If we assume that Euclidean geometry and Newtonian physics are the most reliable repositories of our knowledge about the world, what must be the structure of the human mind that could produce them?" In analogous fashion
I take metaphysical constructions, the Russian novel, Greek
tragedy, and the lyrics of Rilke, Wallace Stevens, and Hoelderlin for granted. And my question then is: "If we assume that
such works as *Hamlet, Richard III, Oedipus Rex, Four Quartets*, Plato's *Dialogues, Don Quixote*, and the plays of Schiller,
Brecht, and Pirandello are among the most brilliant repositories of poetic making and human culture, what must be the
structure of the human minds that could produce them?"

In one sense the results of this book are frankly dualistic, for it sees the age-old quarrel between the sciences and the humanities as deeply motivated, as grounded not merely in the accidents of temperament but in basic commitments founded upon the structure of the human mind. As such it runs counter to a pervasive tendency of our age. Much of contemporary philosophy, as I have shown elsewhere, has been a "revolt against dualism." Whitehead, Dewey, and other have tried to relax the polarities between subject and object, mind and matter, thought and emotion. But the ancient antagonism between the sciences and the humanities which runs back at least to the time of Boccaccio and Chrysoloras—to the Renaissance conflict between the protagonists of the newly-acquired Arabic natural science on the one hand, and the humanist sponsors of the classical revival on the other—does nevertheless in my judgment represent a real and important schism, untouched by fugitive insights that literature possesses "structure" and that science can be "creative." Essentially the purposes of the two enterprises are different, and they are grounded respectively in the nuclear operations of the understanding and the imagination. This is the central presupposition of the theory of knowledge which underlies this book.

C. P. Snow's Rede Lecture of 1959, "The Two Cultures and the Scientific Revolution," has dramatized for our time the gulf between natural scientists and literary intellectuals. His account of their mutual incomprehension, their hostility and dislike, has touched us in a sore place, and his plea for their mutual understanding and reconciliation has been widely heralded and applauded. But there is something suspiciously facile about his solution. It is superficial because it sees the difficulty in terms of human obstinacy and wilfulness rather than in that basic schism of the mind upon which this obstinacy is founded. Naturally one deplores the sharp separation of the sciences and the humanities in education. Naturally one favors a general education for men which shall propound the

values of each. This is not, however, the real point. The real
point is that when you push the superficial intent of science
and the humanities back far enough, you come upon fundamentally discordant approaches to life—to a conflict of basic
philosophies. Positivism is that approach to the world which
minimizes the importance of art, metaphysics, and literature
because it bases all important knowledge upon the results and
the methods of the sciences. Idealism and existentialism, on
the contrary, are philosophies which minimize the results
and the methods of science because they are too often irrelevant to the emotional requirements of man and to the facts
of his human existence.

Deep down, I surmise, Snow himself knows this, and were
he forced to a choice it would, I think, be science. Here is why
I think so. "The Two Cultures" seems to breathe the atmosphere of mutuality, of a magnanimity which envisages science
and literature as a kind of dual monarchy jointly sovereign
for men's minds and sensibilities. But in truth it does nothing
of the sort. For Snow frankly says that humanists are inordinately vain about the traditional nonscientific culture, and
that in the moral life it is the scientists who are the "soundest"
group of intellectuals. In "The Two Cultures" reconciliation
is the manifest content, but it is in his novel *The Masters* that
this Dickens of the atomic age has revealed his latent message.
In this novel (as in some mediaeval morality play) science and
the humanities are given their fictional personifications in the
two rival candidates for the Cambridge Mastership. Jago, the
Senior Tutor in English Literature, is the humanist: at fifty
balding and grey, a man who apologizes too much, is militantly
conservative, loves display. He has much sympathy and emotion, feels deeply and has a passionate pride, but is quick-tem-
pered, mercurial, and unstable—a man whose heart often runs
away with his head.

Crawford, a brilliant biologist and member of the Royal Society, is, in contrast, the scientist: a man of fifty-six with glossy

black hair (the symbolism is most obvious), both cordial and impersonal, authoritative and impassive. He has a calm and steady judgment, is radical and fearless in uttering opinions, is confident, impervious, and self-assured. Whereas Jago is a more feelingful man than his rival, it is Crawford who has the broad, strong, powerful mind. The contrast between these two, Snow seems to be saying, is that between the humanities and the sciences in general, and although he places our initial sympathy on the side of the humanities, imperceptibly but forcefully this feeling is reversed, and we are in the end relieved and convinced of its inevitable rightness when in the contest for the Mastership, the scientist finally wins. To whose strength the governance of this world rightfully belongs—this is a matter upon which Snow the novelist leaves us in little doubt.

There have been in the modern world other attempts to heal the wounds of division between the sciences and the humanities; if not (as in "The Two Cultures") by the delusive device of multiple sovereignty, at least by the attempt to arrogate to science all of the peculiar virtues of the humanities and the arts. This is the obvious strategy of J. Bronowski in his popular little book *Science and Human Values*. Bronowski argues chiefly against "the prejudice of the humanist who takes his science sourly" and who believes that science is "mechanical and neutral." On the contrary, he finds a profound likeness between the creative acts of the mind in art and in science, and with a fine confusion refers to "those imaginative acts of understanding" which exercise the creative mind equally in both spheres. His appeal is to the act of synthesis, and he cites Coleridge's definition of beauty as "unity in variety" to show that science "is nothing else than the search to discover unity in the wild variety of nature." It is wrong, says Bronowski, to think of science as a mechanical record of facts and of the arts as remote and private fancies.

So far there is much with which we may agree, and yet in

the end Bronowski, for all the eloquence of his rhetoric, is unpersuasive. For he is finally forced to say that both science and the humanities contain the same moral values, and that "truth" is not different in science and the arts—only more difficult to communicate in the latter. The position is equivocal, and it comes up against the stubborn facts of scientific and humanistic practice. For science *is* mechanistic in two respects: in its necessary reverence for "matters of fact" and in its basic reliance upon the principle of causation (both characteristic marks of the understanding), whereas the humanities are "anthropomorphic" in a sense which natural science can never allow, and their "teleology" and "drama" (both gifts of the imagination) are far removed from the neutral "causation" of science. The great Kant treated the scientific understanding in his *Critique of Pure Reason* and the humanistic imagination in his *Critique of Judgment,* and the distinction celebrated by this separation is still, I think, eminently sound and right.

Literature, Philosophy, and the Imagination represents a preference for Kant's latter work rather than his former, for the "Third Critique" rather than the "First," for it relates the imagination not to "cognition" but to "purpose." Classical epistemology from Aristotle to Hume views the imagination as an adjunct to "knowledge"—as the necessary bridge between "perception" and "thought." Kant himself in the *Critique of Pure Reason* takes the same position. But in the *Critique of Judgment* the imagination has been transformed. Here it is "creative" rather than merely "reproductive." Here it has its own playful imperatives, originating ideas "beyond the facts," and it celebrates just those aspects of perception which are "purposive" and "organic"—keyed to the needs of the human agent, and creative in organizing our experience into integrated and poetic wholes. It is from this latter portion of Kant's work that my own thinking (as reflected in this book) has taken its origin and its central focus.

2 HAVING STATED that my theme is *the imagination*, my purpose *a defense of the hu-
manities*, and my point of origin *the philosophy of Kant*, it
remains to say a word about the strategy which has dictated
the titles and the contents of the chapters which follow. This
is particularly necessary because of the diffuseness of my subject matter. For I have meant this to be not so much a technical treatise upon the imagination as a *demonstration* of its
functioning and its operations, and these have been concretely
illustrated in the epic and the novel, in the modes of poetic
perception, and in the varieties of the tragic drama. History,
myth, metaphysics, all pass upon my stage, but its center is
firmly held by the forms of literary expression. If then (reluc-
tantly) I should be forced to pin-point its nature, I should call
it an exercise in the philosophy of literature—now and again
lightly touched by the gentle breeze of metaphysics. My illustrations may seem many-faceted, overly rich, even disconnected, but such is the nature of that faculty which they express. The imagination is protean in its shapes, its disguises,
its vehicles. And it is my purpose to suggest some of its rich
and multifarious embodiments—some representative selection, perhaps, of "the treasury of forms" and "the treasury of
significances" which, as Avicenna says, the active Imagination
has the option and the prerogative to inspect.

Although my theory of the imagination originates in Kant,
it is the culmination of a line of development which includes Nietzsche, Vaihinger, Bergson, Santayana, Cassirer—
even Dewey and Gilbert Ryle. And if there seems to be some
similarity between my concept of the imagination and Collingwood's, the fact is that I owe more to Cassirer than to
Collingwood, and probably more to Kant, Nietzsche, and
Santayana than to either. For there is, I think, a certain
emerging unity among these men, stemming from Kant, but
illustrating the fact that philosophy as "a reflection upon ex-

perience" need turn not only to science for its materials. Literature, metaphysics, religion, myth are cultural elements, equal in age and dignity; equal also (if not superior) in their relevance to men's concerns and to the human condition.

In Chapter 2, I have tried to do two things. I have tried to trace very briefly (and I hope not too painfully) the philosophic theory which is the source of a doctrine of the imagination "from Kant to Cassirer." I want to show how it is grounded in Kant; how it develops in his immediate successors—Vaihinger, Nietzsche, and Lange; how the dualism in question reappears in Bergson and Spengler only to find its best expression in Santayana. Those whose primary interest is literature may not be happy with this excursion into the philosophy of the past, but they will do well to note the section with which the chapter ends. For its subject, "the scientific chain of meaning" and "the humanistic complex" states in miniature the entire thesis of my book.

It can be summarized as follows. The human understanding is the source of the enterprise of the natural sciences as the human imagination is the source of that division of human culture which contains literature, metaphysics, the arts, and the humanities. Each of these faculties of the mind is uniquely responsible for its own table of categories, its own alphabet of forms, its own vocabulary of concepts, its own family of meanings. The family of scientific meanings, the vocabulary of the understanding, I have called *the scientific chain of meaning*. Among its concepts are those of "true and false propositions," "prediction," "fact," "error," "causality," and "scientific law," but I have not expanded or developed these notions here. This is not my subject matter, and besides, the learned journals (the exclusive restaurants as well as the soup kitchens of philosophy) are full of it. Problems of causality, statistical inference, theory construction, the nature of scientific explanation—with these topics the analytic tradition and the philosophy of science have dealt, and are dealing, admirably.

In contrast, the family of humanistic meanings, the vocabulary of the imagination, I have called *the humanistic complex*. Among its concepts are those of "appearance and reality," "illusion," "destiny," "fortune," "fate," "tragedy," and "peace." This is very much my subject matter, and to the illumination of these notions as they appear in history, philosophy, and the forms of literature my last three chapters are devoted.

Chapter 3 ("The Teleological Imagination") and Chapter 4 ("The Dramatic Imagination") are reserved for an explication of the most general characteristics of imaginative functioning. As the chief characteristics of scientific thought (and the scientific chain of meaning which it produces) are "impartiality" and "objectivity," so I have found those of the imagination (and the humanistic complex which is its product) to be "purposiveness," "drama," and "organic unification." It is clear, then, that the "teleological" and the "dramatic" imagination are not two separate parts of a single area (as Illinois and Missouri are two adjoining segments of an American map), but rather two separable qualities of a single function (as "sharpness" and "heaviness" might be two separable qualities of a woodsman's axe). They work together, although it is possible to analyze them separately.

My description of the teleological imagination requires a brief presentation of the history of the concept of imagination from Hobbes and Hume to Coleridge and Kant, and it ends with Cassirer's theory of myth, which brings together so much that is crucial for an understanding of the role which imagination plays in the economy of human belief. Purposiveness in the imagination presents human experience as connected, subjective, unified, and these characteristics (drawn from Kant's *Critique of Judgment*) are illustrated in Virgil— by an examination of the function which simile performs in the *Aeneid*.

My description of the dramatic imagination emphasizes the concepts of "action," of "enactment," and of "reenactment," and is illustrated in Gilbert Ryle's notion of "pretending" and in Dewey's emphasis upon "the imaginative rehearsal" of behavior. And this leads naturally and by easy stages to Aristotle's theory of dramatic imitation, of plot, and of the rhythm of dramatic action. The modalities of drama are investigated —in religious ritual, in philosophical dialogue, and in dialectic, and the sources of drama are finally traced to the qualitative rhythms of life which are an inherent feature of all human experience.

Chapter 5 marks a certain break with what has gone before, for it leaves the *theory* of the imagination in order to investigate characteristic forms of literary imagination, concretely expressed in contemporary poetry and in the Russian novel. Here is provided the clearest demonstration in the book that metaphysics and epistemology have literary relevance, that modes of poetic perception and novelistic style are functions of systems of knowing and philosophic points of view. The demonstration analyzes the methodology and poetic practice of Wallace Stevens, Ezra Pound, and T. S. Eliot, and concludes with a stylistic analysis of Dostoievsky and Tolstoy, Joyce and Robbe-Grillet.

The final three chapters (6, 7, 8) are a return to the concept of "the humanistic complex," and present a running argument to show the peculiarities and interrelationships of the family of meanings which it comprises. Chapter 6 explores the distinction between appearance and reality, shows how it is the basis of the metaphysical imagination, briefly traces its history in the pre-Socratics, Plato, Kant, Schopenhauer, and F. H. Bradley, before turning to the application of the distinction to literature. *Don Quixote* and the plays of Pirandello are then used to show the literary play with the problem of illusion and reality, and the chapter ends with a contrast between the metaphysical venture and the scientific enterprise in which the philosophic preference for illusion is exemplified in Nietzsche and Santayana.

Chapter 7 investigates the ideas of "destiny," "fortune," and "fate." Distinguishing fortune from chance, it pursues the idea of fortune as an agency in history according to the notions of Plutarch, Burckhardt, and Machiavelli. But the central notion treated is that of fate. Its occurrence is traced in the early versions of Aeschylus, Hesiod, and Homer. Three historical moments in the appearance of the notion of destiny are described: Stoic Fate in Cicero, the doctrine of Providence in Seneca and Boethius, Romantic Destiny in Hoelderlin, Hegel, and Tolstoy. Finally destiny is presented as a literary idea. Its relation to tragic drama is explained, and the plural perspectives under which it makes its appearance in the modern world are investigated in the modern novel.

My concluding chapter (8), presenting the culmination of my argument, explores the problem of tragedy and the nature of peace. These two concepts are the final notions of the humanistic complex. They mark that point where one of the supreme products of the Western imagination embodies its supreme wisdom of life. The problem of tragedy arises at that moment of perplexity when the interpretation of man's moral world is immobilized between the forces of natural compulsion and his active moral agency. This dilemma I have termed *the ultimate antinomy of the dramatic imagination.* The tragic rhythm of action is examined in its multiple forms, and the doctrine of "reconciliation" is related to the ancient idea of "catharsis." This, at last, permits us to see the intrinsic relation of tragedy as a form of art to tragic action in the midst of life. The tragic categories become mirrors of human importance, and with our comprehension that in the understanding of tragedy lies peace, the humanities are given their rightful place as crucial vehicles for the expression of the moral nature of man.

Two / From Kant to Cassirer: the Scientific Chain of Meaning & the Humanistic Complex

THE MODERN theory of the imagination begins with Immanuel Kant—one of the most brilliant and obscure philosophic minds of the eighteenth century—and finds its notable culmination in the work of Ernst Cassirer, also a German philosopher of genius, who died in 1945. My task in this chapter is to show how the germ of an idea in Kant is transformed by his successors and carried down to our own time. But Kant's ideas are always difficult unless we relate them to his central purpose. Then they become luminous and inevitable. In the following two sections I should like to show briefly the concerns which generated Kant's ideas, and how these ideas lead to the promised land of the imagination—a land which Kant himself did not finally explore, but which he, like some philosophic Moses, viewed from the lofty mountain top of his own speculations about the scientific enterprise.

In the *Critique of Pure Reason* (among the early pages of the Transcendental Analytic) is a passage in which Kant explains the sense in which we may ask for a "deduction" (we should say "explanation") of the concepts of pure reason. He notes that many scientific concepts are employed without being questioned by anyone, since experience is always available to confirm that there are existing objects which conform to them. He then continues: "But there are also usurpatory concepts, such as *fortune*, and *fate*, which, although allowed to circulate by almost universal indulgence, are yet from time to time challenged by the question: *quid juris*. This demand for a deduction [explanation] involves us in considerable perplexity, no clear legal title, sufficient to justify their employment, being obtainable either from experience or from reason."[1]

It is an interesting and a puzzling passage. The phrase "usupatory concepts" *(usurpierte Begriffe)* strikes us as far from clear. *Usurpatory* in what sense? And why the particular examples "fortune" and "fate"? Also, is it really true that these concepts have no clear legal title obtainable either from experience or from reason? If we consider these questions a little more deeply (and also Kant's statement that although the concepts have no clear title, yet they are permitted to circulate "by almost universal indulgence") we may perhaps finally come nearer to a solution of certain problems which have long perplexed students of aesthetics and the philosophy of literature. What is the relation between science and poetry? Does literature give us *knowledge?* In what consists the function and the value of the imagination?

Kant's meaning is not difficult to perceive. The *Critique of Pure Reason* is an investigation into the rational presuppositions of mathematics and the natural sciences. The "matter" of our knowledge in these fields is derived from the senses, and its "form" from the ordering of the Understanding; and by "knowledge" Kant always means those propositions which are reliably established as a part of the corpus of science. The *Critique of Pure Reason* is an examination of what concepts are necessitated by seventeenth- and eighteenth-century science as a going concern, and when Kant in this work also repudiates the legitimacy of metaphysics, and terms all "transcendental" logic a "logic of illusion," he is placing an absolute barrier between science and what lies upon its other side. Upon this other side lie not only metaphysics, but also literature, and it may be that the principles of these two disciplines are related, and that the "logic of illusion" upon which both rest has its own stringent necessities no less than the rational logic of the natural sciences.

"The pure concepts of the understanding" which Kant found necessary for the ordering of science were such ideas as those of "quantity," "quality," and "relation." It seems clear, therefore, what he had in mind when he wrote the words which I have quoted just above. "Fortune" and "fate" are "usurpatory concepts" not merely because they are not to be found among the ordering ideas of science, but, more importantly, because they belong to *a completely different realm of discourse* from the concepts of science. And yet, since they are allowed to circulate "by almost universal indulgence," surely there must be some human utility, some other reason for their employment. What can it be? For if they receive "no clear legal title . . . either from experience or from reason," whence do they derive their almost universal indulgence, and what constitutes their *raison d'être?* These are questions which Kant does not answer here because he is interested only in exploring the presuppositions of exact science. But the by-product of this exploration is the establishment of a dualism in knowledge which is profoundly relevant for the answering of our questions.

Kant himself views the domain of reason with a certain perplexity. He is her best cartographer and yet he is aware that there are segments of her geography which are not finally known. The Preface to the first edition of the *Critique of Pure Reason* begins with the famous words:[2] "Human reason has this peculiar fate that in one species of its knowledge it is burdened by questions which, as prescribed by the very nature of reason itself, it is not able to ignore, but which, as transcending all its powers, it is also not able to answer." That there should be questions which our reason is fated to ask and equally fated never to answer says something very curious about the nature of our reason, and suggests why the Kantian enterprise of exploring its limits so as to provide an exhaustive inventory of what it contributes to science (and science alone) is bound to end in heroic failure. For the *First Critique,* like contemporary Positivism, asks for the elimination of metaphysics, and yet no one is more clearly aware than Kant himself of the essential hopelessness of doing this completely. "There has always existed in the world and there will always continue to exist," he says,[3] "some kind of metaphysics, and with it the dialectic that is natural to pure reason." It seems that Nietzsche has been anticipated, and that there exists some intrinsic *metaphysisches Bedurfnis*—"a metaphysical need" which no positivistic passion can ever finally overcome, because it is native to the constitution of the human mind.

There exists, then, a *necessary* "logic of illusion"—a natural and unavoidable difficulty of pure reason; not one, as Kant says,[4] "in which a bungler might entangle himself through lack of knowledge, or one which some sophist has artificially invented to confuse thinking people, but one inseparable from human reason, and which, even after its deceptiveness has been exposed, will not cease to play tricks with reason and continually entrap it into momentary aberrations ever and again calling for correction."

It is unfortunate for science that reason finds herself so compromised, but there is one trump card which Kant has concealed up his sleeve. What is unfortunate for the scientific interests of philosophers may yet be fortunate for the practical interests of mankind, and a speculative (scientific) reason which fails in absolute purity may yet be justified by the services which it renders to the moral life. As one follows Kant's account of the *antinomies of pure reason* (the contradictions into which reason falls), one sees how carefully the case for moral belief has been prepared. The infinity of the cosmos in space and time versus God's creation of the universe at a moment in time; the *necessity* of the laws of nature versus the *freedom* of the moral self; the *impossibility* of God versus his absolute *necessity* as maker or cause of the world—these are dualisms which contrast the claims of morality and religion with the claims of our scientific reason.

But I think we may now see that Kant was wrong in his presentation of a dialectic of reason which should contrast its scientific *only* with its moral and religious uses. It has been argued with great plausibility[5] that it is Kant's moral philosophy which furnishes the clue to his entire system, but I believe that we can learn most here from a comparison of his philosophy of science with his philosophy of art, and that the really crucial antithesis which Kant presents is the contrast of the scientific reason, not with its moral, but with its artistic employment. From the "dualism" of reason upon which Kant insists much can be learned, but more important for one who would understand the imagination is his contrast of the method of the natural sciences (treated in the *Critique of Pure Reason*) and of the literary arts (implied in the *Critique of Judgment*).

2   WHY WAS it that Kant (unlike Aristotle) did not separate the scientific, the moral, and the poetic activities of the mind in such a way as to clearly distinguish the sciences from the arts? The answer, I think, is twofold. In the first place because his architectonic conception of reason shows him to be obsessed with the primitive "faculty psychology" of his time. And in the second place because his general account of the imagination is too restricted, too confined in its position as a mere instrument in the service of scientific knowledge.

Although Kant's division of philosophy is into scientific (theoretical) and moral (practical), the first guided by the *Understanding* and yielding "concepts of nature," the second guided by the *Reason* and yielding "the concept of freedom," he thought it necessary to find still a third faculty—*Judgment*

—in the family of the higher cognitive powers. But in his *Critique of Judgment* his subject was determined less by looking directly at the world of literature and the arts than by very abstract psychological considerations. How this worked in detail need not concern us here, except that it caused the *Critique of Judgment* to deal with two chief notions rather than one: that of "pleasure" and that of teleology or "purposiveness." Kant's treatment of "pleasure" as a major term of aesthetic analysis was, I am convinced, a mistake, but his analysis of the concept of *purposiveness* is of the greatest importance for an understanding of literature and the arts. It is therefore paradoxical that in the *Critique of Judgment* he utilized the idea of purposiveness as an interesting *addition* to the scientific treatment of Nature.

Although "laws" of nature have their origin in our Understanding, which *prescribes* them to Nature, Kant also thought that there is a *purposiveness* of nature which has its origin solely in our Reflective Judgment. Strict scientific thinking forbids us to ascribe to the parts of nature a purposiveness in themselves, but nevertheless we use the idea of their possessing purpose as a principle for the orderly and connectd representation of natural phenomena in our minds. Kant calls the purposiveness of nature "a transcendental principle of the faculty of Judgment." It is a typically cumbersome bit of Kantian terminology, but if we reflect upon it we shall, I think, see that Kant's "faculty of Judgment" does not really make *logical* judgments at all, but acts very much as Bergson and Cassirer have described *the myth-making faculty* in man.

In our attributing of purposiveness to nature is implied just those maxims of metaphysical wisdom which cannot be demonstrated by the use of scientific concepts, and which, in fact, are clearly in opposition to them. If we take seriously Kant's remark that metaphysics has always existed, and always will, because it is implied in the very *dialectical* (contradictory) *nature* of pure reason, then we must interpret this persistence of metaphysics as due less to the necessities of our

moral experience than to *an inborn propensity toward teleo-*
logical interpretation with which our minds are equipped,
and which, moreover, coexists in equal dignity with the scientific understanding, although engaged in constant warfare
with its conclusions. The real explanation for "the antinomies
of pure reason" is, then, not that they show a moral employment of pure reason in opposition to a scientific, but rather
that they insert the urgencies of teleological explanation into
a domain preempted by the requirements of a mechanistic
science.

The job of the scientific Understanding is to make a connected and unified experience out of our perceptions of
nature, but the purposiveness which Judgment reads into
nature satisfies the same need, although in terms which are
clearly not acceptable to the scientific enterprise. For the presupposition of scientific thinking is *objectivity,* and the assertion that nature has a purpose is inherently *subjective,* since
it says less about nature than about the experiencing subject
who needs such a principle to guide its reflections about
nature. Thus, as Kant saw, we neither ascribe purpose to
nature on the basis of our reason, nor do we learn that nature
has a purpose by observation. "Fortune" and "fate" are (as we
shall see in Chapter 7) ideas which can be defined only with
reference to "purpose." From the standpoint of an exact science they are, indeed, "usurpatory concepts." But if, as Kant
said, they are allowed to circulate by almost universal indulgence, this is because their origin, while not in the scientific Understanding, is, nonetheless, from a faculty of creative
imagination which is as deeply rooted and as worthy of respect as is the Understanding itself. "Fortune" and "fate,"
however foreign they may be to the vocabulary of an objective natural science, are the creations of myth; they express a
purposiveness in the affairs of men within the broader environment of nature. Kant thought that there was something in
the very constitution of our judgments about nature which
made us peculiarly attentive to its teleology, some utility in

the "fiction" of an ideal purpose in nature which satisfied an inherent need of the mind. He attributed the need for purpose to our Judgment. He might better have attributed it to the Creative Imagination.

Why was it that Kant chose to locate this necessity in the first area rather than the second? It is, as I have said, because his treatment of the imagination *(Einbildungskraft)* is warped by his excessive preoccupation with its merely cognitive claims. Kant's account of the process of acquiring knowledge in the *Critique of Pure Reason* (wherein he exhibits the advance of knowledge from particular perceptions to universal concepts) lies under the tacit influence of Aristotle's *De Anima.* Therefore he reads this process as an activity combining a manifold of atomic elements of sensation into a unity so that from this unity ideas or concepts may be extracted. The synthesis of sensory elements into a single sensory *gestalt* is followed by the "reproductive" activity of imagination crystallizing or "fixing" the evanescent imagery in time, thus making possible both recall by memory and the final emergence of the universal or abstract concept from the initial diversity of sensory particulars. Imagination, as the middle stage of knowledge, is thus both "synthetic" and "reproductive," actively contributing to the formation of knowledge (rather than passively mirroring the impressions impinging upon it) but at the same time subservient to the final ideas or concepts which it makes possible. All of Kant's emphasis upon *the synthetic activity* of imagination cannot conceal his basic doctrine that it is instrumental to purely cognitive ends. Such an imagination would be the handmaiden of science, but it could never be the originator of poetry. For while it "combines" and "reproduces," it cannot *create*. It remained, therefore, for Kant's successor (and particularly Coleridge in his distinction between the *Primary* and the *Secondary* imagination) to provide a doctrine of the imagination adequate to the needs of literary criticism and aesthetic theory.

But even Coleridge's account of the poetic imagination

leaves something to be desired. Derived from the Kantian doctrine of synthesis, it sees imaginative activity as a *fusing* or *"esemplastic"* power, drawing upon all the powers of the mind to reconcile the oppositions and discordant qualities of experience. But of the basic *need* which it fulfills, of the way in which it functions to further human values in a way that scientific knowledge never can, Coleridge says little or nothing. For hints about this we must return to Kant's *Critique of Judgment* and what he says there about the idea of purpose.

We have, says Kant, good grounds for assuming a "subjective" purposiveness in nature, for only so is human judgment comprehensible and only so can we combine our particular experiences into a system. But that the parts of nature *really* serve one another or that they fulfill *our* purposes, there is absolutely no empirical evidence. Since, therefore, experience cannot *prove* to us the existence of purpose in nature, Kant says, it must have come from "a rationalizing subtlety *which only sportively* introduces the concept of purpose into the nature of things, but which does not derive it from objects or from their empirical cognition."[6] The language is defective. It is too rationalistic and deliberate. But that "rationalizing subtlety" which "sportively" introduces the concept of purpose into our experience—what better description could one have of the creative imagination? It is true that Kant sees the purposiveness introduced by human Judgment as "regulative" rather than as "constitutive"; that is, he sees it as residing not *in nature,* but *in the mind,* as a principle making our experience orderly in those cases where the rules of a strictly mechanical causality do not suffice. But if he had treated this "bias in favor of purpose" more seriously, he would have made a significant discovery. When we visualize the activities of nature according to the model of the kind of causality which we experience in ourselves (in terms of "aim" or "will" or "purpose"), we deal with nature in a new and nonscientific and interesting way—one which frees us from viewing nature merely as a blind mechanism. We would then, as Kant says, "supply to nature causes acting *designedly,* and consequently place at its basis teleology, not merely as a *regulative* principle for the mere *judging* of phenomena . . . but as a *constitutive* principle of the *derivation* of its products from their causes;" and if we should do this, then "the concept of a natural purpose would no longer belong to the reflective but to the determinant Judgment. Then, in fact, it would not belong specially to the Judgment . . . but as a rational concept *it would introduce into natural science a new causality, which we only borrow from ourselves and ascribe to other beings,* without meaning to assume them to be of the same kind with ourselves."[7]

What Kant here visualizes as a new concept of causality, borrowed from ourselves and our own subjective experience of how we think and behave, and only mythically and metaphorically ascribed to the cosmos or projected into nature, is simply that "purposiveness" which has its source in, and is the characteristic product of, the creative imagination.

3   LET ME make it clear that I do not wish to minimize the importance of Kant's distinction between the "constitutive" and the "regulative" principles of pure reason, nor the special emphasis which he gives to the latter. For it is through this feature of his system that three of his major successors—Nietzsche, Lange, and Vaihinger—have found their subject matter, and, in so doing, directly contributed to the enterprise in which we are now engaged. The partial return to dualism in some modern thinkers (as, for example, Bergson and Spengler) is significantly related to the demarcation of the realms of the understanding and the imagination, and has had its more remote sources of inspiration in F. A. Lange's *"standpoint of the ideal,"* in Nietzsche's emphasis upon man's *"will to illusion,"* and in the *"fictionalism"* of Hans Vaihinger. From these in

turn have sprung the major insights of the chief philosophers of symbolic forms in the modern world—Santayana and Cassirer.

The entire last half of Kant's *Critique of Pure Reason* treats metaphysics as a logic of illusion. This both limits the pretensions of the speculative reason and enormously enlarges the sphere of those moral and religious ideas which are practically necessary in the life of man and through whose "interference" the pronouncements of pure speculative reason have been infected with confusions, contradictions, and logical mistakes. Kant's notion that these difficulties are not importations from outside reason, but difficulties arising within reason itself, suggests the strategy with which they must be handled. If expulsion is unrealistic, there remains domestication. The distinction between the realms of appearance and reality, the idea of the simplicity of the soul, the concepts of human freedom and of the existence of God, are not "hypotheses" in the scientific sense. They cannot be handed over to the understanding to be passed upon by its scientific equipment. But the interesting thing is that *from reason's own standpoint* it is not important that they cannot be established as true. For this "natural dialectic of human reason" has a purpose all its own.

"The ideas of pure reason," says Kant[8] (he means the ideas of God, immortality, human freedom), "can never be dialectical [contradictory] in themselves; any deceptive illusion to which they give occasion must be due solely to their misemployment. For they arise from the very nature of our reason; and it is impossible that this highest tribunal of all the rights and claims of speculation should itself be the source of deceptions and illusions. Presumably, therefore, the ideas have their own good and appropriate vocation as determined by the natural disposition of our reason." The concepts of the simplicity of the soul, of human freedom, of a supreme intelligence, are *mere ideas,* useful devices constructed by the mind to bring about the greatest possible order in our think-

ing. The concept of purposiveness functions similarly.
Objects in our world, the phenomena of nature, must be
viewed *as if* the soul were simple, men were free, God existed,
and Nature were purposive, in order that the systematic unity
of knowledge may be achieved. The ideas which give rise to
the transcendental dialectic are therefore "regulative principles," "as-if notions," "heuristic fictions" for the internal
guidance of the mind. This may seem like pragmatism with a
venegeance, but it is not. For it does not maintain (like James
in some of his less guarded moments) that "that which works"
is "true." It still conceives "true propositions" and "useful
beliefs" as logically different structures of the mind, and
merely claims that many notions which cannot be adjudged
scientifically true have value for the processes of life and for
the successful prosecution of human intentions. And it is just
here, at this point, that the works of Nietzsche, Lange, and
Vaihinger have taken up Kant's suggestion.

Starting out as a commentator upon Kant, Vaihinger
finally exalted the Kantian doctrine of "the heuristic fiction"
into a complete philosophy of As-If. Kant's treatment of "the
dialectic of illusion" convinced him of the basic truth of the
fictionalist position—that "an idea whose theoretical untruth
or incorrectness (and therewith its falsity) is admitted, is not
for that reason practically valueless and useless; for such an
idea, in spite of its theoretical nullity may have great practical
importance."[9] Vaihinger's *chef d'oeuvre* appeared in 1911.
It was therefore able to place the eighteenth-century Kantian
theory of the mind within a Darwinian context, to consider
human thought *instrumentally,* from the point of view of its
operations as a purposive organic function. Thought constructs are not the product of a "Pure Reason" in the Kantian
a priori sense. They are biological phenomena, and in this
light many ideas which appear to be consciously false assumptions (and which may contradict reality or even themselves)
can be seen to be *intentionally* formed in order to overcome
difficulties, and reach an extracognitive goal. "The as-if

world," says Vaihinger, "which is formed in this manner, the world of the 'unreal' is just as important as the world of the so-called real or actual (in the ordinary sense of the word); indeed it is far more important for ethics and aesthetics. This aesthetic and ethical world of 'As if', the world of the unreal, becomes finally for us a world of values, which, particularly in the form of religion, must be sharply distinguished in our mind from the world of becoming."[10]

Vaihinger's position is based ultimately upon a dualistic mode of perception. It is empirical—even phenomenalistic —in its definition of "ultimate reality" as "the sequence of sensations given to mind," but at the same time (with the strategy of all idealisms since Kant) it stresses the creativity of mind in its fiction-constructing activity. There is also here an implicit reference to imagination, wider perhaps than Coleridge's, but, like it, emphasizing a free, creative, and inventive activity which passes beyond the requirements of mere cognitive unification toward broader aims, biologically given, although by no means biologically contained.

Like Vaihinger, Nietzsche owes an enormous debt to Kant, and like Vaihinger also, what he derived, he placed within an evolutionary framework. Both saw clearly that life, no less than science, is not possible without imaginary (if not actually false) conceptions, but what Nietzsche particularly stresses is the distinction between "reality" and "appearance," and the enormous significance which "appearance" has in the productions of science, no less than in those of the arts. He is devoted to an exposure of the pretensions to truth of all analytically-minded men, whether those of a Socrates or a Euripides, and he delights (with the playful malice of the dedicated ironist) in showing the far-reaching implications of "invention," "myth," and above all "falsification" in the life of man. Art is falsification; myth is falsification; poetic creativity is falsification; for each operates by the conscious creation of a world of *aesthetic illusion* which is, however, indispensable for human habitation. There are moments when Nietzsche expresses the very deepest sympathy with "the primitive longing for illusion"; moments when he seems to insist that "delusional concepts" are a salutary, indeed a necessary, element for the preservation of the freshness of human thought. The construction of metaphors, he tells us, is the fundamental instinct of man, and the typical exaggeration of this point (in which he so characteristically revels) appears in the remarkable early fragment (1873) *Ueber Wahrheit und Luege im aussermoralischen Sinn (On Truth and Lying in An Extra-moral Sense).*[11] "Lying in an extra-moral sense" is his ironic characterization of those "untruths" of myth and metaphor which are at once the standard content of art as they are the intentional expression of man's "will to illusion."

To Nietzsche almost nothing is more incomprehensible than how an honest and pure urge for truth could make its appearance among men. "They are deeply immersed in illusions and dream images; their eye glides only over the surface of things and sees 'forms'; their feeling nowhere leads into truth, but contents itself with the reception of stimuli, playing, as it were, a game of blindman's buff on the backs of things" *(ein tastendes Spiel auf dem Ruecken der Dinge zu spielen).* This metaphor "on the backs of things" is striking, and crucial to Nietzsche's meaning, for it implies that which is uncertain, precarious, fraught with lurking danger. And Nietzsche presses it further. ". . . Man rests upon the merciless, the greedy, the insatiable, the murderous, in the indifference of his ignorance—hanging in dreams, as it were, upon the back of a tiger. In view of this, whence in all the world comes the urge for truth?" The urge for truth, he would have said, is only the linguistic correlative of Hobbes' social contract—a conventionalizing of meaning to prevent mutual damage by deception. Man desires it for its agreeable and life-giving consequences, even as he is indifferent to pure metaphysical knowledge, and downright hostile to any truth which might be damaging or destructive. "Only through forgetfulness can man ever achieve the illusion of possessing a 'truth' in the sense just designated. If he does not wish to be satisfied with truth in the form of a tautology—that is, with empty shells—then he will forever buy illusions for truths."

The fact of the matter is that in Nietzsche the classic pre-Kantian notion of truth has undergone a sea change, influenced, I think, by Kant's own ambiguous doctrine of the "as-if" and the "heuristic fiction." In Nietzsche's ironic suggestion that to be "truthful" means only to use "the customary" metaphors, or, in moral terms, means "the obligation to lie according to a fixed convention, to lie herd-like in a style obligatory for all" lies a revaluation of "truth" and "objectivity" which reinstates the fiction not by a sober-minded assessment of its relative utility, but by a malicious attack upon the ultimate sincerity of that "objectivity" which scientific method claims for itself. "What, then, is truth? A mobile army of metaphors, metonyms, and anthropomorphisms—in short, a sum of human relations, which have been enhanced, transposed, and embellished poetically and rhetorically, and which after long use seem firm, canonical, and obligatory to a people. Truths are illusions about which one has forgotten that this is what they are; metaphors which are worn out and without sensuous power; coins which have lost their picture and now matter only as metal, no longer as coins."

It reminds us somehow of Hobbes' doctrine of imagination as "decaying sense," but with the moral of the empiricism exactly inverted and debased. For now it is not imagination that functions as a diminished surrogate for the purity of sense, but science that functions as a decadent substitute for the purity of the creative imagination. Science, I think Nietzsche is saying, is like a coin whose engraving has been worn away. It portrays a world in which all the teleology—all the rich purposiveness—has been rubbed off in the daily commerce of a grimy use.

4 NIETZSCHE AND VAIHINGER have both been profoundly influenced by Kant, but it is in F. A. Lange (who preceded them both) that the most direct link is to be found between Kant's notion of the heuristic fiction working for cognitive unity, and the imaginative transformation of the world. It appears in the remarkable concluding chapter of his massive *The History of Materialism*,[12] strangely entitled (after what has come before) "The Standpoint of the Ideal." Materialism, he asserts, is the lowest, the most primitive, but also the "firmest" stage in the history of philosophic thought. Its certainties are the certainties of science. But now Kant's earlier paradox reappears. The unity of knowledge which makes isolated facts into a science, and science into a system, is the result of a free synthesis, and it is the same unifying activity which also produces the notion of *the Ideal*. Speculation about the ideal has its own rules. Like empirical research, it strives after unification, although it lacks the discipline of the principles of experience. Nevertheless, says Lange, only in "creation" in the narrower sense of the word, in *poetry*, is the ground of reality consciously abandoned. In thought form may have an edge over content, but in poetry it is completely dominant. "The poet in the free play of his spirit creates a world to his own liking, in order to impress more vividly upon the easily manageable material a form which has its own intrinsic value and its importance independently of the problems of knowledge."

The synthetic activity of the mind always works toward the production of unity, harmony, and perfect form in the products of the mind. In art this produces beauty, in ethics universal norms, and in metaphysics a predominance of the shaping, form-giving factor in our picture of the world. But for just this reason the conclusions of science are bound to differ from the constructions of the imagination. Despite the unifying effect of our categories of space and time, despite the formal ordering performed by our systems of logic, the whole world of phenomena (that is, of scientific reality) is bound to appear bizarre, capricious, inharmonious to the point of perversity as compared with the free creations of the arts. Art, for example, turns its back upon evil, suffering, and death *as actually experienced;* not that it shrinks from them as content for its poems and plays, but that in giving them literary "form" it reduces their power to hurt. This (as we shall see in Chapter 8) is the meaning of Aristotle's theory of the tragic *catharsis.* "The more freely synthesis exerts its function, the more aesthetic becomes the image of the world." The imagination turns even the shapelessness of fact and the uselessness of suffering into a world of art.

The analytic method of the natural sciences clings to the particular. But for its world of particularity and pluralism we can feel as little enthusiasm as for a poem which we read not as a complete image (or even line by line), but rather letter by letter. But says Lange, if we embrace the whole as a unity, "then in the act of synthesis we bring *our own nature* into the object, just as we shape the landscape that we gaze at into harmony, however much disharmony in particulars may be concealed by it. All comprehension follows aesthetic principles, and every step towards the whole is a step towards the Ideal."

Naturally (and in what seems to be opposed to Nietzsche's belief) we are *not* deceived. Our urge toward the ideal is not diminished by the knowledge that our reality is no absolute reality, but only appearance. Indeed, the demand here for a *demonstration,* the obsession with confirmation and testability, will only produce the reappearance of materialism to chasten the sense of speculative adventure and render our mental acts chronically earth-bound. *"One thing is certain, that man needs to supplement reality by an ideal world of his own creation, and that the highest and noblest functions of his mind cooperate in such creations.* But why must this act of intellectual freedom always keep on assuming the deceptive form of a demonstrative science?"

This last is the crucial question, and since Lange asks it

rhetorically, it shows that he embraces the dualism of science and poetry candidly and without bad conscience. For he understands that when poetry leaves the ground of reality entirely, and creates a myth, when the creative imagination, by unhesitatingly removing the Ideal into the realm of fantasy, lends it an overpowering force, both achieve values which no literal description can encompass. Man pursues science and credits its extension of knowledge so long as he feels himself imaginatively free. But let him be chained down to what is attainable merely through the senses and the understanding, and he will rebel, giving expression to the freedom of his imagination and his spirit in forms even cruder and more scientifically outrageous than those which a more moderate materialism has previously destroyed. "Let us then," says Lange, "accustom ourselves to regard the world of ideas as figurative representations of the entire truth, as just as indispensable to all human progress as the knowledge of the understanding."

The moral of Lange's "standpoint of the ideal" is thus the same modest assertion of a principle of reciprocal tolerance as is implicit in the "regulative ideas" of Kant, the "appearances" of Nietzsche, and the "fictions" of Vaihinger, for it assumes that art and science make correlative and non-exclusive claims. One cannot deny Darwin because he does not conform to Genesis, nor question the second law of thermodynamics as inconsistent with the divine creativity. And conversely, one cannot logically refute a Mass of Palestrina, or invoke the theory of probability in order to convict a Cimabue Madonna of error.

Nevertheless when A. J. Ayer (in *Language, Truth and Logic*) claims that all utterances about the nature of God are *nonsensical,* and when, conversely, Philip Wheelwright (in *The Burning Fountain*) insists that the expressive statements of religion can rightfully be declared *true* on intuitive grounds, the danger of conflicting jurisdiction (against which Lange so carefully guards) has shown its unwelcome face.

For that narrowing tendency, positivistically inspired, which would purify the language of science by denigrating all non-referential usages has produced its natural antidote: a broadening tendency, viewing all symbolism *qua* symbolism as humanly interesting and significant and even (in the most extreme advocates) as somehow cognitively true. When "the standpoint of the ideal" has been forgotten, then it follows that "semantic positivism" and "symbolic humanism" will fight to the death for the sterile fruits of a merely semantic victory.

In the materialist-idealist controversy of his day Lange saw the serious sign of the times. But what is not only historically interesting, but also prophetic, is the way in which this "metaphysical" issue prefigured the "semantic" battleground of ethical, aesthetic, and religious thought in the contemporary world. Lange not only perceived the conflict, but the clue to its resolution. Therefore he said: "But one thing only can finally bring humanity to an enduring peace—the recognition of the imperishable nature of all poesy in Art, Religion, and Philosophy, and the permanent reconciliation, on the basis of this recognition, of the controversy between scientific investigation and imagination." Here is where Santayana has learned his wisdom!

5   IT IS TIME, I think, to note where we have arrived. Our ultimate interest lies in the contrast between the method of science and the method of the literary arts, between, if you will, the cognitive understanding and the creative imagination. It is a contrast which, like so many, finds its modern origins in the philosophy of Kant; in this case in his division between the "analytic" presuppositions of mathematics and physics, and the "dialectic" of illusion; between the principles which make scientific assertions possible in mathematics and natural science, and "the heuris-

tic fictions" of the mind which have been inserted there by the necessities of cognitive unity and practical reason. And we have also seen how Kant's treatment of this contrast finds its development in the cognate dualisms of his followers: between fact and fiction in Vaihinger, reality and illusion in Nietzsche, the standpoint of materialism and the standpoint of the Ideal in Lange.

It is interesting that the dualism as it finds expression in Kant and his immediate followers is a contrast at the level of *ideas,* of faculties or functions of the mind, and that it locates the issues in a domain which we should roughly classify as *epistemological.* Whereas in our own time, in the field of contemporary philosophy, the same problem has been restated as a problem of alternative functions of language, of alternative possibilities of linguistic use, of the kinds of *words* which are appropriate in scientific, religious, and poetic discourse, and this locates the issues in a domain which we should roughly classify as *semantic.* This is true upon whichever side of the debate one chooses to participate.

The *locus classicus* of the semantic formulation of the problem is, of course, the analysis of the symbolizing functions of language presented by C. K. Ogden and I. A. Richards in *The Meaning of Meaning* (1923). This work presents the famous (but invidious) distinction between the "emotive" and the "referential" uses of language. Language has two major functions; to "designate" and to "express." The first is scientific—the second is not. The distinction between these two uses coupled with an obvious preference for the former is the essence of "semantic positivism," and it provides a strategic vantage point in terms of which "the language of science" may be vindicated while the "pseudo-statements" of religion, poetry, and metaphysics, although permitted their "expressive" virtues, are condemned as cognitively meaningless. This has become the classic positivistic position. Carnap, so far as I know, has never explicitly acknowledged the debt which he owes to the suggestive remarks of Ogden and Richards, but his treatment of "object-questions" in *The Logical Syntax of Language* and elsewhere shows him to have been deeply under their spell. In that work he said: "The suppositious sentences of metaphysics, of the philosophy of values, of ethics . . . are pseudo-sentences; they have no logical content, but are only expressions of feeling which in their turn stimulate feelings and volitional tendencies on the part of the hearer."[13] And what holds for metaphysical and ethical sentences also holds *a fortiori* for the sentences of literature, poetry, and religion.

The most sustained and at the same time the most astute counterattack upon semantic positivism in recent times is that of Philip Wheelwright in *The Burning Fountain: A Study in the Language of Symbolism* (1954). Wheelwright's whole purpose is to defend religion and poetry against the charge of "nonsense," and to assert the thesis "that religion, poetic and mythic utterances at their best *really mean something,* make a kind of objective reference, although neither the objectivity nor the method of referring is of the same kind as in the language of science."[14] But the irony is that in attacking positivism, Wheelwright has succumbed to the same rhetorical strategy as the position he combats. Naturally, he uses it in reverse. Although he asserts that the inquiry upon which he is embarking is partly semantic, partly ontological, the ontological side is largely submerged. This is, of course, inevitable when one meets a semantic argument with semantic weapons. He therefore accepts the *kind* of distinction which Ogden and Richards have made, while recasting it in terms which are rhetorically friendly to poetry and religion.

There are, Wheelwright says, two strategies of language. One works like mathematical logic, the other like music. The first tries to designate with maximum clarity. The second tries to express with maximum fullness. The first he calls mere *steno-language;* the second *depth language.* This is of course *not* the distinction of Ogden and Richards, for theirs makes emotivity and reference into polar concepts, and not the least impressive of Wheelwright's theoretical achievements is his redefinition of the semantic situation in such a way that *emotivity and reference no longer function as contraries, but as independent variables.* This neatly undercuts the positivist position, for it permits the sentences or statements of religion and poetry to be simultaneously emotive *and* referential.[15]

I am not really concerned with the details of the semantic debate, but only with how it indicates the multiple levels upon which our basic dualism is expressible. For I think it is clear that the issue of science and the imagination has at the same time metaphysical, epistemological, and semantic implications, and that it varies according to whether we address it in terms of "things," of "ideas," or of "words." At the level of things it is a distinction between two varieties of experience concerned respectively with *nature* and with *art.* At the level of ideas it is a distinction between two faculties, or (in a less hypostatic formulation) two functions of the mind: *the understanding* and the *imagination.* At the level of words it is a distinction between two strategies of discourse yielding respectively *a language of science* and *a language of literature.* I have suggested that from Kant to Vaihinger the problem has been stated primarily in epistemological terms, and from Ogden and Richards onward primarily in semantic ones. But there is, in addition, a brief period, falling roughly in the interval between Vaihinger and I. A. Richards, when something much more metaphysical, much more cross-sectional, was accomplished, and which, in spite of the sometimes questionable philosophic setting in which it was placed, has implications of the greatest importance for our problem. I am referring to the implicit *metaphysical* dualisms which underlie the work of Bergson and of Spengler.

What is the ultimate meaning of man's philosophy, his religion, and his art? Stripped of all nonessentials, this, I think, is the root problem of Bergson's philosophy. It is true that his attempt to support the tottering enterprises of phi-

losophy, religion, and the arts requires the mediating apparatus of a metaphysics and an epistemology, and that in Bergson
each of these is founded upon an absolute and unrepentantly
dualistic mode of perception. Bergson accepts without question the Darwinian major premise. Man is first of all an
animal, and the basis of his epistemic equipment is the need
to navigate within an environment, and to manipulate practically a universe of intractable solids. This is the essential
purpose of all intellectual functions. But the consequence of
this view of the intellect is that it cuts the realm of human
culture in two: on the one side the practical operations
of even the most theoretical of the sciences; on the other the
metaphysical implications of even the most applicable of the
arts. And this split is founded upon the almost philosophically trite disjunctions of appearance and reality, body and
spirit, analysis and intuition.

In Bergson these disjunctions are reciprocal and mutually
implicative. The transformation of the problem of culture
into the problem of knowledge is accomplished when *analysis*
as the natural geometric method (as the operation of the
understanding) is contrasted with *intuition* as the overflow
of intellectual sympathy (as the operation of the creative
imagination), and then the distinction between intuition and
analysis can be further generalized as the difference in
procedure between the sciences and the arts. Moreover,
although the scientific utilization of analysis is always relative
to interests which are practical, art, on the contrary, recreates
and preserves experience for its own sake, and is therefore an
intimate contact with what can be metaphysically conceived
of only as *the real*. The object of art is to provide unmediated
immersion in the stream of continuity, to permit the individual to enter directly into an accord with nature and with
life. The media of the arts are materials which in ordinary
existence perform utilitarian functions, but which are here
magically transformed so as to suggest the rhythms of nature
and the "music" which underlies reality.

Intuition is the method of knowing in art, as analysis is

the method of knowing in science, but it is important to remember that for Bergson this epistemological distinction hangs upon a metaphysical claim. The universe is split through the center. On the one side lie the phenomena of the living, characterized by real time or *"duration,"* expressing the continuous mobility which is the most generic characterization of the real. On the other side lies appearance, the realm of inert matter, static, governed by *a mechanical time* of infinite repetition, manipulatible but inherently "unreal." If the understanding is the agency of dealing with the phenomenal world (as Kant also thought), and if its mathematical apparatus permits the control of a solid environment, it must at the same time be recognized that it is incapable of penetrating reality, of providing intimations of the metaphysical truth. That is the function of intuition, and among the modes of its expression are those of literature and the arts.

Life, real time, the method of intuition exhaust one area of human experience. Matter, mechanical time, the method of analysis exhaust another. And through this extreme dualism we are brought to see that the contrast between science and literature, treated by Kant's followers in epistemic terms, and by Ogden and Richards' in semantic, has also metaphysical implications. For (as we shall see in Chapter 6) it is somehow inextricably bound up with the problems of appearance and reality.

6 THROUGHOUT the entire massive enterprise which is Spengler's *The Decline of the West* there is not a single reference to the work of Bergson. This is a fact so singular as to rouse our deepest curiosity. For the systems of the two men are so structurally and philosophically isomorphic as to suggest, if not explicit cross-fertilization, at least a common parentage. Spengler, like Bergson, proposes a split down the center of the universe, and,

in harmony with this metaphysical dichotomy, a correspond-
ingly dualistic epistemology and theory of method. Bergson's
metaphysics is founded upon the dichotomy of the world as
life versus the world as matter; Spengler's metaphysics is
founded upon the dichotomy of *the world as history* versus
the world as nature. Bergson's epistemology proposes the distinction between the real time of duration versus the artificial
time of mechanical repetition; Spengler's epistemology proposes the distinction between the idea of *destiny* and the idea
of *causality*. Bergson's methodology contrasts the method of
intuition with the method of analysis; Spengler's methodology
contrasts the technique of *analogy* with the technique of
establishing *mathematical law*. Thus the Spenglerian "world
as history" with its idea of destiny and its technique of analogy
is the functional correlative of the Bergsonian "world of life"
with its idea of duration and its method of intuition. And
their opposites, the Bergsonian "world as matter," with its
idea of mechanical repetition and its method of analysis, and
the Spenglerian "world as nature," with its idea of causality
and its technique of mathematical law, are so similar as to
have been conceived, if not by the same mind, at least according to the same mode of perception.

Although Bergson begins with a consideration of biological
evolution, and Spengler with a treatment of historical process, the opposite of this area of concern is in each case a world
of matter or of nature conceived both in materialistic and in
mechanistic terms. For Bergson and Spengler alike, nature,
matter, mathematical law, mechanical repetition, causality,
and analysis form a single invidious complex against which
are to be set the operations of an artistically and poetically
operative intuition. This intuition offers the possibility of
the unveiling of a metaphysical truth against the background
of epistemic illusion, of the penetration of the sphere of
reality against the counterclaims of scientific appearance.
Here is the heritage of the Kantian dualism at still another
level.

"With all rigour," says Spengler,[16] "I distinguish (as to form, not substance) the organic from the mechanical world-impression, the content of images from that of laws, the picture and symbol from the formula and the system, the instantly actual from the constantly possible, the intents and purposes of *imagination ordering according to plan* from the intents and purposes of *experience dissecting according to scheme....*" Thus, at the outset, is presented a contrast which implies a revaluation of the philosophical enterprise in that it suggests "the intents and purposes of the imagination" as a source for philosophical material over against that of the understanding and its systematic operations. Its metaphysical source is *a Heracleitean conception of process* which rules the insights of Spengler exactly as it does those of Bergson. The former's distinction between "Nature" and "History" indicates the opposition of a range of human possibilities which has at one end "things becoming" and at the other "things become," represented to Spengler by the contrast between Plato, Rembrandt, Goethe, and Beethoven (the artists) on the one hand, and Parmenides, Descartes, Kant, and Newton (the scientists) on the other. *Cognition* (in the most accurate sense of the word) is the act of experience of which the completed issue is called Nature, and the aggregate of things cognized is equivalent to the aggregate of things mechanically defined in so far as they have been brought under law. *Nature* for Spengler is thus *the sum of the law-imposed necessities.* Contemplation or "vision," on the other hand, is that act of experience which is History *because it is itself a fulfilling.* Laws of nature are forms of rigorous (and therefore inorganic) necessity. But *the pure becoming* which is the subject matter of History is incapable of confinement within such cognitive bonds. (Spengler's contrast between Nature and History owes much not only to Goethe, but also to Nietzsche, for it shows that even in science occurs the production of "images.")

It appears then that there are two separate elements in all "world-picturing," that of "form" and that of "law," the first the gift of the imagination, the second that of the understanding, and the more a world-picture concentrates upon Nature, the more likely will be its dependence upon the types of serial order and the molds of law. But the intuitive picture of the world will analogize its operations to the physiognomy and acts of man; it will therefore produce images in the form of drama and of portraiture.

The Spenglerian distinction of the world as history versus the world as nature carries with it the opposition of the *Destiny Idea* and the *Causality Principle* (an opposition which we shall have further opportunity to explore in Chapter 7). The first is expressed in the "emotive" language with which Ogden and Richards have acquainted us—with words like "happiness," "despair," "devotion," "repentance," or "doom," while the second is expressed in the "referential" language of "perception," "description," "classification," "abstraction," and "identification." It is the organic logic of things *felt* in opposition to the inorganic logic of things *understood*. The Destiny-idea, as Spengler says, demands life-experience and not scientific experience, the power of seeing and not that of calculating, depth and not intellect. And this is the source, I think, from which Wheelwright has drawn his distinction between "depth language" and "steno-language." "He," says Spengler,[17]

who expects here, in the domain of the living, to find reasons and consequences, or imagines that an inward certainty as to the meaning of life is the same thing as "Fatalism" or "Predestination," simply knows nothing of the matters in question, confusing experience lived with experience acquired or acquirable. Causality is the reasonable, the law-bound, the describable, the badge of our whole waking and reasoning existence. But destiny is the word for an inner certainty that is *not* describable. We bring out that which is in the causal by means of a physical or an epistemological system, through numbers, by reasoned classification; but the idea of destiny can be imparted only by the artist working through media like portraiture, tragedy and music.

The conception of the world as *heavy with fate* is not incompatible with the world as a *system of causal connections.* One comes from a feeling for life, the other is a method of knowledge. No less a rationalist than Whitehead has said that our belief in the lawfulness of the order of nature comes as much from the instinct of Greek tragedy as from the formulations of Newtonian science. Thus, as if in confirmation of Spengler, it is perhaps possible to say that the *knowledge* of cause and effect is founded upon the *feeling* of destiny. Destiny was passed over, if not in silence at least in perplexity, by Kant himself, who had no use for it in his scientific system of the world founded upon the principle of causality. He called it a "usurpatory concept" receiving no clear title either from experience or from reason (although, as we have seen, there lay in his *Third Critique* the insight for its explanation). This strategy of rejection for mythical notions must always be the program of science, and its opposite the program of literature and the arts. "Pure reason," says Spengler disdainfully, "denies all possibilities that are outside itself. Here strict thought and great art are eternally in conflict. The one keeps its feet, and the other lets itself go. A man like Kant must always feel himself as superior to a Beethoven as the adult to the child, but this will not prevent a Beethoven from regarding the *Critique of Pure Reason* as a pitiable sort of philosophy."[18]

Spengler's need to distinguish between "great art" and "strict thought" is one of the necessities of his system. It not only permits him to distinguish two methodologies appropriate respectively to the understanding and the imagination, but it also fits in perfectly with his emphasis upon a comprehension of "the world-as-history" through a technique of analogies. This in turn places his own work (with its metaphorical style and its elevation of analogy into a canon of historical method) closer to the borders of "great art" than to those of "strict thought." Almost the same could be said for the works of Plato or Nietzsche, Santayana or Bergson. Wherever there is recourse to myth or aphorism, metaphor or imagery, there is some imaginative appeal, and this is particularly apt (as in the case of Spengler or Bergson) where the very content to be illuminated seems inherently recalcitrant to the analysis of "strict thought." Spengler's use of the idea of Destiny with its affinity for time rather than space, and its identification of inner time with the nature of organism, is absolutely Bergsonian, and if he uses analogy to comprehend the workings of destiny, this is no less "poetical" than the intuitive means which Bergson uses to illuminate the nature of "life," "the flux," or "the real."

Yet I have not appealed to Bergson and Spengler as poets, but for the metaphysical dualisms which they suggest in contrast to the epistemological dualism of Kant and his followers, and the semantic dualism of Ogden and Richards, Carnap, and Wheelwright. That Bergson and Spengler propose the dualism only to espouse its intuitive or poetic side is less consequential for our purpose than their original distinction. But there is, in addition, something of value which we may learn from them, and that is a further enrichment of *the vocabulary* which is somehow relevant in the opposition between the method of science and the method of the literary arts. "Appearance and reality," "intuition and analysis," "fate and natural law," "nature and history," "destiny and causality," "the image and the sensation": these are the concepts which not only have appeared, but are *predestined* to appear whenever the issue of the arts versus the sciences comes into question. If we add to this enrichment the Spenglerian insight that destiny, experience, and causal knowledge *each* have their appropriate modes of perception (so that the natural scientist turns instinctively to hypothesis, observation, and mathematics, as the artist turns naturally to investigate man's desiny in the musical score, in the portrait, and above all in the tragic drama) we shall gain some insight into the phenomenon which is the inverse of that cited above. For we shall see (and this will be our chief preoccupation in Chapter

5) not only that there are philosophers who are committed to a content which renders their methods poetical, but also literary artists whose form and style contain an implicit philosophy.

7   IT IS NOW clear, I think, that the insight which originated in Kant's distinction between the logic of the understanding and the logic of illusion, which expressed itself in the work of Vaihinger, Nietzsche, and Lange, in the semantic twists of Ogden and Richards, Carnap, and Wheelwright, and in the ultimate metaphysics of Bergson and Spengler, represents a form of radical dualism. It is an attempt to deal with two aspects of experience which have the paradoxical character that although they are both modes of operating in the world, yet they seem often to yield opposite and conflicting reports of its nature. And this paradox, although it has both semantic and metaphysical aspects, is strongest at precisely that point where it seems to spring from an inner cognitive division, when it is interpreted as a built-in feature of the responsiveness of a human mind situated in nature. This brings us at last to Santayana.

That incoherence and instability, he tells us, which we find in human systems of ideas is hardly to be wondered at when we compare the modesty of our sensory equipment with the cognitive tasks which we attempt to perform. The mind's reach does seem to exceed its grasp; its resources for knowledge are distinctly not commensurate with its ambition. Now, this notion is, indeed, Kantian, but it is Santayana's virtue, I think, that he locates the difficulty not (as Kant did) at the intersection of the theoretical and the practical reason, but at the intersection of the understanding and the imagination. "We have," he says,[19]

memory and we have certain powers of synthesis, abstraction, reproduction, invention,—in a word, we have understanding. But this faculty of understanding has hardly begun its work of deciphering the hieroglyphics of sense and framing an idea of reality, when it is crossed by another faculty—the imagination. Perceptions do not remain in the mind, as would be suggested by the trite simile of the seal and the wax, passive and changeless, until time wear off their sharp edges and make them fade. No, perceptions fall into the brain rather as seeds into a furrowed field or even as sparks into a keg of powder. Each image breeds a hundred more. . . . The mind, exercised by its own fertility and flooded by its inner lights, has infinite trouble to keep a true reckoning of its outward perceptions. It turns from the frigid problems of observation to its own visions; it forgets to watch the courses of what should be its pilot stars. Indeed, were it not for the power of convention in which, by a sort of mutual cancellation of errors, the more practical and normal conceptions are enshrined, the imagination would carry men wholly away,—the best men first and the vulgar after them.

Santayana's assessment of the power of the imagination is perhaps extreme—it is the estimate of a highly imaginative man—but his image of the seeds in the furrowed field or the sparks in the powder keg does greater justice to the creative imagination than is ordinarily accorded. What is most important for our purposes is the sense one derives from him that the imagination is of metaphysical import. The five senses as the original instrument; the understanding as the chief interpretive device, but the play of fancy to overlay and perhaps cloud that interpretation: this is Santayana's picture of the endowment of the human mind. But since the mind's ambition and its need demand the construction of *a map of reality*, a picture of the world, an explanation of itself and the universe, its products are *metaphysical*.

Nor, in the last instance, is the functioning of the imagination for Santayana merely a confusing overlay of the understanding. It is an independent originative source of interpretative pictures; as Nietzsche said, it stamps the everyday metal with its engraving to produce a sharp intaglio. This suggests not merely a clouding of the picture presented by the understanding, but the confrontation of the understanding with an alternative picture. There are, then, not one, but *two* "maps of reality," one of which guides the immediate functioning of the organism, the other also "applicable to life" but in a more remote, perhaps a more "metaphysical" fashion, and each springs from its own cognitive necessity. It is clear that for Santayana (and I think the insight is absolutely valid) imagination and intelligence do not differ in their origin, but only in their validity. "Understanding is an applicable fiction, a kind of wit with a practical use. Common sense and science live in a world of expurgated mythology, such as Plato wished his poets to compose, a world where the objects are imaginative in their origin and essence, but useful, abstract, and beneficent in their suggestions."[20]

Common sense and science live in a world of expurgated mythology—this is the heart of the matter, and if we ask what manner of expurgation has been performed to make the creatures of the imagination more amenable to the requirements of the understanding, we shall have to say (as Santayana did not) that what has been expurgated is not merely all that is "emotive," but particularly *all that has been touched by purposiveness and by drama.* And then, by an application of the method of residues, we shall discover that precisely these two qualities constitute the essence of the creative imagination!

The language of science is rich in concepts which are capable of verification by sense (and therefore infinitely serviceable in practice), while the language of religion, poetry, and metaphysics contains conceptions which, although not "verifiable," are yet "useful, abstract, and beneficent in their suggestions." They are useful because they provide *an interpretation of the world of human interests.* They are abstract in that they are *the formalized patterns of ideal experience.* And they are beneficent because *they combat just those tendencies toward torpor and despair which dangerously attenuate our attachment to life.* It is, Santayana notes, the profounder minds that commonly yield to the imagination, because it is these minds which are capable of feeling the pressure of the problems of life, and who sense the inadequacy of the understanding with only its resources of observation and verification to deal with them. The imagination, as Wallace Stevens says,[21] "is the power of the mind over the possibilities of things" and it is, therefore, the source "of as many values as reside in the possibilities of things." The intuitions which science cannot assimilate remain as the foundations of poetry and religion, and it is unfortunate that religious teachers and metaphysicians are unwilling to admit that their creations are the creatures of the imagination. But whether they call them products of "prophecy," "revelation," or "the higher reason," these are simply "eulogistic synonyms for imagination, implying (what is perfectly possible) that the imagination has not misled us."

But to say this is of course to enter a truth claim, and it is at this point that the jurisdictional battle between science and its alternatives reenters the arena of controversy. It therefore is more fitting for the poet, the prophet, or the metaphysician to be modest in his claim, and to recognize with Santayana that "Faith and the higher reason of the metaphysicians are, therefore, forms of imagination believed to be avenues to truth, as dreams or oracles may sometimes be truthful, not because their necessary correspondence to truth can be demonstrated, for then they would be portions of science, but because a man dwelling on those intuitions is conscious of a certain moral transformation, of a certain warmth and energy of life. This emotion, heightening his ideas and giving them power over his will, he calls faith or high philosophy, and under its dominion he is able to face his destiny with enthusiasm, or at least with composure."[22]

To indulge the imagination is to express something indigenous to man, to bring to the foreground a contagious quality of all individuals, a certain potentiality for reading purpose and drama into the universe which we all share. No scientist, therefore, is entitled to view it with contempt. Pascal called imagination the "mistress of the world." But he did not say this in her praise. He meant that she is promiscuous, untrustworthy, deceptive, and disloyal, the dangerous and eternal enemy of the reason, and in this he was the prophetic forerunner of Ogden and Richards, of Ayer, and of Carnap. But if we wish to correct this positivistic bias, we need not turn completely away from the tradition of analysis, but only to another of its contemporary branches, that of linguistic investigation, and to a relevant and important insight of the school of Wittgenstein and Ryle.

8   THE ORIGINAL insight of which I wish to make use seems to be Wittgenstein's, for in his examination of the linguistic features of various realms of discourse, he was impressed by those similarities between various words in a single realm which he called "family resemblances."[23] Gilbert Ryle has taken over from Wittgenstein the idea of "a family of conceptions" and has elevated it into a tool for dealing with those recurrent philosophical perplexities which he calls "dilemmas." "There often arise," he says,[24] "quarrels between theories, or, more generally between *lines of thought, which are not rival solutions of the same problem, but rather solutions or would-be solutions of different problems, and which, none the less, seem to be irreconcilable with one another.* A thinker who adopts one of them seems to be logically committed to rejecting the other, despite the fact that the inquiries from which the theories issued had, from the beginning, widely divergent goals." The relevance of this formulation for our purpose is, I think, clear. The perplexities of Kant concerning "fortune" and "fate," the quarrels between semantic positivism and

symbolic humanism over the nature of "truth," are obvious illustrations of those "quarrels . . . between lines of thought which are not rival solutions of the same problem, but rather solutions of different problems, and which none the less, seem to be irreconcilable with one another."

But Ryle sees in addition that such "quarrels" really involve *the conflict of two vocabularies, two completely different sets of concepts,* or, as he put it, "the interferences which are unwittingly committed between *different teams of ideas.*" Suppose that one asks: Is there destiny, or does all happen by strict causality? Is there fate, or only prediction? Is the universe dramatic or only factual? The point is that the answers to these questions do not hang merely upon the careful analysis and final definition of such terms as "prediction" and "fate." The three questions are interrelated, their terms are interrelated; it is impossible to deal with the issues raised by one without somehow coming to terms with the others. The nature of this curious conceptual interdependence Ryle saw very well. "I have," he said,[25] "no special objection to, or any special liking for, the fashion of describing as 'analysis' the sort or sorts of conceptual examination which constitutes philosophizing. But *the idea is totally false that this examination is a sort of garage inspection of one conceptual vehicle at a time.* On the contrary, to put it dogmatically, *it is always a traffic-inspector's examination of a conceptual traffic-block, involving at least two streams of vehicles hailing from the theories or points of view or platitudes which are at cross-purposes with one another.*"

Ryle's imagery is, in its own way, as rich and varied as Santayana's, and the profusion of his metaphors should not distract us from the importance of his conception. Whether one visualizes them as "different teams of ideas" fighting it out like stout chaps upon the playing fields of Eton, or "different streams of conceptual vehicles" snarling up the traffic on Regent Street or Charing Cross, the vocabulary of science provides one group of concepts while the vocabulary of religion, literature, and the arts provides quite another. If our preceding historical considerations have taught us anything, it is that the central dualism of ·modern philosophy since Kant (a dualism providing a series of philosophical conflicts, quarrels, and perplexities) produces as its inevitable consequence *the uneasy mutual confrontation of the language of the understanding and the language of the imagination.*

In terms like "true and false propositions," "error," "scientific law," "causality," "chance," "prediction," "fact," "change," "equilibrium," "stasis" we have, then, a series of components in what I will call *the scientific chain of meaning.* In terms like "appearance and reality," "illusion," "destiny," "free will," "fortune," "fate," "drama," "tragedy," "happiness," "peace" we have also a series of components in what I will call *the humanistic complex.* The confrontation of these two provides an excellent illustration of what Ryle has spoken of as quarrels between different lines of thought which are *not* rival solutions of the same problem, but address themselves to different problems; indeed, as I shall add, to different *needs* of our cognitive situation. For it would be a mistake to hold that the scientific chain of meaning and the humanistic complex are mere conceptual bundles without a deeper anchorage in the structure of the mind and *therefore* in the nature of things. The scientific chain of meaning presented below is a characteristic selection from the total language of the understanding, as the humanistic complex is a typical selection from the total language of the imagination, and each represents the linguistic correlative of the performance of a function. And when, in this book, we inquire further into the nature and the purpose of these performances, we shall find ourselves at the heart of those problems concerning the philosophy of literature which I have mentioned before: What is the relation between science and poetry? Does literature give us knowledge? In what consists the function and the value of the imagination?

Let me therefore present in a condensed and schematic form the confrontation which I have suggested:

THE SCIENTIFIC CHAIN OF MEANING	THE HUMANISTIC COMPLEX
(the language of the Understanding)	(the language of the Imagination)
"true" and "false" propositions	"reality" and "appearance"
the problem of "error"	the problem of "illusion"
"causality" and "scientific law"	"destiny" and "human purpose"
"prediction" and "chance"	"fate" and "fortune"
"fact"—"matter of fact"	"drama"—"the dramatic event"
"competition"—"biological growth"	"tragedy"
the "stasis" or "equilibrium" of systems	"peace"

There is an obvious and a crucial difference between the language of the understanding and the language of the imagination, and yet there is a paradoxical similarity between them also. The scientist is concerned with the truth and falsity of propositions, the poet with the appearances and realities of the world, and so the problem which the one deals with under the rubric of "error" the other must consider under the heading of "illusion." Both Einstein and Cervantes are concerned with the nature of "relativity," but scientifically the problem of the tensor calculus is what its application will yield in errors of physical measurement, while the poetic problem of the mind of Don Quixote is the natural history of those illusions which stem from the inability to distinguish fiction from fact. And so throughout our list. The blinding of the unhappy Oedipus is not a matter of "prediction" but of "fate," while, conversely, the incidence of blindness among the new-born to a medical statistician is not a matter of "fate" but of "prediction." The mathematician's account of the continual casting of the dice involves the scientific notion of "chance," but the act by which Desdemona loses her handkerchief to Iago is not an act of "chance" but of "misfortune." And yet, such is the supposedly oppositional character of the scientific chain of meaning and the humanistic complex that positivists (like Reichenbach and Carnap) will insist that to speak of "appearance and reality" is nonsense, and poets (like Eliot and Wallace Stevens) will complain that in a world dominated by the ideology of mechanistic causation, real tragedy is no longer possible.

But our concern is less with the alleged conflict between the specific concepts of "error" and "illusion" or of "destiny" and "scientific law" than with *the general contrast presented by the language of the understanding and the language of the imagination*. The meaning of this contrast can be brought out best, I think, if we ask ourselves what is *the common quality* illustrated respectively by the terms making up *the scientific chain of meaning* and those ingredient in *the humanistic complex*. What is the generic property of terms like "illusion," "destiny," "fate," and "tragedy," and how does this differ from the generic property of terms like "error," "causality," "prediction," and "fact"? If we consider this question in the light of its historical occurrence, we may at first be tempted to answer it in the terms of Ogden and Richards' classic distinction, and to say that the language of the understanding is "referential" while that of the imagination is "emotive." But closer examination will, I think, convince us that this distinction, although not false, is insufficient; it is plausible, but at the same time, since it persuades us to be satisfied with a "property" rather than an "essential characteristic," it manages to conceal what is really there. The essential characteristic of the terms of *the scientific chain of meaning* is not that they are "referential," but that their reference is to *objectivity* and to *factuality*. And the essential characteristic of the terms of *the humanistic complex* is not that they are "emotive," but that such emotivity as they possess is due to their function as vehicles for the expression of *purposiveness* and *drama*.

Appearance and reality, illusion, destiny, free will, fortune, fate, tragedy, and peace:—these terms are tied together by the sense of drama which they evoke and by the purposiveness which is implicit in their use. They therefore point to a specific interpretation of the creative imagination which links it to the particular art form of the drama and to the principles of all teleological judgment. Kant in his *Critique of Pure Reason* attempted an analysis of the faculty of understanding which was to demonstrate the *a priori* conditions necessary for the scientific achievement of objectivity and factuality. And in this book (which attempts the cognate enterprise of providing a critique of the imagination) we shall necessarily discover that the myth-making faculty operates characteristically through *the dramatization of purposiveness* and as such represents *the propensity toward teleological interpretation* in man.

Three / The Teleological Imagination

❘ TO ANYONE interested in the facts of literary or artistic creativity the traditional empiricist accounts of the imagination from Hobbes to Gilbert Ryle are somehow unsatisfactory, strangely meager and thin. Hobbes' theory of imagination as "nothing but decaying sense" requires an identification of imagination and memory which does scant justice to the originative fancy, and his corollary that the vividness of memory varies inversely with the distance in time and place of the original sense experience is a mechanistic mode of explanation which is clearly false to the facts. Nor does his distinction between the simple and the compounded imagination with its theory of creative images as additive properties help our cause. For the conception of the Centaur or the daydreams of the man who "imagines himself a *Hercules* or an *Alexander* (which happeneth often to them that are much taken with reading of Romants)" is presented by Hobbes as a "fiction of the mind" in a sense which is clearly invidious, and which means to preserve us from confusing these erroneous images with the truths of immediate sensory experience.[1]

Nor is Hume appreciably better. He does distinguish (as Hobbes did not) between memory and imagination ("When we remember any past event, the idea of it flows in upon the mind in a forcible manner; whereas in the imagination the perception is faint and languid. . . ."), and he also valuably notes that whereas memory is constrained to preserve the original form and sequence in which its objects were presented, there is a practically unlimited "liberty of the imagination to transpose and change its ideas." He continues:[2] "The fables we meet with in poems and romances put this entirely out of question. Nature there is totally confounded, and nothing mentioned but winged horses, fiery dragons, and monstrous giants." Either Hume has been reading Hobbes, or both have been reading Cervantes, or this is the peculiar way in which the empirical mind works, for the reference in both to the fables to be met with in "romances" indicates a fear of deception likely to be encouraged by the fictional and the fabulous, and, indeed, in any production of literature or fine art where "nature" is liable to be as Hume says, "totally confounded."

For Hume the belief or assent which always attends the memory and the senses (but not the imagination) is nothing but the vivacity of the perceptions they present. This is never a completely reliable criterion for a careful empiricist, since both the memory and the imagination "borrow their simple ideas from impressions and cannot go beyond these original perceptions." And so the danger of confusion remains. Ideas of memory may degenerate in vivacity to such an extent that they may be taken for imaginations, and in the case of habitual liars, contrariwise, "an idea of the imagination may acquire such a force and vivacity as to pass for an idea of the memory, and *counterfeit its effect on the belief and judgment.*"[3] The italics are mine, for I wish to indicate that the words are significant. For Hume no less than for Hobbes the imagination is not so much a source of cognitive delight as a problem. Insofar as it can "counterfeit its effect" upon belief and judgment, it constitutes an epistemic threat—a danger to reliable knowledge.

Gilbert Ryle is the latest epistemologist with whom I am acquainted to deal with the imagination, and, although critical of the details of Hobbes and Hume, he presents an analysis which is, I think, one with them in spirit and which I assume belongs, broadly speaking, to the empirical tradition. Chapter 8 of *The Concept of Mind* deals with this topic, interestingly and in many respects challengingly, but its conclusions can be no more palatable to the aestheticians and philosophers of literature than those of Hobbes and Hume.

From the very beginning they are likely to be mistrustful of the type of mind here at work. Ryle's first chapter is entitled "Descartes' Myth," and while we may at first believe that its provocativeness rests merely upon a metaphor, it soon appears that this is not quite how Ryle himself sees it. Descartes's "myth" is not the myth of Homer or Cassirer; it is not an antique fable or the rationale of the ritual of primitive man. Ryle's own usage makes this unambiguously clear. Descartes's myth is "the official *doctrine*," "the official *theory*"; it is "the *dogma* of the Ghost in the Machine," it is "a category *mistake*." But to put it this way is also a misuse of language. A myth is not a *doctrine*, nor a *theory*, nor yet a *mistake*. These are terms which belong to the language of science; they are not the language appropriate to the mythical imagination. But, far from being a mere metaphor, this usage has been elevated by Ryle himself into a canon of method. In his Introduction he tells us: "A myth is, of course, not a fairy story. It is the presentation of facts belonging to one category in the idiom appropriate to another. To explode a myth is accordingly not to deny the facts but to re-allocate them. And this is what I am trying to do."[4]

But we must respond: On the contrary! A fairy story *is* one species of what the genus myth comprehends, and "the presentation of facts belonging to one category in the idiom appropriate to another" is just what a myth *is not*. It may seem that this is a definitional issue, a futile quarrel over the meaning of a word where, obviously, either party has the right to define the word as he wishes provided only that the stipulation be unambiguous. But I think there is more to it than this. I think that Ryle's usage indicates that he has made a mistake, and that it is a category mistake. For what Ryle says he is interested in is to explode the myth, and when attention to his argument indicates that this is for him equivalent to *showing that an accepted theory is false* (and that a falsehood has, unfortunately, become an accepted belief) we must reply that, ironically, he has himself committed the very error from which he is most passionately concerned to save us: *he has presented facts belonging to one category in the idiom appropriate to another.* Exploding a myth is not proving that a theory is false (if, indeed, a word like "exploding" is justified in the domain of myth at all), for, as we have seen, whereas the criteria of truth and falsity are eminently appropriate in the scientific universe of discourse, they are unsuitable to the realm of discourse of the mythological. Ryle's confusion stems from the fact that he has illegitimately appropriated a term from the humanistic complex to illuminate the scientific chain of meaning.

When Ryle does finally get to the imagination, he has some interesting things to say. He wants mainly to puncture the habit of ascribing some "other-worldly reality to the imaginary, and then to treat minds as the clandestine habitats of such fleshless beings." This causes him to assert a series of theses of the following order. (1) What we call imagination involves less of what we call "seeing" or "picturing" than what we call "pretending." (2) There are multiple functions of imagination, and thus no single "common nuclear operation" which is to be found in each of its exemplifications. (3) Memory is not a process of searching for pictures but of presenting or narrating that which has been learned. The last is not precisely to our point, but I hope to show later that in both (1) and (2) Ryle, even where possibly substantively mistaken, is on the trail of something of real importance. At any rate, in the course of the presentation of these points, Ryle does a considerable amount of remedial epistemology. He criticizes (tellingly, I think) Hume's distinction between impressions and ideas, he practically demolishes the theory that imaginary picturing is looking at reproductions of sense data, and he almost persuades us that it is false to believe that the relation of a visual image to a visual sensation is "like the relation of an echo to a noise, a bruise to a blow, or a reflection in a mirror to the face reflected."[5] But setting Hume right and reproving naïve empiricism is, after all, very much the same enterprise by means of which Hume sets Hobbes right, and naïve empiricism reproves naïve rationalism. It is polemical for the sake of correction.

The empiricist account of the imagination is needlessly thin because it is like the endeavor of those specialists in public health who are so obsessed with the prevention of epidemics that they do not explore comprehensively the positive regimen which is the high road to general health. The psychology of avoidance is valuable, but it is the negative way. Ryle himself, like Hume, is so devoted to "exploding" our myths, "vaccinating" us against false theory, and guarding us against "cognitive malpractices" that he only incidentally touches upon those features of the creative imagination which we need to understand for a reasonable interpretation of the ultimate meaning of literature and the arts. Empiricism (and Ryle with it) is oriented to the prevention of epistemological error. But no mere antisepsis of the imagination can hope, I think, to understand the humanistic complex and the area of human experience for which it stands.

2 THE EMPIRICIST mistrusts the imagination because it seems to threaten the clarity of the understanding, but his account of imaginative functioning is still dominated by the same mechanistic principles in terms of which the understanding is itself explained. This is why the empirical beginnings of Hobbes, Locke, and Hume passed so effortlessly into the associationism of Hartley and

James Mill. Any merely empirical treatment of the imagination as an adjunct of cognition will see it as a "changing," a "transposing," or an "associative" power, but hardly as a "creating," a "forming," or a "synthesizing" one. For the shift to the latter we must wait for the idealist tradition and particularly for Kant. But Kant himself (as we have already noted) was too obsessed with the theory that imagination is a mere instrument in the service of theoretical knowledge to explore its independent claims. The imagination for him produces a synthesis which is an expression of spontaneity, and is thus not merely a reproductive activity entirely subject to the empirical laws of association. Its place *between* the sensibility and the understanding shows its mediating function and its transitional utility. It produces knowledge, not poems or objects of imitation.

It was the purpose of Coleridge's theory of the imagination to take over from Kant the creative or formative quality of imagination and to elevate it to an independent status outside of the process of mere cognition. This he does through his distinction between the Primary and the Secondary imagination.[6]

The imagination then I consider either as primary, or secondary. The primary Imagination I hold to be the living power and prime agent of all human perception, and as a repetition in the finite mind of the eternal act of creation in the infinite I AM. The secondary Imagination I consider as an echo of the former, co-existing with the conscious will, yet still as identical with the primary in the *kind* of its agency, and differing only in *degree*, and in the *mode* of its operation. It dissolves, diffuses, dissipates, in order to re-create: or where this process is rendered impossible, yet still at all events it struggles to idealize and to unify. It is essentially *vital*, even as all objects (*as* objects) are essentially fixed and dead.

The essential quality of the secondary imagination is its *plasticity;* in this it is to be distinguished from "Fancy," which is, indeed, little more than "a mode of memory emancipated from the order of time and space" which can playfully rearrange those fixities of sensation received in the course of our perceptual experiences. It seems clear from the surrounding pages of the *Biographia Literaria* that Coleridge is not proposing a new epistemology, but simply an expansion of the basic Kantian terms which might serve the purposes of literary criticism—which might make intelligible the guiding principles of a new poetics. For if Fancy is merely an associationism of the mind, while Imagination represents its essential creativity as the "esemplastic power"—the bringing into oneness—it should be possible to describe and evaluate objects of imitation or works of art according to the degree of unity which they exhibit. Thus, for example, Shakespeare's *Lear*, quite apart from the curious symmetry of its plot construction and the repetitive duality which only buttresses its dominant theme, carries a series of allusions that massively reinforce the two cognate images which are the focus of the play—the contrast between "nature" and "the unnatural" and its physiological correlative, the contrast between "sight" and its privative "blindness." From Lear's "Out of my *sight!*" to Kent in the first scene to his "I'll *see* that straight" (also to Kent) in the very last, the play provides a perfect "organic unity" of images. But in a conceited lyric of Abraham Cowley or Richard Lovelace, although there is gaiety, wit, and profusion of images, they work only as a mere federation—a loose aggregate of externally related metaphors. And so, in Coleridge's view, would it be in larger works also. Where experience is atomized, where the "slice of life" point of view prevails, there the Fancy will be manifest. But in whatever example of epic or drama is expressed "an integral view of life," the Imagination is at work.

It is clear that this emphasis upon "integration" or "organic unification" is crucial to Coleridge's critical theory, and that it makes poetry (both the product and the process) rest upon a theory of the imagination. A poem differs from a work of science in that its immediate object is pleasure rather than truth, but it differs also from all other types of composition by the way in which it emphasizes "such delight from the *whole"* as is compatible with gratification from the component parts. The poetic or imaginative power *as such* is dominated by "the sense of wholeness." "The poet, described in ideal perfection, brings the whole soul of man into activity, with the subordination of its faculties to each other according to their relative worth and dignity. He diffuses a tone and spirit of unity, that blends and (as it were) *fuses*, each into each, by that synthetic and magical power, to which I would exclusively appropriate the name of Imagination."[7]

From Coleridge onward in British philosophical thought (and particularly in Bradley and Bosanquet), the theory of imagination has become a theory of mental functioning in general, claiming finally even for the understanding the esemplastic function which Coleridge reserved for the imagination alone. And finally in our own time Brand Blanshard, in affirming that "invention is merely purpose assuming authority over the course of ideas," invokes that Bosanquet for whom the principles of logic and the principles of aesthetics exemplify the same ultimate commitment. "Our contention in short, is nothing less than this, that in the mind of the successful thinker the spirit of logic itself is at work leavening the unformed mass, and that in the mind of the creative artist the spirit of beauty is at work, supplying both ends and means. A 'nisus toward wholeness' as Bosanquet would call it, is everywhere the spring of thought."[8] It seems almost gratuitous to add that for that contemporary Coleridgean, T. S. Eliot, Bosanquet's "nisus toward wholeness" becomes the very criterion which distinguishes the poetic mode of experience from that of the common man. "When a poet's mind is perfectly equipped for its work, it is constantly amalgamating disparate experience; the ordinary man's experience is chaotic, irregular, fragmentary. The latter falls in love, or reads Spinoza, and these two experiences have nothing to do with each other, or with the noise of the typewriter or the smell of the cooking; in the mind of the poet these experiences are always forming new wholes."[9]

The idealist correction of the narrowness of the empirical

estimate of the function and scope of the imagination is valuable, and I shall subsequently try to show in detail how the "nisus toward wholeness" upon which it insists does express a crucial aspect of the imagination viewed as a teleological instrument. But in correcting the epistemological atomism of the empirical position, idealism proceeds to compound an opposite felony. In insisting upon the similarity in spirit of logic and aesthetics, Bosanquet, like the empiricists (but of course in a directly opposite fashion) succeeds in blurring the crucial distinction between the imagination and the understanding. The empiricist sees them both as illustrating the mechanistic principle. The idealist sees them both as functioning in the pursuit of organic wholeness. But this is to compromise the cognitive dualism to which our previous distinction between "the scientific chain of meaning" and "the humanistic complex" has called attention. The language of the understanding suggests a mechanical mode of functioning which is admirably suited to a universe of logical interrelations. The language of the imagination points to an organicity which operates so as to provide an aesthetic counterpart of human needs which a universe of impersonal logical relationships must necessarily ignore. And this becomes slowly apparent only as we direct our attention less to the descriptive question: How in fact does the imagination work? than to the normative question: What is the value of imagination? and indeed to the further question: Why should there have been an imagination at all?

But to be able to ask this question presupposes the idealistic revolution. For it was the suggestions of Kant and Schelling, augmented by Coleridge's peculiar genius, which led to the passage from the "reproductive" to the "productive" conception of imagination and from the more primitive treatment of imagination as combination, arrangement, and grouping to the more poetic treatment where the function of imagination was "to invent" rather than "to perceive." When imaginative invention becomes familiar as the process which

creates metaphors, allegories, and symbols, then for the first
time the ambiguous notion of the "image" becomes less that
of an Aristotelian "phantasm" than of a Coleridgean literary
device. This in itself has considerable significance. It marks
the passage from the notion of "the visual image" (which is
"the copy of a sensation") to the "figure of speech"—what I. A.
Richards speaks of as "a double unit involving a comparison."[10] When this transition has been made, then we are beyond the literal boundaries of time and space and into that
obscure twilight zone where the imagination has become a
vehicle for the creation of fictions rather than a tool for the
apprehension of an objective reality. To pass from the "realistic" to the "projective" outlook is to sense the relevance of
the creative imagination to the necessities of human feeling.
It might even be urged (as Ribot did) that in all problems of
the creative imagination, the emotional element is the primal,
originating factor. All invention presupposes a want, a craving, an unsatisfied impulse; therefore the urgencies of poetry
are akin to those of myth, legend, and prophecy. Thus arises
the fruitful suggestion that in addition to the shaped substance of poetic imagery, primitive myths and religious conceptions grow out of the fertile soil of imaginative need. The
suggestion has its roots not only in Coleridge, but in the
leading figures of the German romantic movement. But its
flowering appears in our own time in the philosophies of
Santayana and particularly of Cassirer, and it is to his culminating work that I should now like to turn.

3 THE ENORMOUS value of Cassirer's work
lies in the way in which his meticulous investigations of symbolic forms are guided by the twin guard-
ians of a critical and a cultural interest. Kant is never far
from his horizon. When he wishes to distinguish between
myth, empirical science, and mathematics, the Kantian frame

is before his mind, and the "immediacy" of the mythical image, the "classificatory" nature of the scientific structure, and the "purity" of the mathematical concept suggest at once to him the threefold operations of the sensibility, the understanding, and the reason. But Cassirer's endeavors are informed by much more than the attempt to construct a "critical" epistemology. Here the influence of Kant must share its kingdom with that of Hegel (supplemented, of course, by Vico and Schelling). A critique of reason in the formal eighteenth-century pattern is supplemented by the attempt to construct a philosophy of human *culture* (in the spiritual rather than the sociological sense) as the nineteenth-century German romantics hoped to do. The outcome of Cassirer's *The Philosophy of Symbolic Forms* and his shorter, but more comprehensive, *An Essay On Man* is, therefore, not unlike that of Hegel's philosophical corpus—it is an attempt to produce a kind of "phenomenology of the human spirit." But whereas Hegel is limited by the requirements of his logic, and the disdain of empirical materials which his logical *a priori* imposes, Cassirer in his philosophy of culture can draw at will upon the vast resources of psychological, ethnological, historical, and linguistic researches which the decades since Hegel have produced. He is not the slave of the empirical materials, but he is lavish in their use as adjuncts to his essentially philosophic enterprise.

It must be admitted at the outset that Cassirer's work does not contain a unified and thoroughly articulated theory of the imagination. We shall not, for example, find him (as we shall Bergson) directly attempting to answer the question: Why should there have been an imagination at all? or giving the imagination its due function within the setting of evolutionary necessity. Rather Cassirer addresses himself to the descriptive question: How in fact does the imagination work? But in so doing, he does not completely avoid the problem of evaluation either. Unlike the positivistic tendency first exemplified in Comte (which assumes a hierarchy of cultural development by which mankind gradually sloughs off fictions, mythical beliefs, and animistic modes of thought until at last the scientific method has become the exclusive criterion of reliable knowledge, and man confronts empirical reality—"the facts"—directly, and without the deceptive glass of his feelings, desires, and subjective images and ideas), the effect of Cassirer's treatment of symbolic forms is the recognition that they are permanent qualities of human mentality. This suggests not only a tolerance of all these various cultural forms for their distinctly human quality, but a willingness to discern utility in the multiple ways in which mentality operates in making sense out of the human experience. Thus even the patient and attentive concern with the question: How in fact does the imagination work? implies the belief that the imagination has value.

If Cassirer does not propose a general theory of the imagination (literally employing the word itself), he does provide its equivalent in his conception of *the symbolic system*, that "new dimension of reality". which defines the human situation in contrast with its merely animal origins.

No longer in a merely physical universe, man lives in a symbolic universe. Language, myth, art, and religion are parts of this universe. They are the varied threads which weave the symbolic net, the tangled web of human experience. . . . Physical reality seems to recede in proportion as man's symbolic activity advances. Instead of dealing with the things themselves man is in a sense constantly conversing with himself. He has so enveloped himself in linguistic forms, in artistic images, in mythical symbols or religious rites that he cannot see or know anything except by the interposition of this artificial medium. His situation is the same in the theoretical as in the practical sphere. Even here man does not live in a world of hard facts, or according to his immediate needs and desires. He lives rather in the midst of imaginary emotions, in hopes and fears, in illusions and disillusions, in his fantasies and dreams.[11]

Nor is this world of "imaginary emotions," hopes, and fears formless and chaotic, a crude mass of superstitions or gross delusions. It has structure and conceptual form, although the language in which it expresses itself is not the language of the understanding—what I have called the scientific chain of meaning. For, as Cassirer says, "side by side with conceptual language there is an emotional language; side by side with logical or scientific language there is a language of poetic imagination."[12] It is this "emotional language"—the language of poetic imagination—which constitutes the humanistic complex.

But in the diversity of the multiple products of art, myth, and religion is it possible to discern a unity of function, or must we agree with Ryle that although there are multiple functions of imagination, there is no single "common nuclear operation" which is to be found in each of its diversifications? In answering this question Cassirer wishes (in good Kantian fashion) to preserve for imagination a unity of form and genesis, while at the same time repudiating the scholastic theory of the mind as *object* which, even in the faculty psychology of the eighteenth century, seemed to reify and substantialize what was in fact a *power* and not a substance.

The philosophy of symbolic forms starts from the presupposition that, if there is any definition of the nature or "essence" of man, this definition can only be understood as a functional one, not a substantial one. . . . Man's outstanding characteristic, his distinguishing mark, is not his metaphysical or physical nature—but his work. It is this work, it is the system of human activities which defines and determines the circle of "humanity." A "philosophy of man" would therefore be a philosophy which would give us insight into the fundamental structure of each of these human activities, and which at the same time would enable us to understand them as an organic whole. *Language, art, myth, religion are no isolated, random creations. They are held together by a common bond.* But this bond is not a *vinculum substantiale*, as it was conceived and described in scholastic thought; it is rather a *vinculum functionale*. It is the basic function of speech, of myth, of art, of religion that we must seek far behind their innumerable shapes and utterances, and that in the last analysis we must attempt to trace back to a common origin.[13]

What is that common bond which unites language, myth, religion, and art? What is the basic function and the common origin which they share? If in Cassirer's work these questions are not given an explicit answer, they are implicitly covered in that section of his philosophy of symbolic forms where his thought is at its most original—in his critique of the mythical consciousness. In the explication of myth—its forms, its matter, its inner logic—Cassirer provides a phenomenology of imaginative working whose relevance to religion and art becomes increasingly clear. Of the three, it is myth which is the anterior construction, and one aspect of the dialectic of culture is the natural history of imaginative functioning as it passes from myth to religion and from religion to art. The concluding section of *Mythical Thought* (*The Philosophy of Symbolic Forms:* Volume Two), entitled "The Dialectic of the Mythical Consciousness," is a brilliant formulation of the ontological problems growing out of the passage from myth to religion, and if the passage from religion to art is only hinted at in Chapter 9 of *An Essay on Man*, this is because the work in which it was to be definitively expressed, the *Aesthetics* (which was to have been Cassirer's culminating achievement) he did not live to complete.

The mythical consciousness is engaged above all in the construction of a world of pure imagination, and, just as myth is an indirect expression of the nature of reality, it is also in a certain sense a preparation for philosophy. But insofar as the myth (as for example in Plato) seems to stand over against the process of rational argument, it is an impediment to the rational factor in the reflection upon experience in which philosophy engages. The quarrel between Plato and the Sophists (whom he never tired of ridiculing and opposing) is, therefore, in some sense a dramatic conflict between the claims of the imagination and of the understanding. The mythical imagination may not be subject to those forms of rationality by means of which the understanding orders the empirical manifold of original sensations, but it is nevertheless far from producing a composite of "meaningless" ideas and "arbitrary" fictions. It must be viewed as *a teleological instrument,* a structured and far from arbitrary presentation of a picture of the world—representing the earliest form of aesthetic fantasy, but serving not to *mirror* the external world so much as to *master* it: to hold it at arm's length and to keep it in its place. My dichotomy of "mirroring" and "mastery" is used advisedly. Mirroring suggests doing justice to the objective claims of that which powerfully exists in its own right. Mastery suggests adapting, forming, bending to the requirements of a subjective necessity. The typical primitive examples of mythical thinking are demonic objects, haunted places, strange clouds or other shapes in nature hinting at the ominous and the portentous. Together in their unorganized heterogeneity they constitute *a suggestive universe* where the "suggestiveness" indicates good or evil, safety or violence, life or death. The world is mysterious, magical, holy. It is a plenum of tabooed objects, demonic powers, miraculous interventions. All this is only to say that it is *full of purposes and saturated with values.* And this empire of practical responses and of imaginative rendering of impressions is an altogether different edition of mentality from that of the understanding, which patterns the material world by logic, classes objects neutrally according to their objective properties and relations, and claims the laws of causality as its own.

4 "THE PHILOSOPHICAL understanding of myth," says Cassirer,[14] "begins with the insight that it does not move in a purely invented or made-up world but has its own mode of *necessity* and therefore, in accordance with the idealist concept of the object, its own mode of reality." Out of the need to master the external world grows a second form of "objectivization" which myth itself accomplishes, and thereby permits consciousness to free itself from passive captivity to sensory impressions and to

create a special world of its own in accordance with its own needs. If the primitive origins of myth arise in an uncriticized intuition of the magical force inherent in all things, this is less representative of a primitive form of cognition than of a propensity to construe the universe itself according to the model of affectivity and will. This is perhaps in no small degree the reason for its failure to make the usual sharp empirical distinctions: between the world of dream and the world of waking reality; between the condition of life and the condition of death; between the principle of causality and the principle of casual association. But the relation between the realm of affectivity and will and the problem of mastery is very close. Nature, as the primitive knows, yields nothing without ceremonies. And those magic and mysterious rites which assure fertility, or secure identification with the powers that be, perform an effective action in that mode of imitation to which can be traced the impulse of all dramatic art.

But perhaps the most crucial distinction between the logic of the understanding and the "logic" of the imagination is illustrated in the contrast between "the lawlike" and "the arbitrary," "the necessary" and "the contingent" as this contrast is applicable to mythical and scientific thought. The mythical imagination has no place for the concept of "the accidental." Sickness, misfortune, catastrophe, death are never accidental, but due to magical intervention or malign influence.

In this light, mythical thinking seems to be so far from an arbitrary lawlessness that on the contrary we are tempted rather to speak of a kind of hypertrophy of the causal "instinct" and of a need for causal explanation. Indeed, the proposition that nothing in the world happens by accident and everything by conscious purpose has sometimes been called fundamental to the mythical world view. . . . *Myth . . . begins with the intuition of purposive action*— for all the forces of nature are for myth nothing other than expressions of a demonic or divine will. This principle constitutes the source of light, which for myth progressively illuminates the whole of reality and outside of which there is no possibility of understanding the world.[15]

It is just here that the Kantian philosophy (as I have suggested in the preceding chapter) moves curiously between the poles of scientific and imaginative thought. The *Critique of Pure Reason* explores the scientific understanding as it subsumes the individual event under the molds of uniformity which make possible the emergence of scientific law. But the *Critique of Judgment* moves in the atmosphere of another category entirely. The guiding concept here is the principle of purpose, and the principle of purpose from the standpoint of the first *Critique* would be merely the principle of "the lawfulness of the accidental."

Cassirer's comparison of the empirical-scientific and the mythical world view makes it evident that apart from the crucial distinction between factual neutrality and· purposiveness, they do not make use of essentially different categories in the Kantian sense. Space, time, and number (for example) also qualify the mythic world. It is, however, clear that they are employed with a difference. "It is not the quality of these categories but their *modality* which distinguishes myth from empirical-scientific knowledge."[16] Thus in mythical representation space is *magical,* time is *spiritual,* and number is *sacred.* Unity also works differently in the two spheres. For science it means the unity of the world as a hierarchy of laws or of the corpus of science as a graded series of propositions ordered by increasing generality. For myth there may be a hierarchy of forces and of powers, but the basic distinctions and differentiations upon which scientific unification depends are here discarded or lost. "Things which come into contact with one another in a mythical sense—whether this contact is taken as a spatial or temporal contiguity or as a similarity, however remote, or as membership in the same class or species—have fundamentally ceased to be a multiplicity: they have acquired a substantial unity."[17]

It is the strategy not only of the mythical, but also of the *mystical*, which is but the mythic impulse given its furthest religious extension, and it is reminiscent of the form of perception which again and again shows itself in Eliot's later poetry.

> Time present and time past
> Are both perhaps present in time future,
> And time future contained in time past.
> If all time is eternally present
> All time is unredeemable.
> What might have been is an abstraction
> Remaining a perpetual possibility
> Only in a world of speculation.
> What might have been and what has been
> Point to one end, which is always present.[18]

Here the simple temporal series of past, present, future (historically accurate in terms of calendar location or physically related as instants registered on chronometers or by the correlation of light signals) becomes a mystical unity in which distinctions are purposefully and meaningfully blurred in order to present an enigma—the unity of the temporal viewed as the intersection of time and eternity. "To be present in," "to be contained in," "possibility" and "end" working with the fullest of controlled ambiguity suggest the scientific paradox (but the mythic commonplace) of plural dimensions dissolved into unity. Mythical thinking transforms this paradox into a fine art. And what Cassirer calls "this characteristic law of the *Concrescence or coincidence of the members of a relation in mystical thinking*"[19] holds not only for the category of *time*, but also for *quantity* and *relation*. The mythical world view not only blurs the distinctions of past, present, and future, but systematically fails to maintain the distinction between a whole and its parts or between a thing and its attributes.

For mythical thought the categories of space, time, and number operate with an analogous logic. It is fundamental to Cassirer's whole point of view that the contents of the mythical consciousness are joined into a whole, and that they "form a self-enclosed realm and possess a common totality" whereby they are distinguished from the contents of ordinary empirical existence. This characterization of "an isolated, self-sufficient realm of discourse" holds for the imagination from the most primitive and magical of its levels to the highest manifestations of the religious and aesthetic impulse. There is "revelation" and "mystery" and "sacredness"; these are but the qualities of phenomena viewed with exclusive relevance to human emotion and human purpose. A virtually Pythagorean identification of number and value finds its analogue in an equal identification of value with space and time. The mythical intuition of space is clearly distinguishable from the abstract properties of the extensive continuum given in pure cognition by the way in which it (the former) is grounded in the human feeling from which it is inseparable. The understanding may require a concept of space and time as "pure" and "empty" forms of sensuous intuition, but for the mythical consciousness they are never either pure or empty, but great mysterious forces which govern all things.

If, as Cassirer believes, there are, indeed, different types or strata of spatial and temporal experience,[20] it is important to distinguish (1) the *perceptual* space of physiological optics from (2) the *abstract* space of Democritus and Newton, and from both of these (3) the *organic* space (or the space of possible action) upon which the mythical world view is founded. Space for the primitive mind is like a magnetic field filled with nameless dangers which is nonetheless a line of direction through which the courses of action must be charted and pursued. It is related to fearfulness and peril or to safety and the promotion of life. Neither objective, abstract, nor directly measurable, such space has egocentric and anthropomorphic characteristics. Immediately related to practical action for the primitive, it may be subtilized and refined into poetic forms of the symbolic imagination of the kind which have also left their imprint upon the European literary tradition.

However rudimentary as science, Plato's doctrine of the receptacle (the *Timaeus*), Aristotle's idea of place (*Physics*, Book IV) and Democritus' conception of the void (*De Rerum Natura*) represent the approach of the understanding to the cosmological problem. But in Homer and his literary representation of reality appears the expression of that same legendary and imaginative space which Cassirer has attributed to the mythical imagination. Victor Bérard spent his life in charting the navigations of Odysseus through the literal geography of the Mediterranean world as we know it,[21] and we are indebted to him (as any scientific age must be) for showing the rugged contours of fact emerging from the mists of myth. But to be assured that the stones which Polyphemus-Vesuvius hurled at the departing Greeks are the islands of Ischia and Procida off the bay of Naples, that the Ferracine promontory with its sanctuary of Feronia is Circe's Isle, and that it was somewhere between Capri and the Sorrento mainland that the Sirens sang their reckless song, is to jar us rudely away from the inherent qualities of the Homeric world. Even if it should be true (as Bérard believes) that the *Odyssey* is a typical Phoenician *periplous* (mariner's logbook) transposed into Greek verse according to certain very simple and typically Hellenic principles, we do not like to be reminded (particularly if we are romantic) of the creaking machinery which controls the stage. To recognize as techniques the anthropomorphic personification of objects, the humanization of natural forces, and the specific Hellenization of the raw materials distracts our attention from the Homeric *drama* in which the weary human adventurer seeks Home, and where the parable of the eternal return is told in terms of a space full of fateful objects (be they rocks, promontories, or straits) and the dynamic movement which is the restless ecstacy of the wine-dark sea. Homeric space is no Democritean void or Newtonian matrix of mathematical relations. It is a plenum of magical powers—friendly in Aeolus, cruel with Scylla and Charybdis—but meaningful because heavily laden with value properties and infinitely relevant to the purposes of the hero. "Space" for Odysseus means the alternative possibilities of life endangered or life secure, and its challenge is to his wisdom or to his folly.

The principles of the presentation of imaginary space become even more explicit when we turn to Dante. For *The Inferno* is no empirical journey mythologized, but a constructed artificial space in which the furniture of the imaginary landscape becomes the living symbol of a moral hierarchy. Inert matter is here given the vitality of organic life, as organic life becomes the repository of spiritual decay. The violent against their fellow men choke and drown in the river of boiling blood, while the violent against themselves are the gnarled and twisted branches on which the Harpies feed. Blood and ice, mud and excrement, biting wind and crushing rock, suffocating water and scorching fire proclaim the magic whereby the innocent four elements of Aristotle's *De Generatione et Corruptione* are transmuted into devilish instruments or parables of evil. And as we follow the contours of hell across the raging rivers, skirting the fiery pits and down the violent precipices of sharpest rock, we have the practical devices of mythical thought converted into the literary devices of the pure imagination. Perhaps not completely pure, for the representation of reality can never be completely abandoned. Even the similes of spiritual portraiture remain those of the natural world. The carnal sinners troop by as flying cranes or starlings; as frogs flee from their enemy the serpent, so the fallen angels pass before the poet; the uneven sepulchres of the heretics are like the stagnant waters at Arles or at Pola; the banks of Phlegethon are like those of the rivers at Bruges and at Padua; Brunetto Latini, though a shade, runs like a racer at Verona; as the Venetian shipbuilders boil the clammy pitch in their arsenal, so in boiling pitch are the Barrators engulfed; as a peasant looking down into the valley at twilight sees the twinkling fireflies, so the poet observes the flickering flames of the eighth chasm.

And just as Victor Bérard charted the voyages of Odysseus from Troy to the pillars of Hercules, so there have been those who have attempted to trace through the evidence of Dante's similes in *The Divine Comedy* the actual route of the wanderings of the exiled Florentine poet in the north of Europe, and his life experiences in the countryside of his birth. But this misplaced naturalism is as philosophically inappropriate to the epic of Dante as to that of Homer. For what we ought to recognize here are the mythic categories of space and time removed from their original location as the matrix of primitive practical activity, only to reappear poetically transmuted in the major works of the European imagination.

5 I HAVE suggested (and an analogous suggestion appears in Cassirer also) that myth, religion, and poetry form the great triad of the humanistic complex which is grounded in the necessary workings of the human imagination. But to note that these three are all examples of the imagination at work is perhaps to blur important distinctions between them. These distinctions depend less upon differences in the products of a nuclear operation of mind than upon differences of attitude by which these products are accompanied. It is easy to demonstrate that the mythical categories of organic space and time reappear in Homer and Dante as qualities of the literary imagination, but also easy to forget that in the primitive world view these categories determine the decisions of men and eventuate in fateful forms of action, whereas in literature they merely constitute the structure of a world of make-believe poetically contemplated. It is easy likewise to point to the common mythic elements in poetry and religion without sufficiently emphasizing that in the latter these organize a system of belief—even a

system of epistemic commitment—whereas in the former (poetry) we have merely that temporary "as if"—that "willing
suspension of disbelief for the moment" of which Coleridge
spoke. Within this trilogy of myth—religion—poetry many
confusions are possible. Santayana (as we shall see), by neglect-
ing the religious claim to being a system of true belief, can
blur beyond the possibility of distinction the boundary between the domains of religion and poetry. On the other hand
the Romantics (men like Schlegel and Novalis) could see no
difference between myth and reality, poetry and abstract
truth. So that when Novalis says "Poetry is what is absolutely
and genuinely real. . . . The more poetic the more true," he
is, in effect, denying the crucial distinction between the understanding and the imagination upon which a reasonable
epistemology must be based.

Cassirer himself is not completely satisfactory in this matter of imaginative relationships. His treatment of poetry is
undeveloped. His account of mythical thinking is perhaps the
heart of what he has to offer us. He is least precise in his
treatment of religion. Nonetheless if we attend to his account
of religion as it emerges from myth, we shall arrive at an important conclusion concerning the essential purpose behind
the functioning of the religious imagination.

Cassirer's failure to distinguish clearly and distinctly between myth and religion is perhaps less a failure of analysis
on his part than a characteristic ambiguity in the subject matter. It is precisely his point that in fact the two are hardly
distinguishable. "The further back we follow it toward its
origins, the less the content of religious consciousness can be
distinguished from that of mythical consciousness. The two
are so interwoven that they can nowhere be definitely separated and set off from each other. If we attempt to isolate
and remove the basic mythical components from religious
belief, we no longer have religion in its real, objectively historical manifestation; all that remains is a shadow of it, an
empty abstraction."[22] The fact is that the archaic images of

the mythical fantasy continue to reappear in religious dogma long after their original ritual meanings have been lost, and this holds true whether one is dealing with a religion of action like Mohammedanism, a religion of suffering like Christianity, a culture religion like Confucianism, or a pure nature religion like Taoism. If there is a contrast between religion and myth, it lies in the fact that religion introduces distinctions of which the unified mythical world view is incapable: first the epistemological one—that between illusion and religious reality; and second the semantic one—that between the symbol and the religious reality for which it stands. If myth points to a unidimensional world of total magic potency, the religious world is based upon a dualism of mundane objects and their transcendent spiritual significance. "What appears to the common, profane view as the immediately given reality of 'things' is transformed by the religious view into a world of 'signs.' The specifically religious point of view is indeed determined by this reversal. All physical and material things, every substance and every action, now become metaphoric, the corporeal, imaged expression of a spiritual meaning."[23] The all-embracing totemism of preliterate Australia has become the stratified symbolic consciousness of the mediaeval mind.

But what is important here is less the distinction between the mythical and the religious imagination than the ideology, the *motivation* which they express in common. What, in short, is the function which they perform in the life of man? For Cassirer the most fundamental feature of myth and religion is the deep conviction they express of the fundamental *solidarity of life*. Nature is a single domain in which everything is alive. Every animal, every plant participates in the vast society of the living. And it follows (although differently in the two cases) that for both the Australian aborigine and the mediaeval Christian the feeling of the indestructible unity of life is so strong and unshakable as to deny and defy the fact of death. Many mythical tales are concerned with the

origin of death. The conception that man is mortal, by his nature and essence, seems to be entirely alien to mythical and
primitive religious thought. . . . If anything is in need of
proof it is not the fact of immortality but the fact of death.
And myth and primitive religion never admit these proofs.
They emphatically deny the very possibility of death. In a
certain sense the whole of mythical thought may be interpreted as a constant and obstinate negation of the phenomenon of death. . . . Primitive religion is perhaps the strongest
and most energetic affirmation of life that we find in human
culture."[24] In this passage we find an important clue to the
major utility of the mythical and the religious imagination.

Myth and religion are both *objectifications*. They are the
way in which bare emotion is transformed into an expression,
into an *image*. And this transformation is expressed most
characteristically in those emotions related to death.

Myth, and religion in general, have often been declared to be a
mere product of fear. But what is most essential in man's religious
life is not the fact of fear, but the *metamorphosis* of fear. Fear is a
universal biological instinct. It can never be completely overcome
or suppressed, but it can change its form. Myth is filled with the
most violent emotions and the most frightful visions. But in myth
man begins to learn a new and strange art: the art of expressing,
and that means of organizing, his most deeply rooted instincts, his
hopes and fears.

This power of organization appears in its greatest strength when
man is confronted with the greatest problem—that of death. . . .[25]

The myths of death are universal. They appear among the
tribes of central Australia described by Spencer and Gillen,
in the Trobriand Islanders reported by Malinowski, in the
sacred writings of the Manicheans, and in the central mystery
of the Christian religion. And in all these guises and mutations they perform a common service.

Primitive man could not be reconciled with the fact of death; he
could not be persuaded to accept the destruction of his personal

existence as an inevitable natural phenomenon. But it was the very fact that was denied and "explained away" by myth. Death, it taught, means no extinction of man's life; it means only a change in the form of life. One form of existence is simply exchanged for another. . . . In mythical thought the mystery of death is "turned into an image"—and by this transformation, death ceases being a hard unbearable physical fact; it becomes understandable and supportable.[26]

In a sense we have here a solution of the central problem of the imagination. Its original utility is that through it *"the mystery of death is turned into an image,"* and all that follows from this for religious thought, as well as the many transformations through which imagination passes in order to create the modes of poetry and the forms of art, must be interpreted as generous mutations (which culture makes possible) of an original impulse almost "biological" in its functioning. And to put it this way—to pass from the level of symbolic forms to that of evolutionary necessity—is to be cognizant less of the suggestions of Cassirer than of those of Bergson. In the two passages from *The Myth of the State* which I have just quoted, there is an unmistakable Bergsonian flavor. Such suggestions do not appear in *The Philosophy of Symbolic Forms* written two decades earlier, and it is a fair assumption, therefore, that this insight, which supplies a missing link (and therefore, in a sense, completes *Mythical Thought*), has been derived from *The Two Sources of Morality and Religion*.[27]

The chief originality of that book is that in it Bergson, by giving biology the widest possible meaning, can conclude that all morality, whether that of pressure or aspiration, and all religion, whether that of institutional conformity or mystical communion, is, in essence, *biological*. The problem of religion is this: It is "absurd," yet it is universal. Why? Or, stated more impersonally and as a comment: "L'homo sapiens, *seul être doué de raison, est le seul aussi qui puisse suspendre son existence à des choses déraisonnables.*" It is not merely primitive mentality which is here in question. Men today also permit themselves as reasonable beings to be guided by superstitions and by myths.

These representations which appear as "images" may be classed as a whole as imagination, and it is "myth-making" or "fictionizing" which produces them.

Let us take, then, in the vaguely and doubtless artificially defined realm of imagination, the natural "cut" which we have called myth-making and see to what use it is naturally put. To this faculty are due the novel, the drama, mythology together with all that preceded it. But then, there have not always been novelists and dramatists, whereas humanity has never subsisted without religion. Very likely, therefore, poetry and fantasy of all kinds appeared as extras, benefiting from the fact that the mind knew how to make myths, but religion is what accounts for the myth-making function: that faculty standing to religion in the relationship of effect and not of cause. Some need, individual perhaps, social in any case, must have required from the mind this type of mental activity. Let us ask what this need was. It must be noted that fiction, when it has the power to move us, resembles an incipient hallucination: it can thwart our judgment and reason, which are the strictly intellectual faculties. Now what would nature have done, after creating intelligent beings, if she had wanted to guard against certain dangers of intellectual activity without compromising the future of intelligence?[28]

For Bergson, literature and mythology are the *consequences* of religious need, the largesse of a general myth-making faculty (*la fonction fabulatrice*) which addressed itself in the first instance to producing vivid and insistent images *not to assist the understanding* in its work, but rather *to seduce the intelligence away from* its natural operations. But what is the utility of this seduction? What dangers had "nature" to contend with in the very functioning of intelligence itself?

If it is indeed true that "religion is a defensive reaction of nature against the dissolvent power of intelligence," then we must ask in what quality or potency of intellect does this dissolvent power reside? The answer is twofold. The vital impetus of life has turned all creatures except man *away* from the image of death. Man alone knows that he must one day die, and, as Heidegger has shown, this dread in the face of death, while it may produce philosophic reflection, does so as an act of desperation. Religion, as we have seen, "denies" and "defies" the fact of death. In this lies its counterclaim against intelligence. As Bergson says:[29] "Looked at from this second standpoint, religion is a defensive reaction against the representation by intelligence of the inevitability of death."

But there is a further point as well. Intelligence is a tool-making and a tool-using instrumentality. It is an agency of adaptation, a means for the realization of human purposes. But intelligence, as it views its successes and its failures in the world, might well succumb to a certain natural depression. There are times to be sure when it achieves brilliantly, but more when it fails miserably. To what accidents are we not exposed? How the unforeseen and the incalculable supervene upon even the best of human planning! The understanding has no option but to operate in the modality of cause and effect, but it must grant a depressing margin to the contingent and the unforeseen. So much so that even as rigorous an advocate of strict determinism as Freud was forced in his moment of truth to exclaim: "Dark, unfeeling and unloving powers determine human destiny. . . ."

For the average man, unprotected by Freud's inner strength, by his stoicism, what must such a conclusion mean? Depression at this knowledge of how things really are. Perhaps paralysis of the optimistic centers of purposive striving. But reinforcements come from nature. For the vital impulse is also optimistic. And so in the face of this logic of the intelligence which requires us to postulate a world of neutral but frustrating causes and nonfriendly powers, a "logic" of the imagination will postulate a world hospitable to human desires because it expresses the will of a supreme power essentially friendly to human purpose. Religion is this "logic" of the imagination, and it is, as Bergson notes,[30] a series of "defensive reactions of nature against the representation by the intelligence of a depressing margin of the unexpected between the initiative taken and the effect desired."

The facts of existence as they are processed by the understanding lead to two conclusions inimical to *l'élan vital*: the presumption of failure and the inevitability of death. Against this pessimism the religious imagination makes its dramatic counterclaim: the existence of a cosmic sympathy and the illusoriness of death. Such a conclusion is religion's evolutionary purpose. And if the imagination, later, in poetry and drama, in epic and art, travels far toward a transcendence of this immediate, solid, religious practicality, we must nonetheless never allow ourselves to forget that this is the center from which it has begun its journey.

6   THERE IS something a little forbidding in Bergson's account of static religion—something a little too practical and pat, as if in this age of mechanization and glossy instruments, even the rituals of sacredness which bear the burden of our intuitions of the holy should be reduced to a calculus of their marginal utility. But Bergson surely does not intend to be understood in this fashion. The "utility" of the myth-making faculty is not meant to compromise religion or poetry as to their metaphysical claims. These must be considered independently and on other grounds. But to *place* the imaginative activities of the mind, to indicate (in Bradley's phrases) "their station" and "their duties" is the first step in a process of evaluation, and poetry itself, no matter how far it has advanced from the primitive center, must welcome and encourage our knowledge of the utility of its efforts. "There is, in fact," says Wallace Stevens,[31] "a world of poetry indistinguishable from the world in which we live, or, I ought to say, no doubt, from the world in which

we shall come to live, since what makes the poet the potent figure that he is, or was, or ought to be, is that he creates the world to which we turn incessantly and without knowing it and that *he gives to life the supreme fictions* without which we are unable to conceive of it." This, although merely implicit, is perhaps utility enough. But a moment later a more explicit utility has become the subject of the poet's argument. Stevens is talking specifically about "nobility," but the passage is ambiguous. It might, and probably does, refer equally well to this moral quality, and to the poetic imagination which is its vehicle. "It is a violence from within that protects us from a violence without. It is the imagination pressing back against the pressure of reality. It seems, in the last analysis, to have something to do with our self-preservation; and that, no doubt, is why the expression of it, the sound of its words, helps us to live our lives."

Stevens' image of "the imagination pressing back against the pressure of reality" is valuable because it serves again to set the functioning of the imagination against that of the understanding. The understanding gives way before the pressure of reality; it is, indeed, itself a kind of cognitive "reality principle" which deals with the world on the world's own terms. It is not accidental that Freud, who originated this terminology, countered this activity by that of "the pleasure principle," which, often thwarted at the level of overt activity, expresses itself in the substitute gratification of unrestrained fantasy. The imagination is the center of the life of fantasy and whether in myth, in religion, or in art, it presses against reality with all the force and energy of its own subjective claims.

When in 1605 Sir Francis Bacon published his *Advancement of Learning*, included in the "Survey of Learning" which formed his second book was a consideration of poetry, which he saw as an art used "to give some shadow of satisfaction to the mind of man in those points wherein the nature of things doth deny it." The world is inferior to the soul of man; in magnitude, rareness, variety, and goodness. And "so as it appeareth that poesy serveth and conferreth to magnanimity, morality, and to delectation . . . therefore it was ever thought to have some participation of divineness, because it doth raise and erect the mind by submitting the shows of things to the desires of the mind; whereas reason doth buckle and bow the mind unto the nature of things."

Bacon's *Advancement of Learning* and Stevens' *The Necessary Angel* have more than three hundred years between them, but they both presuppose an understanding (Bacon calls it "reason") which "doth buckle and bow the mind unto the nature of things." When Stevens speaks of the fantasy "pressing back against the pressure of reality" and Bacon of poetry as elevating the mind "by submitting the shows of things to the desires of the mind," both are describing the nuclear function of the teleological imagination.

I have called the imagination *teleological,* and have dwelt upon the fact that it is "purposive." But this attribution is ambiguous. The imagination can be purposive in two distinct senses; in the sense of Bergson's treatment, or in the sense of Cassirer and of Stevens and Bacon just above. It can in its total cognitive role perform a function which is implicitly directed toward a larger end, or it can internally, in its specific functioning, operate according to a principle (Kant would have said a "concept") of purposiveness. The first might be called extrinsic, the second intrinsic purposiveness. Both kinds have been suggested here. When Bergson speaks of the myth-making faculty as a defensive reaction of nature against the dissolvent character of the intelligence, he is pointing to the *extrinsic* purposiveness of the imagination. He is saying that it, like intelligence, is the creation of an evolutionary process which has originated the faculties of the mind for the express performance of certain acts of adaptation. Bergson and Dewey alike hold to this instrumental theory of cognitive operations within the environment of animal nature, and their attempt to present the "why" of mentality has certain important values. But it is a theory which blurs the distinction between the imagination and the understanding, because in the *extrinsic* sense both the understanding and the imagination are teleological—both are the expression of natural purposes. But my primary concern here is the distinction between the operations of understanding and imagination, and this is what the concept of *intrinsic* purposiveness permits. For this *intrinsic* purposiveness, this operation according to an implicit concept of purpose, is precisely what the imagination contains and the understanding lacks. It is what Cassirer means in showing how the categories of space and time in mythical thought are drenched with purposiveness, and what Bacon speaks of as submitting the shows of things to the desires of the mind. This is exactly what the understanding does not do. But for light upon this *intrinsic* teleology (of thought or feeling guided by the concept of purposiveness) we must turn to its *locus classicus*—the *Critique of the Teleological Judgment* of Kant.

For Kant the universal laws of nature have their ground in our understanding, which "prescribes" them to nature, but this prescription operates only in the formulation of particular empirical laws and not for their systematic relatedness. If there is a purposiveness of nature in its manifoldness, this the understanding cannot assert; it can only in its unity operate *as if* this were the case. The "purposiveness" of nature is, therefore, a concept which has its origin in the reflective judgment and not in our inspection of the individual objects in nature. Purposiveness is thus a concept neither of the speculative nor of the practical reason, but only represents the peculiar way in which we must proceed in reflection upon the objects of nature so as to ensure that our experience of nature shall be a thoroughly connected experience. For Kant, as for Whitehead, purposiveness is related to connectedness. The problem is again to make a connected experience out of those perceptions of nature which can be ordered according to an infinite variety of empirical laws. For Kant there is a close relation between the notion of a harmony in nature and the need of the understanding for finding universal principles, but we can, I think, project this need beyond the operation of the understanding to that of the imagination. And in this further generalization we shall still be deeply indebted to Kant's insights. If there is something in our judgments upon nature which makes us attentive to its purposes as it affects our understanding, there is also something in the concept of ideal purposiveness which is basically relevant to the needs of imagination as well. Why this is the case, we may also learn from Kant.

If the purposiveness of a thing as represented in perception is not attributable to the object itself, it must be bound up with some subjective element. Here Kant expresses his conviction that "the object is only called purposive when its representation is immediately combined with the feeling of pleasure," so that this is at bottom an "aesthetical" representation of purpose. And further: that this "susceptibility to pleasure from reflection upon the forms of things" (*die Empfänglichkeit einer Lust aus der Reflexion über die Formen der Sachen*) indicates a purposiveness of the subject.

The understanding must order the forms and combinations of nature in accordance with the laws of a mechanical causality, and here it is not merely that the understanding *does not* utilize the principle of purposiveness, but that it *cannot* according to its own principles do so. In Santayana's words, it is of the essence of science that it shall "live in a world of expurgated mythology." Therefore, as I have suggested in the preceding chapter, it can have no commerce with "appearance and reality," "illusion," "destiny," or "fate." These, in Kant's terms, arise only "when we represent to ourselves the possibility of the object after the analogy of that causality which we experience in ourselves."[32] Purposiveness means a new kind of causality *which we only borrow from ourselves and ascribe to external nature or experience in general.* The freedom of man's moral nature (in contrast to the deterministic causality of the external world) suggests a general purposiveness which the imagination can project outward upon nature. This projection (as Cassirer has shown), is the basic mechanism of mythical thought. For man's imagination knows how to give to things a conformity with his own arbitrary fancies for which the understanding can have nothing but suspicion and contempt.

In harmony with what principles does purposiveness function? According to Kant the basic principle here is that of *organic unity*. For a thing to have a natural purpose in the first place, its parts must be possible only with reference to the whole. "An organized being," says Kant,[33] "is then not a mere machine, for that has merely *moving* power, but it possesses in itself *formative* power of a self-propagating kind which it communicates to its materials though they have it not of themselves; it organizes them, in fact, and this cannot be explained by the mere mechanical faculty of motion." The internal purposiveness of organized objects (in nature or created by art) is one in which every part is reciprocally end and means. Here (and this holds for the "fatefulness" of drama or the "unity" of the impressionist landscape) nothing is without purpose, vain, or to be ascribed to a blind mechanical agency, and if this seems to give rise to an antinomy, it is perhaps not quite, as Kant thought, because we confuse a fundamental proposition of the "reflective" with one of the "determinative" judgment. Paraphrasing his own principle,[34] we should say instead: *All appearance of an antinomy between the maxims of the proper physical (mechanical) and the purposive (teleological) methods of explanation rests therefore upon this: that we confuse a fundamental need of the understanding with a fundamental need of the imagination.* Purposiveness arises from a subjective principle that we have learned from art (i.e. of a causality according to a guiding idea), and even when, as in mythical thought, we apply it to nature, the analogy with artistic agency is never completely lost. It is for this reason that the problem of a causality acting

with design ends for Kant in the ambiguous marshes of theology—in the rational but inconclusive consideration of a
supreme Being *productive* in a way analogous to the causality
of a humanly productive intelligence.

7 THE CONSIDERATIONS above, drawn from
Kant's third *Critique,* are, I think, of the
highest importance. Unfortunately they are abstract. Suppose,
therefore, that we ask: How does that purposiveness which
we only borrow from ourselves and ascribe to external nature
function in the poetic imagination? How does the poet *work*
to construct a universe governed by the principle of organic
unity? Almost any poet with *the cosmological sense* will serve
here. I have already appealed to the practices of Homer and
Dante. This time I will turn to Virgil.

Hidden away in the writings of St. Augustine is a famous
passage in which he charts the geography of the mediaeval
universe. The totality of it all, he says, is divided into three
parts. First there is the realm of things *below man:* rocks and
trees, mountains and rivers, climate and weather, plants and
animals—the realm of Nature. Second there is the realm of
things *on the level of man:* family life and social activity,
moral responsibility and political action, war and peace, conquest and defense—the realm of the Human. Third there is
the realm of things *above man:* God in his perfection and
power, the saints and the saved, values in their holy authority
—the realm of the Divine. But one does not have to be a
believer in Christian theology to see in this the portrayal of
any cosmology which attempts to do justice at once to the
natural, the human, and the supernatural in experience. In
Homer and in Dante alike there is the "thickness" of a cosmos which sees human action operating within a "natural"
setting and guided by divine influences from above. And if
Shakespeare's drama is less immediately cognizant of this

thickness, and more self-contained within the domain of the human, yet even here the supernaturalism of Hamlet and the Roman plays, and the intrusive Nature of *As You Like It, Lear,* and *The Tempest,* reinforce the cosmological distinction.

How does a poet transform such a cosmos according to the pattern of necessity imposed by the teleological imagination? How, in short, does he show that the three realms do not run their separate and concurrent ways, but deeply merge and interpenetrate? The classical method is the poetic assertion of purposiveness—of organic unity—exhibiting the cosmos as a system of universal order. Thus Pope in the eighteenth century:

> What if the foot, ordained the dust to tread,
> Or hand, to toil, aspired to be the head?
> What if the head, the eye, or ear repined
> To serve mere engines to the ruling Mind?
> Just as absurd for any part to claim
> To be another, in this general frame:
> Just as absurd, to mourn the tasks or pains,
> The great directing Mind of All ordains.
> All are but parts of one stupendous whole,
> Whose body Nature is, and God the soul. . . .

Pope's conception of "the ruling Mind" is very Greek, very Platonic, and his metaphor of Nature as the body of God is a type of pantheism which Spinoza would have understood, although it would be an offense to the more conservative Christian tradition. But his central insight is precisely that form of purposiveness which Kant celebrates in the *Critique of Teleological Judgment.*

But there is another method as well: not poetry as philosophical assertion, but poetry as the oblique presentation of a *Weltbild,* showing with all the metrical resources of a Wordsworth or a Blake that nature is alive, or in the dramatic fashion of a Dante or a Euripides how the divine breath enters into and inspires the actions of men. But it is in the gentle romanticism of Virgil's *Aeneid* that the method reaches its apogee. Here we can see in all its simplicity the central device for its accomplishment—the organic reiteration of the mediating simile.

Virgil's romanticism is twofold: inspired at once by those omens and portents which Roman superstition imposed upon the hardy Greek structure of the Olympian gods, and by the sense of the brooding presence of a "countrified" nature, native in one whose youth joyfully roamed the Mantuan hills. The problem of purposiveness here is simple—to dramatize it at all levels by the devices of a mutual reference—to see nature in human terms, to see men in natural terms, to see the gods in both. The Virgilian simile works as the vehicle of this constant interplay, imperceptibly at first, more artfully as we continue, until the massive reiteration has at last produced in us the poetic certitude of an organic world.

In the first pages of Book I we are prepared not merely to see nature in human terms, but to find it personified in a divine or superhuman presence. First Juno the avenger seeks out the powerful Aeolus to solicit his intervention against the tribe she hates.[35]

> Brooding, burning,
> She sought Aeolia, the storm-clouds' dwelling,
> A land that sweeps and swarms with the winds' fury,
> Whose monarch, Aeolus, in his deep cave rules
> Imperious, weighing down with bolt and prison
> Those boisterous struggling roarers, who go raging
> Around their bars, under the moan of the mountain.

But no sooner has this been accomplished, and the winds of Aeolus blow up a monstrous storm, than Neptune the sea god in anger calms with his trident the unruly waves and the swollen sea.

> Sometimes, in a great nation, there are riots
> With the rabble out of hand, and firebrands fly
> And cobblestones; whatever they lay their hands on

Is a weapon for their fury, but should they see
One man of noble presence, they fall silent,
Obedient dogs, with ears pricked up, and waiting,
Waiting his word, and he knows how to bring them
Back to good sense again. So ocean, roaring,
Subsided into stillness, as the sea-god
Looked forth upon the waters, and clear weather
Shone over him as he drove his flying horses.

The wind and the sea are divine principles, but divinities
who exercise essentially human prerogatives. The king of the
winds is like a prison warden who releases his charges at will.
The king of the sea quells the waves as a nobleman cows a
rabble which has gotten out of hand. In short, the powers of
nature are assimilated to the images of human mastership.
But Virgil also, contrariwise, constantly compares the examples of human industry to the examples of the insect world.
Approaching Carthage and looking down from rising ground,
Aeneas sees the industrious Carthaginians building and maintaining their city.

. . . the busy Tyrians toiling
With stones for walls and citadel, or marking
Foundations for their homes, drainage and furrow,
All under ordered process. They dredge harbors,
Set cornerstones, quarry the rock, where someday
Their theater will tower. They are like bees
In early summer over the country flowers
When the sun is warm, and the young of the hive emerge,
And they pack the molten honey, bulge the cells
With the sweet nectar, add new loads, and harry
The drones away from the hive, and the work glows,
And the air is sweet with bergamot and clover.

Later in Book IV this image of Aeneas and his men happily
approaching Dido's realm is balanced by the delight of the
Trojans as they prepare for their tragic departure.

And then the Trojans
Bend, really, to their work, launching the vessels

> All down the shore. The tarred keel swims in the water,
> The green wood comes from the forest, the poles are lopped
> For oars, with leaves still on them. All are eager
> For flight; all over the city you see them streaming,
> Bustling about their business, a black line moving
> The way ants do when they remember winter
> And raid a hill of grain, to haul and store it
> At home, across the plain, the column moving
> In thin black line through grass, part of them shoving
> Great seeds on little shoulders, and part bossing
> The job, rebuking laggards, and all the pathway
> Hot with the stream of work.

Not only are the forces of nature like prison wardens and patricians, but conversely, the actions of men share in the instinctive organicism of the natural world. Architects and artisans are like bees. Sailors and shipwrights are like ants. And this characterization of masses of men is supported by those similes of nature, terrifying or pathetic, which sketch in a few phrases the actions and passions of men and women. In Book II at the burning destruction of Troy, the terrible Greek warrior stands as an image of panic and death.

> Before the entrance, at the very threshold
> Stood Pyrrhus, flashing proudly in bronze light,
> Sleek as a serpent coming into the open,
> Fed on rank herbs, wintering under the ground,
> The old slough cast, the new skin shining, rolling
> His slippery length, reaching his neck to the sun,
> While the forked tongue darts from the mouth. . . .

And in Book IV again, the image of the lovesick Dido is presented in terms, borrowed from nature, of pathos and pity.

> Alas, poor blind interpreters! What woman
> In love is helped by offerings of altars?
> Soft fire consumes the marrow-bones, the silent
> Wound grows, deep in the heart.
> Unhappy Dido burns, and wanders, burning,
> All up and down the city, the way a deer

> With a hunter's careless arrow in her flank
> Ranges the uplands, with the shaft still clinging
> To the hurt side. . . .

In the similes of Aeolus the warden, Neptune the haughty patrician, the Tyrians busy like bees, the Trojan sailors like ants, Pyrrhus the serpent, and Dido the wounded deer, we have the clues to the Virgilian creation of the organic universe, to that dramatization of purposiveness in which the creative imagination achieves its work after the model set down in Kant's *Critique of Judgment*. The *Aeneid* is far away from the pristine workings of the myth-making faculty as it innocently reveals itself in Homer and in Hesiod. It is the product of sophistication, of the consummate art of a silver age, but the devices have not radically changed—they have but become more consciously artful. Nature still remains the magnetic field of Homer's *Odyssey* although the gods have changed their names, and the stakes are not the security of Home, but the establishment of a noble destiny for the Roman race. But, if anything, the organicity has but proclaimed itself more strongly. The Homeric epithet is at least a tribute to the demands of poetic fixity (it is the attribute which gives the personal substance its artistic permanence), but the Virgilian simile blurs the distinctions between the natural, the human, and the divine. It runs together, so to speak, it *dissolves* the boundaries of experience into a single realm of discourse where life vibrates like a plucked string, and where the mechanical causality of the understanding has been banished before the insistent claims of a rich teleology.

8 THE UNIVERSE of Virgil's *Aeneid* reveals the workings of the imagination, precisely as the *Critique of Judgment* has implied, in its connectedness, in its subjectivity, in its organic unity. (These three are in a partial sense dimensions of purposiveness.) The story of Aeneas, from the moment when, Sicily hardly out of sight, he approaches Africa to the final moment when he sends the

spirit of Turnus moaning to the shades, is a tale which grows in familiarity, selfishly solicits our feelings for the hero and his destiny, while it wraps the customary legend in the charms of novelty. The Virgilian world is a world of living nature, such as we might find in the poetry of Wordsworth or the metaphysics of Whitehead or Schelling, and its paraphernalia of prophecies, omens, and sacred places shows how the poetic object becomes a sympathetic repository for the discarded furniture of the mythical imagination. And in all this it contrasts with the exertions of the understanding in its scientific employment, as it tries to hold before itself a representation of the world as a pure mechanism dominated by the logic of a strict causality of constant conjunction. I say "tries," because the expurgations carried out by the scientific method require a constant effort, and are then only partially successful. Mythical thought, as Cassirer has obliquely noted, still exerts its hold upon us, and our common-sense perception of the world is permeated to a degree of which we are hardly conscious by purposive and anthropomorphic elements. If, indeed, as (following out the logic of Pragmatism) Charner Perry has suggested,[36] common sense was formed for the guidance of practice, and therefore apprehends and portrays the environment as opportunities or obstacles to human action, in contrast to the natural sciences, which have freed themselves from teleology and thus avoided the projection into the description of nature of the romanticisms and peculiarities of the human point of view, then the partial successes of natural science only furnish a contrast by which the anthropomorphic and teleological claims of the imagination are emphasized. If we represent the world as operating by forces or energies which we interpret by analogy to our own motor experiences (as for example in Bertrand Russell's romantic early "A Free Man's Worship," where matter itself is "blind" and "restless"—a living reproach to the methodological purity of this charming if crusty old positivist), then that science which tries to see the world as neutral phenomena, fixed and factual if not material and dead, is bound to be defeated in this universal aim by the omnipresent imagination. D. G. James said it perfectly when he characterized *naturalism* as "the effort of the imagination to overcome itself, to commit suicide, a feat which it cannot encompass."[37]

When Ribot in his famous essay of 1900 *Sur L'imagination créatrice* (now largely, and I think unfortunately, forgotten) tried to find another mode of mental functioning to compare with the creative imagination, he chose that of *voluntary activity*. Imagination in the intellectual order, he concluded, is the equivalent of will in the realm of movements. He justified this comparison with arguments which, although he did not, he might have drawn from Kant. Both creative imagination and voluntary activity are in the domain of subjectivity. Imagination is subjective, personal, anthropocentric. It moves from within outward toward an objectification, just as the understanding contrariwise is objective, impersonal, and guided from without. Both imagination and will have a teleological character. They either act or portray action always with a view to some end, being thus the very opposite of the understanding, which pursues neutrality and limits itself to description or to proof. Finally, both the will and the imagination strive for expression: the will in *an act* which completes its deliberations in the realm of practice, the creative imagination in *a work* which is objectified so that it shall exist not only for its creator, but for everybody. And while the act is a motor activity, a *movement,* the imagination expresses itself in an *analogy,* a mechanism of thinking which is protean in its creativity: producing images, resemblances, metaphors, personifications, similes, allegories, transformations, and metamorphoses, and finally transmuting the materials of mere perception into inventions and organic wholes.

Wallace Stevens secures Ribot's insight for poetry:[38] "There is always an analogy between nature and the imagination, and possibly poetry is merely the strange rhetoric of that parallel: a rhetoric in which the feeling of one man is communicated to another in words of the exquisite appositeness that takes away all their verbality." And in greater detail: "The study of

the activity of resemblance is an approach to the understanding of poetry. Poetry is a satisfying of the desire of resemblance. . . . Its singularity is that in the act of satisfying the
desire for resemblance it touches the sense of reality, it en-
hances the sense of reality, heightens it, intensifies it." And
D. G. James completes Ribot's insight in a language less reminiscent of Plato than of Coleridge or Kant:[39] "Poetry arises
from the felt need for an augmentation of life . . . a desire to
encompass life and by encompassing it, to master it. . . . To re-
create the world in a perfect unity of imaginative pattern is
its end—a labor which springs from the feeling of helpless-
ness and impotence in the face of an initially disordered and
confused mass of experience provided by the secondary imagination."

The technique of analogy working toward the creation of
ever larger artistic wholes—this is the *modus operandi* of the
teleological imagination. And in its dependence upon obscure
emotions and hidden elements of feeling (expressed often in
vivid qualities of language and mythic personifications) it is
to be distinguished from the neutral factuality of the understanding. The creative imagination in its mythical guise exploits the "suggestiveness" of nature. It says: "Brooding
Selene kisses the sleeping Endymion." And the understanding
counters dryly and without comment: "It is night." Which is
true? The comment of the understanding, surely. But to settle
the claim of "truth" is to invoke a concept which is itself a
product of the understanding, and the candor with which we
must answer upon this issue neither compromises nor pre-
judges the larger issue of intrinsic value. In saying this I have
been following in the footsteps of D. G. James, who also says:[40]
"I have sought to emphasize that the imagination can never
hope to free itself of scepticism, and that to claim that the
imagination can give us what can be known for truth is an
extravagance which cannot be upheld." But at the same time
I have not ruled out the relevant reply of Wallace Stevens:[41]
"We have been a little insane about the truth. We have had
an obsession. In its ultimate extension, the truth about which

we have been insane will lead us to look beyond the truth to something in which the imagination will be the dominant complement."

In the literal sense the issue of truth does not basically concern the imagination, but if it did, one could say that whereas the understanding by its nature seems committed to a correspondence theory of truth, the imagination is rather governed by a criterion of coherence. If myth and religion are the consequences of imaginative need, and if this implies thinking by analogy with ourselves, so that myth and religion either attribute life to all things or deal with them only as they can be assigned vivid qualities, the extent of this attribution in some sense determines the credibility of the resultant creation. "Illusion" always means that we are the victims of a *partial* imagination, whereas "myth" is the product of the *total* imagination at work. Myth-making, as we have seen from Cassirer, is a constructive activity applying itself to everything and radiating in all directions. It springs from the need of man to reflect and reproduce his own nature in the environment surrounding him, and if its first application is that "thinking by analogy" which vivifies everything after the human model, and attempts to represent everything according to initially arbitrary resemblances, it ends in a total representation symbolically displayed, whether as a religion, a metaphysics, or an artistic vision of the world.

The categories of such a world are teleological through and through. If the concept of space is in question, it is a "purposive space," full of possibilities, the "receptacle" for a nature alive in the fashion of Whitehead, Wordsworth, or Virgil. If the concept of time is in question, it is a "purposive time," directed, prophetic, heavy with fate, and pointing to the climaxes of destiny in the manner of Homer, Sophocles, or Spengler. But, above all, purposive space and time are the dimensions of *action*, and particularly *dramatic* action. At this point the "teleological" imagination becomes the "dramatic" imagination, and it is to the problem of the latter that I should now like to turn.

Four / The Dramatic Imagination

SINCE THE decline of the influence of the Cartesian revolution of the seventeenth and eighteenth centuries and the ascendancy of the influence of the Darwinian revolution of the nineteenth, the status of the categories of thought and action has been reversed. The alleged supremacy of thought has been challenged by the pragmatic revolt, with the consequence that if action has not been elevated above thought, at least we have all been persuaded that the categories are mutually implicative and require one another. Bernanos (surely no pragmatist) speaks for Dewey and common sense alike when he says: "A thought which does not result in an action is nothing much, and an action which does not proceed from a thought is nothing at all." But the interesting thing is that this pragmatism has entered no less into our psychological presuppositions and anthropological methods of explanation than into our theoretical formulations. It appears, therefore, not only in James and Peirce and C. I. Lewis, but in Robertson-Smith, Jane Harrison, and Cassirer.

To understand religious representations, so the theory goes, we must understand religious actions. Jane Harrison put it clearly as early as 1903:[1] "What a people *does* in relation to its gods must always be one clue, and perhaps the safest to what it *thinks*. The first preliminary to any scientific understanding of Greek religion is a minute examination of its ritual." Motives find expression more in acts than in images, and this, anthropologically conceived, means that the "mythic" and the "ritualistic" are but the warp and the woof of the religious fabric.

This insight is also of the greatest importance for our view of the imagination, and no less so because it but reinforces what is implicit in the theory of Aristotle's *Poetics*. The tragic drama is the *imitation of an action,* a presentation of persons acting and doing, while the epic is a poetic imitation which is *narrative in form.* Clearly, Nietzsche was not so very far from the spirit of Aristotle when he saw the work of Homer as an art of Apollonian images, and that of Aeschylus as growing from the ritual Dionysian frenzy. "Perceiving" and "enacting" retain their polarity for the ancient as for the modern consciousness.

For the interpretation of primitive religious life, the *Poetics* provides a central metaphor. For if myth constitutes its *epic* element, so ritual provides its *drama.* A similar possibility is available, I think, for the imagination. If myth cannot be described as bare emotion (because it is the *expression* or *formal pattern* of emotion), no more can ritual. In either case *the formative element* produces an artistic object, and similarly, the imagination or forming actuality of perception may create the teleological products of an authentic imagery or the dramatic products of a sublimated reenactment.

It is to explore the meaning of *enactment* in imaginative terms that we turn from the teleological to the dramatic imagination. But here we must avoid the danger of substantializing a function. Cassirer has already shown that if myth and ritual are distinguishable, they are also inseparable. The world of myth is a dramatic world. Homer's Aegean space (no less than the space of the sorcerers of Dobu) is a space of actions and forces and conflicting moral agencies. And a Hegel or a Brunetière (who saw the collision of strong forces or conflicting powers as the very essence of the tragic drama) would, therefore, have had no difficulty at all in agreeing that drama is mythical and that myth is dramatic. Therefore we may follow an old strategy of Dewey. By the "teleological" and the "dramatic" imagination I do not mean two entities separable as adjoining parts of a geographical area, but two distinguishable uses of a central instrument. I am concerned, therefore, less with the dramatic imagination than with the dramatic *in* imagination. And for light upon the dramatic quality of the imagination we can not do better perhaps than initially to turn to Dewey himself.

There is, I think, in Dewey no comprehensive and unified treatment of the imagination. To the few consecutive pages in *Art as Experience* (pp. 267-275) and *Human Nature and Conduct* (pp. 189-194) devoted to this topic, one must add the fragments to be found in *Experience and Nature,* and that is all. But there is something further to be learned even from this scanty material. In addition to an underwriting of Coleridge's "esemplastic" theory, which has already been subsumed under "teleology," there are two new interesting ideas. First, that the imagination is *the moving point of a perpetual intersection* between the self and its world, its inner and its outer vision. And second, that its driving ambition is *the pursuit of the new*.

Although it is easy to view imagination as pure revery or pure fantasy, it is also, says Dewey, "an organ of nature," for it is "the appropriate phase of indeterminate events moving toward eventualities that are now but possibilities."[2] But, in the beginning, Dewey sees this movement—as do Cassirer and Jane Harrison—as the insight that for the primitive mentality "nature yields nothing without ceremonies."

Devotion to rites, stories and revery springs on its magical side from practical desire to control the contingent; but in larger measure it embodies the happiness that attends the sense of successful issue from the uncertainly hazardous. *Imagination is primarily dramatic, rather than lyric, whether it takes the form of the play enacted on the stage, of the told story or silent soliloquy. The con-*

stant presence of instability and trouble gives depth and poignancy to the situations in which are pictured their subordination to final issues possessed of calm and certainty. *To re-enact the vicissitudes, crises and tragedies of life under conditions that deprive them of their overt dangers, is the natural role of "consciousness,"* which is tamed to respect actualities only when circumstances enforce the adoption of the method of labor, a discipline that is fortunate if it retain some of the liberation from immediate exigencies which characterize dramatic imagination.[3]

"Imagination is primarily dramatic"—this is the sum and substance of what we may learn from Dewey, although this dramatic character is explored in terms of the twin concepts of "novelty" and "organic unity." It is the use of the first which shows how revery pales in importance compared to the "intersective" function.

Reference to imagination is pertinent. But the reference is too frequently used to disguise and avoid recognition of the essential fact and the problems involved in it. Imagination as mere revery is one thing, a natural and additive event, complete in itself, a terminal object rich and consoling, or trivial and silly, as may be. Imagination which terminates in a modification of the objective order, in the institution of a new object is other than a merely added occurrence. It involves a dissolution of old objects and a forming of new ones in a medium which, since it is beyond the old object and not yet in a new one, can properly be termed subjective.[4]

And yet this novelty, like the Bergsonian "memory," contains the old as it invents the new. It is "the grace of sense" of which Eliot speaks:[5]

> . . . a white light still and moving,
> . . . concentration
> Without elimination, both a new world
> And the old made explicit, understood. . . .

In *Experience and Nature,* as we have seen, Dewey lapsed sufficiently from his usual mode of expression to call imagination an "organ of nature" as if it, like the understanding, was somehow substantive, but in *Art as Experience* he has recovered himself and returned to his usual strategy (of which Cassirer would have approved) of turning substances into functions and faculties into operations upon, or qualities of, experience. As in *A Common Faith* he treats not "religion" but "the religious *in* experience," so here he calls attention not to "imagination" but to "the imaginative *in* experience." Imagination is a quality of creation, a mode of perception of the integral whole, the discovery of the new.[6]

More perhaps than any other phase of the human contribution, it has been treated as a special and self-contained faculty, differing from others in possession of mysterious potencies. Yet if we judge its nature from the creation of works of art, it designates a quality that animates and pervades all processes of making and observation. It is a *way* of seeing and feeling things as they compose an integral whole. It is the large and generous blending of interests at the point where the mind comes in contact with the world. When old and familiar things are made new in experience, there is imagination. When the new is created, the far and strange become the most natural inevitable things in the world. There is always some measure of adventure in the meeting of mind and universe, and this adventure is, in its measure, imagination.

Dewey has also been reading Coleridge, and he quotes Coleridge on the "esemplastic" function of imagination with approval, but here again he wishes to transform Coleridge's clear statement that imagination is a "power" into the generalized notion of a mode of experience so that "an imaginative experience is what happens when varied materials of sense quality, emotion and meaning come together in a union that marks *a new birth in the world.*" This union represents a fusion of what Dewey speaks of as the opposition between inner and outer vision in the artist. The interaction of the two is imagination, and from it the work of art is born. That it is creative (in the sense of being opposed to habit or routine) is clear. But that it is to be restricted to aesthetic experience Dewey wishes to deny. If imagination be conceived as the gateway through which meanings find their way into a

present interaction, then all conscious experience has by
nature some degree of imaginative quality. For imagination
is then simply the conscious adjustment of the old and the
new. But here again Dewey's actual language is instructive.
For this is "experience *enacted*," not merely "had," and this
recalls at once the Aristotelian concept of drama as *the imitation of an action*. The drama here is *the drama of the new*.

The gap between experience mastered and experience to
come means risk, means a venture into the unknown. Thus,
for Dewey, "the novel" and "the purposive" merge into
"imagination" as a barrier against recurrence, complete uniformity; the routine and the mechanized which are the assumptions upon which the predictive operations of the understanding are based. To be sure, Dewey does not contrast *the
understanding* which produces the scientific chain of meaning with *the imagination* whose workings provide the humanistic complex (as I have done in Chapter 2). Indeed, his
whole way of thinking is opposed to such sharp dichotomizing
of experience, but what he has to say about imagination fits
with it very well. Aesthetic experience *is* experience in which
the imaginative element predominates. The work of art,
unlike a machine, operates imaginatively in a world of physical existences to unify experience. And here Dewey is led far
beyond Coleridge to an organicism which equates the imagination with the "totalizing" function. Art shows us the immediate wholeness of *all* experience, and the imagination is
not a special faculty, but "that which holds all other elements
in solution."

From Dewey's brief, and not entirely consistent, treatment
of imagination we can, I think, usefully extract two elements:
that of *novelty* and that of *dramatic enactment*. The latter is
probably of primary importance. Even in his own metaphysics
it is of independent significance. Man, he says in *Experience
and Nature*,[7]
combines meanings, like fire, nearness, remoteness, warmth, comfort, nice, pain, expansion, softening, so that fire enters into new
interactions and effects new consequences. By an *intra-organic re-*

enactment of partial animal reactions to natural events, and of accompanying reactions to and from others acquired in intercourse and communication, means-consequences are tried out in advance without the organism getting irretrievably involved in physical consequences. Thought, deliberation, objectively directed imagination, in other words, is an added efficacious function of natural events and hence brings into being new consequences. For images are not made of psychical stuff; they are qualities of *partial* organic behaviors, which are their "stuff."

To see that "images" are the qualities of partial organic behaviors is to theoretically reinforce the insights about myth and ritual which we have already found in Jane Harrison and Cassirer. But the notion of "intra-organic re-enactment of partial animal reactions" leads to a treatment of imagination as dramatic in quite another sense, namely, that publicized by the philosophers of contemporary Oxford. It leads in the direction of the idea of *pretending* as developed by John Austin and Gilbert Ryle.

2 RYLE'S TREATMENT of imagination in Chapter VIII of *The Concept of Mind* has two aspects (some might be tempted to say is beset by two difficulties). First, there is his *ex parte* argument, behavioristically inspired, that we understand imagination best when we conceive of it as incipient or truncated *performance*. Second, there is his failure to decide finally whether the imagination which he wishes to explicate is the indispensable adjunct of cognition or the independent originative source of works of art. The first is *imaging,* which, as we have seen, is that theory of imagination that dominates Kant's *Critique of Pure Reason.* The second is *imagining,* the notion which, as we have also seen, is implicit in the account of purposiveness in Kant's *Critique of Judgment.*

Ryle is primarily interested in *imaging,* because, true to his sources in the British empirical tradition, he wants to under-score its prior insistence that "cognitive malpractices are notoriously due to the pranks of undisciplined Imagination." This, combined with his Wittgensteinian prejudice against "the inner," leads him to parody the doctrine of imaging as "seeing." Paradoxically, he wishes to outlaw the old Baconian metaphor of *the mind as theater,* as the shadowy habitat of the fleshless and clandestine beings which we speak of as "imaginary." The metaphor of "mental vision" disturbs him. Hence he insists that although "picturing" or "visualizing" may have their psychological utility, yet pictures *are not* hung in the gallery of the mind. "Imaging" occurs, he says, but the images are not "seen." "Pictures" is not a single genus of which "photographs" are one species and "mental pictures" are another. To put it this way is, at once, to dispel a danger-ous theory often tacitly assumed that "imagining" is to be described as "the seeing of pictures with a special status," and to provide ammunition against the sense-datum theory of per-ception, to which Ryle is clearly opposed.

But if we are to deny the Miltonic image of the "mind as its own place" where mental pictures are "seen" and mental voices "heard," and if "imagining" is not the special activity of such a mind, then what is it? Ryle's pluralistic answer is instructive.

There are hosts of widely divergent sorts of behaviour in the conduct of which we should ordinarily and correctly be described as imaginative. The mendacious witness in the witness-box, the inventor thinking out a new machine, the constructor of a ro-mance, the child playing bears, and Henry Irving are all exercising their imaginations; but so, too, are the judge listening to the lies of the witness, the colleague giving his opinion on the new inven-tion, the novel reader, the nurse who refrains from admonishing the 'bears' for their subhuman noises, the dramatic critic and the theatre-goers.[8]

Now, "narrating falsely" as a witness, "originating" a new machine, "creating" a fiction, "playing" as a child, "acting" on the stage, as well as "hearing" the witness, "observing" the new invention, "reading" the novel, "watching" the children play, and "participating in" the business on the stage as a theater-goer, different as they are superficially, have one thing in common: they are all eminently *dramatic*. And the fact that even the separation of the active and the passive element, between "actor" and "beholder," has been so consistently maintained, suggests the metaphor of the theater. Ryle wishes to denote by his examples an invincible pluralism, but the same varieties of imaginative effort only serve to indicate stoutly the very point which Ryle wishes to deny—that there *is* one common nuclear operation of the imagination, and indeed that it is *histrionic*.

If there is no "faculty" of imagination *(Einbildungskraft)* as Kant supposed, yet there is an imaginative aspect of certain types of experience where actor and spectator participate in the performance, and where the essence of the performance is not a dedication to factuality or the literal communication of truth, but the creation of an illusion which shall serve its own intrinsic function. In the end Ryle himself perceives this clearly, for the second half of his treatment of imagination is devoted to an analysis of that particular human activity of simulation or dissimulation, of playing a part, of make-believe, which he calls "pretending."

But here again Ryle's analysis is rendered one-sided, if not definitely mistaken, by the supremacy of logical and cognitive considerations. If there are multiple motives for pretending, still they all have in common that they perform actions in "a hypothetical and not a categorical manner," so that for a single action there must be a dual description which records the difference between what is directly done and what is obliquely accomplished. Ryle is particularly interested in those forms of pretending which are involved (or may be involved) in theorizing and planning: making assumptions, entertaining propositions, toying with ideas, considering alternatives. At this point, although his language is analytical

rather than descriptive, there is little to distinguish Ryle's
theory from that of Dewey. Indeed, Ryle's treatment might
have profited considerably by some pointed references to the
pages in *Human Nature and Conduct* in which these matters
are discussed. For Dewey in his investigation of the nature of
ordinary judgments of practice begins with the idea that
"deliberation is a dramatic rehearsal (in imagination) of various competing possible lines of action." Thus, as he says,[9]
"deliberation is an experiment in finding out what the various lines of possible action are really like" and "the trial is in
imagination, not in overt fact. The experiment is carried on
by tentative rehearsals in thought which do not affect physical
facts outside the body." For Dewey then, as for Ryle, "pretending" has important implications for cognition and for
choice, and the latter may even be defined in terms of the
former. "What then is choice? Simply hitting in imagination
upon an object which furnishes an adequate stimulus to the
recovery of overt action."[10]

The last stage of Ryle's argument consists in the practical
identification of the "imaging" of the epistemologist and the
"pretending" of the actor. He wishes to show that "pretending," "fancying," and "imaging" are more or less the same
thing. Although it is true that "playing" and "pretending"
are used generally for "deliberate, concerted and rehearsed
performances" whereas "fancying" and "imagining" stand for
"those activities of make-believe into which people casually
and even involuntarily drift,"[11] the real difference is not that
of the deliberate and the involuntary, but rather that of the
overt and muscular representation of deeds, and what Dewey
has called above "the tentative rehearsals in thought which
do not affect physical facts outside the body." For Ryle it is
all "make-believe"; only one must distinguish the make-
believe externally observable and that internally performed
but externally invisible and inaudible. Here too, as in Dewey,
there is a continuity of the inner and the outer in experience,
with the latter serving as the basic point of reference. Imag-

ination is not a visual sensation, it is *a performance,* and its inner operations represent outer action either temporarily inhibited or at long last finally begun.

Ryle's treatment of "pretending" must be distinguished from the more *ad hoc* and subsequent examinations of Professor Austin and Miss Anscombe.[12] Austin is concerned with showing the "limits of pretense," how, in short, "there is necessarily involved in pretence or shamming, the notion of a limit which must not be over-stepped." Pretense, as he shows, is always "insulated from reality," and while this insight might have been valuable in distinguishing the understanding from the imagination, and even the "as-if" element in all poetry and drama upon which Coleridge insisted, he does not use it for this purpose. He chooses to stress the "shamming" side of pretending, and therefore is led off the track to find the essence of pretending as the intention to disguise some "real" feeling or notion or behavior. When Miss Anscombe follows this with a more extended analysis of pretending as "an intention-dependent concept," she has added little to what is already (in comparison with Ryle) specific but barren.

Ryle's equation of imagination and "pretending" is suggestive, but his limitation of "pretending" to the cognitive activities of planning and theorizing is far narrower than Dewey's equivalent treatment. For Dewey understands admirably that the stringent necessities of problem-solving involve constraint and fatigue, and that art and play are the *moral necessities* which are "required to take care of the margin that exists between the total stock of impulses that demand outlet and the amount expended in regular action. They keep the balance which work cannot indefinitely maintain. They are required to introduce variety, flexibility and sensitiveness into disposition."[13] Hence, also, he can refer to "the immense moral importance of play and of fine, or make-believe, art— of activity, that is, which is make-believe from the standpoint of the useful arts enforced by the demands of the environment."

Play and the make-believe which is fine art are forms of pretending which illustrate the dramatic imagination at work, and if, as Dewey believes, they effectively modulate human nature, "softening rigidities, relaxing strains, allaying bitterness, dispelling moroseness, and breaking down the narrowness consequent upon specialized tasks,"[14] then we have here in *Human Nature and Conduct* a version of that *catharsis* which Aristotle found to be the effect of tragedy, but broadened beyond the implications of the medical metaphor into a form of purification adequate to the strains of a complex culture. Nor is Dewey satisfied with this merely negative account of the psychological functioning of the arts. If art releases energy and focuses and tranquilizes it, it also adds fresh and deeper meanings to the usual activities of life. The arts, and the impulse of play to which they are closely allied, both "aim at reducing the domination of the prosaic." This is but to say that they provide that richness and vitality of meaning, that intensification and vividness of experience which is *dramatic* in the highest degree. Dewey, unlike Bergson, can never escape the essential pragmatism of his Darwinian inspiration. For him "any imagination is a sign that impulse is impeded and is groping for utterance." But the conversion of direct energy into imagination produces an activity which shapes material and generates excitement. And this also is a form of drama.

3   IT IS not really difficult to assimilate the concept of illusory reenactment or of "pretending" to the commonplaces of literary and dramatic practice. When Shakespeare in the fourth act of *Henry V* presents the intimate, yet strangely distant, conversation of the incognito king with John Bates, Alexander Court, and Michael Williams upon the eve of the battle of Agincourt, we know it as a species of pretending, although these very men may then have been alive, and the battle was indeed fought in the year

1415. When Schiller in the third act of *Maria Stuart* brings Mary and Elizabeth dramatically and fatefully face to face in the park of Fotheringay (although there is not the slightest shred of historical evidence that they ever met) we accept the pretense as a negotiable fiction. When Hugo von Hofmannsthal in *The Letter of Lord Chandos* simulates an epistle which the younger son of the Earl of Bath wrote to Francis Bacon, Baron Verulam, in the summer of 1603, we cherish the claim of complete incoherence as an apology for the abandonment of a literary career, although we attribute it in spirit to a youthful Viennese poet rather than to an Elizabethan nobleman. Even when Thucydides in his *History of the Peloponnesian War* reports verbatim speeches of Pericles which he never heard, and which may not even in literal fact have been delivered, we nevertheless accept the pretense both as "necessary" and as "probable" in the sense laid down in the ninth chapter of the *Poetics*. "Pretending" *is* of the essence of the atmosphere of art and the relinquishing of reality (as this is certified by the criteria of the understanding) is its major presupposition.

This is what Coleridge had in mind in his lecture "The Progress of Drama" of 1818, where he said apropos of a stage setting: "The true stage illusion in this and in all other things consists—not in the mind's judging it to be a forest, but in its remission of the judgment that it is not a forest," and it is but a restatement for the drama of that "willing suspension of disbelief for the moment" which he elsewhere declared constitutes "poetic faith."

Not all dramatists presuppose so extreme a distanciation, so clear a separation between the illusion and the reality. Hugo von Hofmannsthal once quoted with approval the following passage from Lucian:[15]

When every spectator becomes one with what happens on the stage, when everyone recognizes in the performance, as in a mirror, the reflection of his own true impulses, then, but not until then, success has been achieved. Such a dumb spectacle is at the same time nothing less than the fulfillment of the Delphic maxim 'Know thyself,' and those who return from the theatre have experienced what was truly an experience.

Bertolt Brecht proposes a Marxist activism which turns the theater into a breeding ground of action:[16]

It is not enough only to ask from the theater insights—informative images of reality. Our theater must in addition excite the desire to understand, must stimulate a pleasure in the transformation of reality. The spectators must not merely witness how Prometheus Bound is freed, but must have actually excited in themselves the urge to free him. All the pleasures and impulses of the inventor and the discoverer; all the triumphant feelings of the emancipator must be learned from our theater. [1953]

This is the very antithesis of that separation of theatricality and practice upon which Aristotle insisted, and suggests one good reason why Brecht subtitled the *Writings on the Theater* (from which the quotation is taken) "a non-Aristotelian theory of the drama."

The Aristotelian theory of the drama does indeed, as Brecht intimates, reduce the incitement of the passions; otherwise it would have had to acknowledge those very dangers in the arts against which Plato's strictures had been directed. But in Aristotle's *Poetics* are first classically formulated those principles of the dramatic imagination which stress "illusory reenactment" as with Dewey or "pretending" as with Ryle.

Drama is "the imitation of an action," and while this leaves both of the major terms in the definition themselves undefined, the *Poetics* does by implication suggest certain important relationships between them. As artistic imitators, the essential procedures of Sophocles and Aristophanes are alike, "for both imitate persons acting and doing. Hence, some say, the name of 'drama' is given to such poems as representing action."[17] The chief contrast in the "manner of imitation" which distinguishes tragedy from epic is that while the latter narrates or "tells about" at second remove, the former *embodies* the story, it *enacts* the plot, it makes of language itself a form of *gesture*. The dramatic, in short, is a form of *kinematics* in which organic sympathy is *so immediately solicited* that the categories of "same" and "other" lose their customary force. As Paul Goodman quite rightly puts it: "Sympathy seems to be a recognition of the other and of the sameness of the other and one's self. The passions and mirth of drama are not sympathic; there is not enough other; we identify ourselves with the directly presented and quickly moving plot, and feelings take us by storm."[18]

But to say that the feelings take us by storm is perhaps less important than to emphasize the directness of the presentation and the swiftness in the movement of the plot, for the essence of the dramatic imagination lies in the dimensions of *immediacy* and of *movement*. Immediacy is secured by the mimetic effort, and by the limitation of the time span of effective action, which heightens, essentializes, and concentrates the activity. In life, as in Newtonian mechanics, one might say, time flows equably, and beginnings and endings are never and always. But to demand that the tragic drama should endeavor "as far as possible to confine itself to a single revolution of the sun" is but to secure by mechanical means alone that maximal concentration of activity which distinguishes the infinite duration of a continuous chronology from the encapulated passion of the dramatic event. It means (in Aristotelian terms) the contrast between the infinite "story" and the finitude of "plot."

In one sense this is the precise distinction between "nature" and "art," between the *apeiron* of the *Physics* and the *olon kai teleion* of the *Poetics,* and it emphasizes the manner in which the ordering activity of the dramatic imagination prepares those selected "incidents" or "episodes" whose organic unity constitutes the plot. Speaking relatively and very roughly (but in a fashion which we shall subsequently be forced to modify) "experience," or the given manifestations of the "stories" of real life, is boundless and without limit, as amorphous as it is continuous. Events succeed one another in nature with neutral regularity, and, in fact, the featureless continuity of the causal sequence is the device which the understanding utilizes to present a "Nature" thick with its "constant conjunctions" or "functional correlations," but bland in its references to past and future, and, therefore, without a face.

In contrast, the work of art is shaped, limited, complete in itself—a unity of the poet's making. Aristotle says it clearly. The drama "is an imitation of an action that is serious, complete, and of a certain magnitude." And again: "But most important of all is the structure of the incidents. For tragedy is an imitation, not of men, but of an action and of life, and life consists in action, and its end is a mode of action not a quality." And finally: "The Plot, then, is the first principle, and, as it were, the soul of a tragedy. Character holds the second place."[19]

Aristotle's distinction between plot and character is not meant to be a rigorous disjunction (indeed, as he says elsewhere in the *Poetics*, the objects of imitation are "men in action"), and I have not meant to emphasize it so much as the shaping work of "imitation" and that "action" which is the raw material of the dramatic art. For I wish to show that the *Poetics* with its doctrine of imitation casts important light upon the nature and working of the dramatic imagination. In this effort I am, I think, in the camp of those who, like Erich Auerbach, Kenneth Burke, Francis Fergusson, and Richard McKeon, believe that the concept of imitation has direct relevance for contemporary aesthetics, and substantially against those like Wilhelm Dilthey, Benedetto Croce, and R. G. Collingwood, who do not.

It is perhaps now a commonplace of the history of philosophy that the aesthetics of the ancient world is built around the concept of *imitation*, that of the eighteenth century around the concept of *imagination*, that of the contemporary world around the concept of *expression* (as in Croce) or *communication* (as in Dewey). This should be eminently clear by a comparative reading of, say, Aristotle's *Poetics,* Kant's *Critique of Judgment,* and Dewey's *Art as Experience.* But to see that problems in the arts can be alternatively stated as problems of imitation, of imagination, or of communication, does not mean that the resources of any one approach need be neglected even if another is chosen as central. But just such a procedure seemed to be the consequence of Dilthey's theory. He argued that imagination (creation) was the central aesthetic concept, and that since the dramatic practice of Goethe and Schiller the concept of imitation which dominated the ancient world had outlived its usefulness.[20] My own inquiry is in the spirit of Dilthey, for it takes the concept of *imagination* as central, and thus finds its chief theoretical resources in the *Critique of Judgment,* and in the modern investigations which have been inspired by the Kantian conclusions. But I do not therefore abandon the alternative traditions. From those who have philosophized around a concept of "imitation" or of "communication" there is much to learn both directly and indirectly. And if one turns to them consecutively, there is, perhaps, an unconscious dialectical commentary upon the tradition which one oneself espouses. It is therefore not completely by accident that I have first turned to Dewey and Ryle, and then to Aristotle, for illumination concerning the dramatic character of the imagination of which they implicitly or explicitly speak, although it is neither the major category of their epistemological investigations nor the necessary center of their aesthetic concerns. Let us, then, return to the *Poetics.*

4   IT IS wholly characteristic of Aristotle's naturalism that he should find the origin of the arts in a quality of human "nature"—that the successes of the artifices of "making" should ultimately rest upon the

exercise of a natural power. The grounding of creativity in
natural impulse provides a commentary likewise upon the
nature of dramatic imagination:[21]

Poetry in general seems to have sprung from two causes, each of
them lying deep in our nature. First, the instinct of imitation is
implanted in man from childhood, one difference between him
and other animals being that he is the most imitative of living
creatures; and through imitation he learns his earliest lessons; and
no less universal is the pleasure felt in things imitated. We have
evidence of this in the facts of experience. Objects which in themselves we view with pain, we delight to contemplate when reproduced with minute fidelity: such as the forms of the most ignoble
animals and of dead bodies. The cause of this again is, that to learn
gives the livliest pleasure, not only to philosophers but to men in
general; whose capacity, however, of learning is more limited.
Thus the reason why men enjoy seeing a likeness is, that in contemplating it they find themselves learning or inferring, and saying
perhaps, 'Ah, that is he.' For if you happen not to have seen the
original, the pleasure will be due not to the imitation as such, but
to the execution, the colouring, or some such other cause.

The urge to mimicry, the impulse to copy, represent, transform, caricature, exaggerate, reenact, is an original impulse
of our active natures, only equaled by the passive pleasure
which we feel as spectators. Built into the nature of man,
therefore, are the conditions of theater, alternately histrionic
and participative. As the *Politics* envisages the political process as that of "ruling and of being ruled," so the *Poetics* envisages the imagination as alternately "playing the part" and
"witnessing the performance." And if the pleasures of enactment are kinaesthetic and lively, no less are those of perception which rest upon *re*-cognition, and hence the element of
universality.

This latter is important. For it is closely bound up with the
native delight in formalization here suggested by Aristotle
and later to provide us with a clue to the understanding of
that paradox—"the tragic pleasure." The cares and catastro-

phes, the miseries and the monstrosities of life, reproduced with creative fidelity, and formalized in art, become objects of intense pleasure. Here is at once a poetic rationale for the reproductive imagination and the epistemic function it performs. The discrimination of similarity (recognition) is a foundation of all learning, since only through it is the discovery of the universal possible. But even where this "educational urge" is absent, the intrinsic character of formalization (spatial organization or chromatic detail) will provide satisfaction for the imaginative powers.

The creative process is for Aristotle closely patterned upon the duality of the imaginative powers, upon the serial "moments" of "playing the part" and "witnessing the performance." Whereas in Kant the chief emphasis of the aesthetics is upon the subjective response (and hence the concern is with a critique of *judgment* and of *taste*), the chief emphasis in Aristotle is upon the poetic *object,* upon the *work* to be made. Thus whereas the *Critique of Judgment* is (although in a very rarified sense to be sure) a guide to the intricacies of aesthetic perception and a statement of principles which might intrigue the connoisseur, the *Poetics* is a manual for the practicing dramatist. And, in the normative inquiry which this entails—in the course of a legislation for the poetic process—Aristotle suggests once again how the dramatic imagination has both a *visual* and a *kinetic* component. In this case the reference is not to natural powers, but to the activity of dramatic construction; to the *pretending* and the *rehearsal* which are inseparable from the *making* of the playwright.

In constructing the plot and working it out with the proper diction, the poet should place the scene, as far as possible before his eyes. In this way, seeing everything with the utmost vividness, as if he were a spectator of the action, he will discover what is in keeping with it, and be most unlikely to overlook inconsistencies. . . . Again, the poet should work out his play, to the best of his power, with appropriate gestures; for those who feel emotion are most convincing through natural sympathy with the characters they represent and one who is agitated storms, one who is angry rages, with the most life-like reality. Hence poetry implies either a happy gift of nature or a strain of madness. In the one case a man can take the mould of any character: in the other, he is lifted out of his proper self.[22]

Here again are those natural powers which are the presuppositions of theater combined in the preliminaries of the poetic work. The playwright in his imagination must be both actor and audience, and the assumption of this double role presupposes both kinetic and perceptual elements in the dramatic imagination. The "appropriate gestures" with which the poet should work out his play are simply the prototype of Dewey's "reenactment," and "the happy gift of nature" or "the strain of madness" which contribute the mimetic skill can be attributed either to the superb actualization of a natural power, or to an intuitive creativity so intense that it seems to be less a natural endowment than a gift of the gods.

Much of the most important material which we can derive from Aristotle concerning the dramatic imagination is in *Poetics* VII-XIV, which is an extended treatment of plot *(mythos)*. We hear from Aristotle constantly that the plot is the soul of drama, that the true poet is the maker of plots rather than of verses, and we conclude (rightly, I think) that the essense of the dramatic is somehow to be revealed in the treatment of this element. In the famous comparison (VII, 4) between any beautiful object artificially constructed and any living organism (which indicates in a few words the logic of Kant's later division of the third *Critique* into a treatment of the aesthetic and the teleological judgment) Aristotle shows how the teleological relationship of whole and parts is a necessary criterion of the beautiful, and he explicates this "organic" relationship in terms of size and orderly arrangement of parts. Magnitude and order thus become the foundation for the unity and sense of the whole. But the organic metaphor obviously has a dual application—to parts coexisting simultaneously in space, and to parts succeeding one another serially in time. Whereas the first is primarily the realm of the teleological imagination, the latter is the realm of the dramatic. The organic unity of the tragic plot consists in the fact that it has a beginning, a middle, and an end, and this cliché of experience is, at the same time, the first principle of the dramatic imagination. Aristotle explicates the requirement of wholeness (unity) in the plot by an application of the "law of probability and necessity" which governs the sequence of the "events," "incidents," or "episodes" which compose it, and it is this which in the first instance governs the definition of proper serial order. A beginning is, therefore, "that which does not itself follow anything by causal necessity" and an end is "that which itself naturally follows some other thing . . . but has nothing following it." As Paul Goodman rightly sums it up: ". . . in the beginning anything is possible; in the middle things become probable; in the ending everything is necessary." In *Richard II*, for example, from the conflict between Bolingbroke and Mowbray in the first scene, anything can follow. By Act III even Richard himself sees probability in the passage "From Richard's night to Bolingbroke's fair day." In Act V his murder by Exton (or another) is inevitable.

But to see the sense in which we have here the essence of the dramatic, we must pass from the epistemic statement to its emotional correlative. The concepts of "possibility," "probability," and " necessity" are *logical* relations, modalities, part of the apparatus of the understanding as it relates propositions and surveys the natural world. But to these merely logical relations there are indeed psychological correlates. "Possibility" means liberty, means freedom of choice, means suspense. "Probability" means the narrowing of choice, the acceleration of movement, and hence a heightening of dramatic focus. "Necessity" means absence of choice, absence of suspense, means, in short, conclusion. Thus the Aristotelian cliché of the beginning, the middle, and the end, involves a deeper reference to passion, involvement, and concern. The beginning of the play means the rousing of excitement (this, indeed, is its peculiar problem). The middle of the play means the maximizing of excitement. The end of the play means the dwindling of excitement. This is why the dramatic experience is inevitably associated with the rhythms of tension and release.

In Aristotle all of this psychological suggestiveness is present, but expressed in an idiom whose primary reference is the tragic plot. Every tragedy falls into two parts; "Complication" *(desis)* and "Dénouement" *(lusis)*, and the moment which separates them, "the turning-point" *(metabasis)* or climax, marks the moment of greatest dramatic excitement. Complication winds up the emotions like a tautened spring; the *metabasis* brings maximum involvement, but also release, and the denouement that return to the plateau of ordinary emotion which rounds off the dramatic experience.

To this general formula Aristotle adds a series of dramatic devices closely allied to the characteristic emotions of the dramatic experience. These latter are the tragic feelings of pity, terror, and surprise, and the devices which service them are "reversal" *(peripeteia)*, "recognition" *(anagnorisis)* and "the tragic incident" *(pathos)*. Reversal means a change in the direction of the action of the play with an ironic reference to the opposition of fact and intention. There is reversal when events boomerang, when the recoil of the gun upsets the hunter, when acting with one intention, one accomplishes the reverse of that intended. It is, therefore (as so often employed in *Oedipus Tyrranus*), the basis of dramatic irony. Recognition is the change from ignorance to knowledge, the moment of truth, the instant of dramatic perception when a Lear is left with the knowledge of his former blindness, a Creon with the knowledge of his stubborn folly. The tragic incident is the destructive or painful action, such as death on the stage, mutilation, bodily agony, and it is here that the pity and terror of the spectators reaches its curiously cathartic

climax. Nor is this by the spectacle alone, for the inner structure of the plot, its narrative devices even, should be sufficient
to present the tragic incident.

Aristotle's terms for the elements of the dramatic imagination (complication, turning-point, denouement, reversal, recognition, climactic incident) have become the coinage of all
critical talk concerning the theater. For they are the fruit not
merely of a rational, but also of an inductive study of the
Greek play and its audience. But that structural sense which
sees emotion as the function of logical relationships, and thus
comprehends the mutual implication of feeling and form, is
nowhere better expressed than in those abstracted plot synop-
ses which Aristotle provides respectively of the *Iphigenia in
Tauris* and of the *Odyssey*.[23]

A young girl is sacrificed; she disappears mysteriously from the
eyes of those who sacrificed her; she is transported to another country, where the custom is to offer up all strangers to the goddess. To
this ministry she is appointed. Some time later her own brother
chances to arrive. The fact that the oracle for some reason ordered
him to go there, is outside the general plan of the play. The purpose, again of his coming is outside the action proper. However he
comes, he is seized, and, when on the point of being sacrificed, reveals who he is. The mode of recognition may be either that of
Euripides or of Polyidus, in whose play he exclaims very naturally:
—'So it was not my sister only, but I too, who was doomed to be
sacrificed'; and by that remark he is saved.

Thus the story of the Odyssey can be stated briefly. A certain man
is absent from home for many years; he is jealously watched by
Poseidon, and left desolate. Meanwhile his home is in a wretched
plight—suitors are wasting his substance and plotting against his
son. At length, tempest-tost, he himself arrives; he makes certain
persons acquainted with him; he attacks the suitors with his own
hand, and is himself preserved while he destroys them. This is the
essence of the plot; the rest is episode.

In each of these we have the same rhythm of complication,
turning-point, denouement. In each case the recognition and

the reversal are counterparts of a single action. Orestes reveals who he is and by the comment on his doom he is saved. Odysseus likewise reveals who he is, and at this very moment destroys those who would destroy him. Further comment is hardly necessary. The *Poetics* is the fountainhead of the Western dramatic tradition, and it is a rich and permanent storehouse for our knowledge of the dramatic imagination.

5 IN THE preceding section I have cited the *Poetics* less as a text in aesthetics than as a manual of ancient theater in which, if we read between the lines, we shall find much that will throw light upon the quality of the dramatic imagination. In the *Poetics,* I think, are to be found both the analysis of what alike in experience and in the art work is inherently "dramatic," and in consequence also those mechanisms (elevated into principles) which are the technical repository of the tragic dramatist. The simple and the complex plot, recognitions and reversals, the tragic incident and the tragic error are all ingredients in the production of the tragic pleasure, and, interpreted with sufficient generality, their joint consideration produces a kind of phenomenology of dramatic experience.

To apply the principles of the *Poetics* to the corpus of Western literature would illuminate the phenomenology, but it would be an infinite task. Instead I should like to take a single principle of the dramatic imagination and elaborate it in a very limited area for the light which it casts on the working of what for want of a better phrase we might call "the dramatic instinct." This is the principle of "reversal" as it satisfies the moral impulse; that is, as it expresses itself in the dramatic concept of villainy and its ultimate outcome.

The underlying idea here is that of *nemesis,* one of the simplest and most pervasive of dramatic notions. In essence it expresses the moral demands of justice in a world all too recalcitrant to its insistent claims, and here it makes a purposive and sublimated reappearance in the work of art. "Nemesis" in literature is the mechanism of retribution, not as the decision of the court of law (although in the *Merchant of Venice* or the *Eumenides* it may be so), but as implicit in the working out of the natural order. For the Greek mind it was that principle of elasticity in human life which permitted a final snapping back from moral dislocation, and thus the assertion of a principle of equilibrium in the moral universe. In Christian thought it is the analogue of divine judgment, noting the link between sin and retribution, and making it explicit in the work of art. But whether in the Greek drama, or in any drama touched by Christian piety, it is in this relationship that the moral imagination finds its purest pleasure. It is a pleasure which the drama only stimulates: there is perhaps no effect more deeply satisfying than that which emphasizes the point that "as a man soweth, so shall he reap."[24]

In the dramatic presentation of nemesis, no one since the Greeks has performed the task as boldly and as skillfully as Shakespeare. *The Merchant of Venice* may owe much to the romantic suspense of the story of the three caskets, but it is the story of the cruel and subtle Jew, bitter and obsessed, but humbled at last and brought low by a cunning (if not an intellect) equal to his own, that feeds the dramatic appetite. The same mode of perception is at work in *Richard III*, where "the bloody dog let loose in a sheepfold," having brought down Clarence, Anne, Grey, Rivers, Dorset, Buckingham, and Hastings in morbid and deformed ambition, finds his own final retribution in the taunting ghosts before the eve of the battle, and the final agony of Bosworth field. The dramatic historiography of the War of the Roses may have been Shakespeare's manifest theme, but its latent vision is that of the nemesis of villainy and the moral fulfillment of a blood-stained earth at last returned for tillage.

But I do not wish to dwell upon the dramatic uses of nemesis in Shakespeare. Instead, I should like to turn very briefly to the story of Don Juan Tenorio, whose nemesis has become one of the peculiar obsessions of world literature. The complete literary genealogy is beyond my purpose, but I should like to compare the legend in what are perhaps its three greatest exemplifications: its entry into the Western tradition in 1630 in the Spanish play of Tirso de Molina, *El Burlador de Sevilla* (The Trickster of Seville), its revival in Molière's play of 1665, *Don Juan ou Le Festin de Pierre,* and finally its culminating expression in Mozart's masterpiece of 1787, *Don Giovanni* (with libretto by Lorenzo Da Ponte).

In Molina's original, Don Juan is primarily a youthful and impudent trickster. In the first act, which takes place in Naples, he rapes the Duchess Isabel, who is expecting instead her lover, the Duke Octavio. Forced to flee Italy, he is washed up on the shore of Tarragona and proceeds to seduce the country maid Thisbe, who has rescued him from the sea. He then sets fire to her hut and flees to Seville. In the second act, he by a similar trick surprises Doña Ana, the beloved of his friend the Marquis of La Mota, and then in turn surprised by her father Don Gonzalo, kills him in a duel, leaving his friend La Mota to be arrested for the crime. The scene then shifts to the countryside near Dos Hermanas where preparations are in progress for the wedding of the peasant couple Batricio and his Aminta. By a ruse (he swears before God to marry her) he seduces Aminta also.

Meanwhile the Duchess Isabel has come to Spain and by chance meets Thisbe, who tells her of Don Juan's treachery. We are now well into the third act. Don Juan and his lackey Catalinón seek sanctuary in a church in Seville, in a private chapel of which stands the stone statue of Don Gonzalo, whom Don Juan has murdered. Don Juan impudently invites the stone statue to supper, and the next night at the inn where Don Juan is supping, the stone statue enters, frightening Catalinón half out of his wits, and returns an invitation to Don Juan to dine with him the following night in his chapel. Don Juan accepts the invitation, and the next evening, true to his word, Don Juan comes to the church, sups with the statue, gives it his hand, and in this act falls dead. Amid thunderous noise, the tomb sinks with Don Juan and the statue, leaving Catalinón to creep out of the wreckage. Meanwhile all of Don Juan's victims (Isabela, Ana, Thisbe, Aminta, Octavio, La Mota) have assembled at the Spanish court to demand justice of Alfonso, King of Castille. Catalinón enters, and reports the end of Don Juan. So finally by royal decree Octavio and Isabel, Ana and La Mota are to marry, and all ends happily.

Molière's adaptation of the Don Juan theme is very different in spirit from Molina's original. There is less movement of plot, but there is deeper characterization. Above all there is that kind of satirical disquisition directed against all the usual *bêtes noires* (physicians, false piety, the hypocrite) for which Molière is famous. The play opens with Sganarelle, Don Juan's valet, talking with Gusman, the servant of a certain Doña Elvire whom the Don has married and abandoned. Sganarelle maligns Don Juan and says he has left Dona Elvire forever. Don Juan enters with a new affair in the offing, and Sganarelle upbraids him to his face. Don Juan puts off the scolding with blasphemy, and Sganarelle warns him of the final punishment of heaven. Doña Elvire enters, and Don Juan repulses her politely but firmly before he exits. She is left swearing revenge.

The second act opens in the country by the sea with the two rustic lovers Pierrot and Charlotte. The former has rescued Don Juan and Sganarelle from the sea, and he complains that Charlotte does not love him sufficiently. As he leaves, Don Juan enters, and makes love to Charlotte, promising in the process to marry her. Pierrot returns only to be given a comic beating by the Don, and as he exits, another peasant girl, Mathurine (whom Don Juan has also promised to marry) enters. In the ensuing jealous argument between Charlotte and Mathurine, Don Juan slips away. It now appears that he is being hunted by a posse headed by the two brothers of Doña Elvire, Don Carlos and Don Alonso, seeking revenge for their sister. To disguise himself Don Juan forces Sganarelle to change clothes with him. Molière's third act opens with a discussion between Don Juan and Sganarelle in which the Don blasphemously denies all belief in heaven, hell, the devil, and the after-life. Sganarelle counters with a perfect statement of the teleological argument, but the conversation is interrupted as Don Juan hastens to the rescue of a man nearby set upon by brigands. It turns out that he is Don Carols, Doña Elvire's brother, and, not recognizing Don Juan in his disguise, he explains his errand of revenge. At this moment Don Alonso, the other brother, comes in and recognizes Don Juan, whom he wishes to kill immediately, but Carlos persuades him to postpone their revenge. The brothers leave, swearing to kill Don Juan on sight should they see him again. Nearby in the forest is the tomb of the Commander whom Don Juan has killed, topped by a stone statue of the dead man. Don Juan as a joke forces Sganarelle to invite the stone statue to supper. The statue twice nods its head in assent. Don Juan and Sganarelle exit hastily.

The fourth act begins with Don Juan at supper. First comes in an importunate tradesman asking for his money. He is disposed of in Molière's best satirical vein. Then Don Juan's father, Don Louis, enters and upbraids his son for his sins. As he leaves, Doña Elvire enters. Bringing the warnings of heaven, she begs him to repent, but he arrogantly refuses and she goes out. Don Juan is now feasting (with Sganarelle surreptitiously stuffing his mouth with morsels from the table) when a loud knock is heard. The door bursts open and the stone statue of the commander comes in to invite Don Juan for supper the following night. Don Juan accepts and the statue retires. The final act opens with Don Juan promising his father that he has repented and will turn over a new leaf, but hardly has his father left when he tells Sganarelle that this has only been a ruse. Hypocrisy, he affirms, is both fashionable and eminently useful. Don Carlos enters to ask if the Don is now ready to return to his sister, but Don Juan with

mock piety says that heaven would not permit the resumption
of so sinful a union. Don Carlos exits, but a specter appears
and warns him to repent. Again he refuses, and at this
dramatic moment the stone statue makes its final appearance.
It asks Don Juan to give it his hand and as he does so, amid
thunder and lightning, the earth engulfs them both.
Sganarelle is left lamenting the loss of his wages.

It is unnecessary to detail the way in which the Mozart-
Da Ponte version of the plot borrows from both Molina and
Molière. Molina emphasizes in Don Juan the sexual prof-
ligate; Molière the blasphemer against heaven. Mozart-
DaPonte retains both elements. The lackey in all three
versions (called Catalinón in Molina, Sganarelle in Molière,
Leporello in Mozart) is a stock comic figure, as are the two
rustic lovers (Batricio and Aminta in Molina, Pierrot and
Charlotte in Molière, Masetto and Zerlina in Mozart), whose
relationship is temporarily destroyed by the Don. Da Ponte has
borrowed Doña Anna and Don Octavio from Molina and
Doña Elvíra from Moliére, but this leads to some overelabora-
tion of a plot already in Molina and Molière complicated
enough.

None of this, of course, can give any conception of the
musical marvels which Mozart's genius has added: Doña
Elvira's indignant entrance aria in E Flat Major, Don
Giovanni and Zerlina's immortal duet *"La ci darem la mano,"*
Doña Anna's outraged and convincing demand for revenge
("Or sai chi l'onore"), the champagne aria, and the other
scenes leading from musical miracle to musical miracle.
Da Ponte has retained some clarity in Act I, but the beginning
of Act II is a madness of plot confusion redeemed only by the
music, which never falters from Leporello's invitation (E
Major) to the stone statue in the cemetery to the wonderful
penultimate scene in D Minor (beginning with the Commen-
datore's *"Don Giovanni a cenar teco"* and ending with
Leporello's agonized "Ah!" with its accompanying descend-
ing minor scale) which provides what is surely the most

dramatic and powerful seven minutes in the whole of musical literature.

The Molina, Molière, and Mozart versions of the Don Juan legend differ in plot, in characterization, and in atmosphere, but it tells us something about the dramatic imagination that they are alike in the invitation to the stone guest, and the climactic episode in which the statue takes Don Juan by the hand, squeezes the life out of him, and, finally, accompanied by the rough mutiny of the elements, drags him to his damnation.

In Molina's *Trickster of Seville*, as the stone statue sinks into the earth with Don Juan amid the rumble of thunder it intones: "Such is God's justice. What is done is paid for," and the King of the Castile, adding his healing words to Cata-linón's hysterical account, concludes: "Just punishment from Heaven has been dealt." In Molière's *Le Festin de Pierre*, Sganarelle's final words are: *"Voilà par sa mort un chacun satisfait: Ciel offensé, lois voilées, filles séduites, familles déshonorées, parents outragés, femmes mises à mal, maris poussés à bout, tout le monde est content . . . [avec] l'impieté de mon maître puni par le plus épouvantable châtiment du monde."* And the final D Major ensemble of remaining characters in *Don Giovanni* proclaims that it is the doom of the wicked that their end is made to match the life they have lived:

> *Questo e il fin di chi fa mal;*
> *E de' perfidi la morte*
> *Alla vita e sempre ugual.*

Spanish renaissance, French classicism, Austrian baroque; each asserts its characteristic point of view, but the nemesis of villainy is a constant in each of these exercises of the dramatic imagination. Philosophers from Kierkegaard to Camus have dwelt upon the meaning of the legend, and it is clear that the ambiguous character of the Don, exemplar of unnatural sensuality or of impiety, lends itself both to a pagan and to a Christian interpretation. But whether we see here the daring, romantic, and theatrical machinery of seduction at work, or the gross, immoderate expression of an unselective sexuality, or the cynical, atheistic, and Machiavellian defier of the laws of God and man, it is the climactic conclusion which counts. Things "beyond nature" intervene to work the downfall of a character himself profoundly "unnatural." And in the intrinsic appropriateness of this moral nemesis is to be found one of the pervasive principles of the dramatic imagination.

6 IN THE preceding sections I have approached the problem of the dramatic imagination through the concepts of Aristotle's *Poetics,* chiefly that of "plot" and of the actions and passions by means of which any plot is constructed and developed. But here I wish to suggest that the idea of "the dramatic" is an analogical concept, applicable at once to the theater, to religious belief, and to the rational operations of mentality. If there is a drama consequent upon the mimetic instinct, why should there not equally be a drama of discourse and of ideas? This is the conclusion to which we are led by a consideration of both the themes and the techniques of Plato's dialogues.

The conclusion is confirmed by the phenomenology of poetic experience. The lyric presupposes but *a single person.* For it is a *vox clamantis in deserto*—a cry; the personal outpouring of the feelings of a heart full to overflowing. Such a cry may be overheard, but it is not intrinsic to its nature that it must be. The epic presupposes two persons. It is the story which one man tells to another. Narrative is of its essence, and it is inconceivable that any story should be told without its proper audience. Lyric is not properly *discourse* at all. Epic *is* discourse, but directed from a single source. The drama presupposes *three persons.* It is conversation overheard: the dialogue between two or more persons in the presence of a third. This is why the Platonic dialogue (as Aristotle almost seems to have noted in the *Poetics*), if it is not strictly "theater," yet shares with the dramatic experience certain important qualities. Philosophic dialogue may be conceived either as the conversation which the soul holds with herself or as the conversation which those who participate in the fellowship of reason hold with one another. In either case the *form* of the enterprise is one with the inner movement of the thought which it expresses. The dramatic imagination, therefore, has its cognitive tasks also, and these are suggested by that passage from idle *conversation* to formal *dialogue,* and from formal dialogue to *dialectical method* as this movement is exemplified in the works of Plato.

Woodbridge defined the Platonic enterprise as "the dramatization of the life of reason," and he remarked that here mind itself is put upon the stage to play its part as a character. In the Platonic dialogues intellect "is lifted out of its practical efficacy and let play. It exhibits its humor and pathos, its comedy and tragedy. It often goes down to its own defeat, defeated by circumstances and its own subtlety, broken off by the inevitable intrusion of affairs, mastered by irrational impulse or seduced by the stories men tell themselves to bolster up a faith they cannot establish by reason."[25] Greek thought, before it is stabilized in the Lyceum and in the scientific treatises of Aristotle, lives the life of discourse, whether this occurs in the shade of a plane tree by the banks of the Ilissus just outside the city walls (as in the *Phaedrus*), at the house of a nobleman within the city (as in the *Symposium* and *Protagoras*), on the steps of the law courts (as in the *Euthyphro*) or at the home of a rich metic at the Piraeus (as in the *Republic*), and the quality of the Platonic philosophy is exhibited less in the static paragraphs of the printed page than in "the dramatic quality of uttered speech with its impact on the ear and its ready stimulation of gesture and posture of the body, its hesitancies and rushings, its sayings and unsayings, its eloquence and its silence."[26]

As one reduces the progressive argument of the *Republic* (with its two climaxes in Book IV and Book IX) to the clearest structure, or as one follows the subtle and complicated argument of the *Theatetus* with its digressions and interludes, its intermissions and breakings of attention, one sees that rational argument also must have a "plot," and when in the *Phaedrus* (264a) Plato asserts (in language anticipating the organicism of the *Poetics*) "that every discourse ought to be a living creature, having a body of its own and a head and feet" and that "there should be a middle, beginning, and end adapted to one another and to the whole," we have not only enunciated an imperative of rhetoric, but a principle for the logical development of argument which can find no more excuse for the jerky, the episodic, and the disconnected in the works of philosophic reason than in the works of the dramatic artist.

But Plato's discourse of reason requires not only the controlled unity of "plot," but also a controlled opposition in "character." The outright antagonism of Socrates and Thrasymachus in the *Republic* only paves the way for the more moderate dialectic of a Glaucon and an Adiemantus. The contrast of mind in a Socrates and a Protagoras is as germane to the *Protagoras* as the issue of the hedonistic ethics which they debate, and the opposition of the views of Gorgias, Callicles, and Polus to those of Socrates in the *Gorgias* displays the valences of temperament in terms of cynicism, patience, and intemperance as well as the differences between the standpoints of rhetoric, politics, and philosophy on the questions of moral integrity and power.

The crucial concept here is *opposition,* for when this is pressed home beyond the accidents of temperament and the momentary hostilities of casual conversation, and has become self-conscious as a rigorous method for the exploration and establishment of meaning, then dialogue has passed over into *dialectic.* The Platonic dialectic is always social, always related to conversation, always insistent upon the method of question and answer as a procedure (in Plato "the dialectical method"—*he dialektike methodos*—is almost equated with "the power of conversing" or "the art of discussion").[27] It is therefore not at all surprising that it should be so firmly rooted in "character" as well as "plot"; that it should be related to the personalities of the disputants as well as to the structure of contrasting arguments. It is true, of course, that a Platonic dialogue may often conclude with a tentative, or merely provisional, outcome (sometimes with the implicit suggestion that a dogmatic outcome is less humanly and philosophically significant than the quest itself), but this too is only to appropriate for the life of discourse a principle to be drawn from dramatic experience: namely, that the climax is in itself of no intrinsic value, since it is the action leading to it and away from it which constitutes the play.

Dialectic is an art of inquiry rather than of demonstration. It seeks to discover what are the real issues and to *illuminate* them by showing the contrasting views concerning them which are possible. When conclusion is reached, it is less by rigid demonstration than by a natural assent of the participating mind—a kind of "self-evidence," or when a position is abandoned it is because it has been convicted of an inconsistency palpable to all.

From Plato's dialectical investigations and from his treatment of dialogue as the drama of the life of reason certain general conclusions about dialectic can be drawn: (1) Dialectic is a process of operating within the realm of discourse. (2) It is a form of controversy or disputation where sides are drawn and partisanship is presupposed. (3) It is a mode of oppositional thinking which requires an appeal to defined meanings, first principles, or ultimate presuppositions in order either (a) for reconciliation to be achieved, or (b) for ultimate irreconcilability to be made self-evident.[28] We might sum it up by saying that dialectic is the *precipitation of an opposition of meanings in discourse,* and that in this oppositional element lies the drama of the life of mind.

The climax of Mozart's *Don Giovanni* occurs at that over-powering moment when the forces of retribution and revolt come into immediate conflict:

STONE STATUE:	*Pentiti, cangia vita!*
	E l'ultimo momento.
DON GIOVANNI:	*No, no, ch'io non mi pento;*
	Vanne, lontan da me!
STONE STATUE:	*Pentiti, scellerato!*
DON GIOVANNI:	*No, vecchio infatuato!*
STONE STATUE:	*Pentiti!*
DON GIOVANNI:	*No!*
STONE STATUE:	*Si!*
DON GIOVANNI:	*No!*

This principle of dramatic opposition likewise haunts the life of thought whether in the *Gorgias* of Plato, the *Sic et Non* of Abelard, or the *Logic* of Hegel.

It is no part of my concern to trace the history of dialectic throughout the development of Western thought. It should be enough to say that this dramatic and oppositional mode of thinking has a perennial fascination, although its moments of greatest intensity have, indeed, come in the works of Plato, mediaeval scholasticism, and Hegel. The Platonic moment is perhaps the purest, not merely because the theme of almost every Platonic dialogue is that opposition of opinions which arises in the course of conversation, to be either clarified or abandoned, but because the dialectical process is understood to be endless, new controversies taking their origins from the partial resolutions of the old. A preoccupation with dialectic is the task of a lifetime, and we are not surprised, therefore, when in *Sophist* (253e) we have a necessary identification of dialectical mastery and the rightful love of wisdom. For Plato the philosopher and the dialectician are one.

How this Platonism is transmuted into the scholastic method is another complex and difficult story. The disputa-tions of an Anselm and the fiery controversial nature of an Abelard turn into a consideration of the alternative render-ings of Scripture and the multiple possibilities of theological interpretation. Thus the *Dialogus de Veritate* and the *Sic et Non* may equally be considered sources for Peter Lombard's *Libri Sententiorum,* and this in turn stimulates those typically mediaeval debates of philosophical and theological theses, the profusion of *Quidlibetae* and the endless *Questiones Disputatae* with which the Middle Ages are saturated. And if the *Summa Theologica* of Aquinas, with its "Question," "Objections," "On the contrary," "I answer that," and "Reply to objections" pretends to the dogmatic and the demonstrative closer to the science of Aristotle than the dialectic of Plato, yet the *form* of the argument testifies to a dialectical principle never finally overcome.

Hegel returns the modern world to dialectic, but, like Aquinas, in a sense which goes far beyond the modest cognitive claims of the Platonic dialogues. Hegel distinguishes clearly between formal logic and dialectical method, but in such a way as to generalize the method beyond its employment in conversation or dispute. For Hegel it is the intrinsic pattern of all intellectual activity and (since for him thinking and reality are identical) of all natural change as well. Thus, wherever there is opposition or change, duality, diversity, or contradiction, there is the material for dialectical thinking. But for Hegel, unlike Plato, the dialectic proceeds by means of a finite hierarchy and ends with a coping stone to crown the tower of ascending trilogies. In Hegel there is a last resolution and a final synthesis of truth. But for Plato the conversation never ends, which is to say that it ends as it begins, with a "likely story" or a mere "suggestion of ours concerning Being" or perhaps in no seizure of Being other than the philosophical enrichment of having undergone the dialectical experience itself.

But it is not my purpose to evaluate the forms of dialectic. All that I wish to emphasize is that the oppositional mode of perception upon which it is founded is dramatic through and through, and that here, in the theater of mind, as outside in the theater which real actors inhabit, we shall find the productions of a dramatic imagination.

7 ANDRÉ GIDE is a literary figure to whom we must always listen with respect, and he was a dramatist of some note, but his view of the theater suggests a considerable cynicism. "The theater," he said,[29] "is really an extraordinary thing. People like you and me assemble at night in a hall to see others pretend to passions that we have no right to have—for our laws and our morals forbid. . . . Could that be partly the reason for our pleasure in the theater: to hear those voices ring out which conventional morals are apt to muffle?" Gide suggests that the drama may be in conflict with current morality, and that its "pretense" is therefore anti-ethical in essence. But I want to suggest something which is both the opposite of this and very obvious —that the dramatic imagination may be used for purposes which are profoundly moral, and, in fact, that this is what happens where "the dramatic" has reference not to the theater, nor the drama of the mind, but to religion.

In this idea we return once more to Jane Harrison's emphasis upon religious ritual. Ritual is by definition reenactment. Reenactment is inherently dramatic. Therefore the dramatic imagination must have its religious, no less than its intellectual and its secular, relevance. There is something important here to be learned from Nietzsche. In *The Birth of Tragedy* he insisted that art owes its continuous evolution to the Apollonian-Dionysian duality, and that the union of the Apollonian plastic arts and the nonvisual art of music inspired by Dionysus produced Attic tragedy. He might have said the same of the developed religious consciousness, which has a doubly imaginative source: on the one hand that immediate reading into the universe of form (that full delight in illusion which is completely expressed in the myth-making faculty as Cassirer has explored it) and on the other that active, mimetic concern with ritual reenactment which inspired the Dionysian celebrations of the dying god and the sowing of new seed. Religion has also its Apollonian cosmology, a bright image of the origin of the world and the deployment of its mysterious forces. And it has its Dionysian theatricality wherein the celebration of *the unforgettable event* means the periodic re-presentation of its essence in dramatic form. There is the myth of Hesiod's *Theogony* and the myth of *Genesis*. And there is in the Christian world the ritual dramatization of birth, death, and rebirth in the Christmas and Easter events, as there was in ancient Athens the ritual celebrations of the *Diasia* in honor of Zeus, the *Thesmophoria* beloved of Demeter and her daughter Kore, and the *Anthesteria* devoted to Dionysus. But myth and ritual alike, whether pagan or Christian, are both inherently dramatic.

Religion, as Gilbert Murray has said, deals with the unexplored, the uncharted areas of human experience, and it does so by emotional, almost subconscious forms of apprehension. Thus, the Olympian gods are the almost-Apollonian images which Nietzsche spoke of—artist's dreams of ideals, and aspirations composed of half-forgotten traditions, make-believe, and allegory. Religious "truth" could then hardly be other than a set of creeds and definitions which are little more than metaphors, attempts to use human language for purposes to which it does not readily lend itself. Consider, for example, the Greek and the Hebrew accounts of the drama of creation. Here is *Genesis* I, 1-7.

In the beginning God created the heaven and the earth.

And the earth was without form, and void; and darkness was upon the face of the deep. And the spirit of God moved upon the face of the waters.

And God said, Let there be light: and there was light.

And God saw the light, that it was good: and God divided the light from the darkness.

And God called the light Day and the darkness he called Night. And the evening and the morning were the first day.

And God said, Let there be a firmament in the midst of the waters, and let it divide the waters from the waters.

And God made the firmament, and divided the waters which

were under the firmament from the waters which were above the firmament: and it was so.

Here is Hesiod's *Theogony* II.

First of all the Void (Chaos) came into being, next broad-bosomed Earth, the solid and eternal home of all, and Eros the most beautiful of the immortal gods, who in every man and every god softens the sinews and overpowers the prudent purpose of the mind. Out of Void came Darkness and black Night, and out of Night came Light and Day, her children conceived after union in love with Darkness. Earth first produced starry Sky, equal in size with herself, to cover her on all sides. Next she produced the tall mountains, the pleasant haunts of the gods, and also gave birth to the barren waters, sea with its raging surges—all this without the passion of love. Thereafter she lay with Sky and gave birth to Ocean with its deep current, Coeus and Crius and Hyperion and Iapetus; Thea and Rhea and Themis and Mnemosyne; also golden-crowned Phoebe and lovely Tethys. After these came cunning Cronus, the youngest and boldest of her children; and he grew to hate the father who had begotten him. . . .

In some respects the accounts are singularly alike. Certain "elements" of creation are common in the two stories: the void, heaven (sky) and earth, night and day, darkness and light. But if these dramatic oppositions are common, the dramatic "act" of creation is not. The Hebrew account makes of creation almost a *decision,* an *act of will* which eventuates in a divine *imperative: Fiat lux.* And once the original decision has been made, the subsequent work is also *decisive* in the etymological sense of that word—as a "cutting off." "Cutting off," "separating," "dividing" almost rules the first few paragraphs. The light is divided from the darkness, and the firmament is divided from the waters.

The Greek metaphor is completely different. If the Hebrew guiding idea is that of will and moral imperative, that of the Greek is sexual passion; of that Eros "who in every man and every god softens the sinews, and overpowers the prudent purpose of the mind." Creation for the Hebrew is an act of *decision;* for the Greek it is an act of *procreation.* Light and Day are the children of Night and Darkness, Earth lay with Sky and gave birth to Ocean as to Themis (law) and Mnemosyne (memory). So the Greek drama of religious personification continues.

Thaddeus Zielinski has told us[30] that for the Greeks not one religion existed, but three: the poetic religion, otherwise called mythology; the philosophical religion, or the way the gods are understood in the Academy, the Lyceum, the Stoa, and by Epicurus; and the citizen's religion which bound the Athenian freeman by the cults to which he belonged and the ceremonies in which he participated. For our purposes the first and third are the most important. They roughly correspond to the general distinction between myth and ritual, and they show respectively religion as "the deification of nature" and religion as "the consecration of work" (the phrases are Zielinski's), both of which contain dramatic elements.

For the ancient Greek the sense of the mysterious life of surrounding nature was the foundation of religious feeling. Nature is not dead but instinct with spiritual powers, and each natural object has its indwelling spirit, its god or goddess. Not only Demeter, Zeus, and Poseidon for the major elements, but each tree has its dryad, and Artemis, goddess of the groves, as their queen, each spring flowing from a crevice in the rocks has its naiad, each river its river god, and even the high wastes of Hymettus or Pentelicon, where naked rock or prickly herbage has supplanted fields and forests, has its oreads who spin their invisible fabrics as they sing their inaudible song. And as the earth has its deities, so have the heavens and the seas. Father Zeus and Mother Earth are the major forces, and when the heavens fructify the earth with light, rain, and warmth, it is the congress of male and female element which join to create the life of nature. Such a religion is a drama of living personification from which Greek science itself was never finally able to escape, and if the cosmology of Plato's *Timaeus* and Aristotle's *Physics* contains elements of both teleology and drama, this is because they were also under the influence of mythological elements inextricably fixed in the Greek mind. No one, perhaps, has seen this better than Whitehead.[31]

Every philosophy is tinged with the coloring of some secret imaginative background, which never emerges explicitly into its trains of reasoning. The Greek view of nature, at least that cosmology transmitted from them to later ages, was essentially dramatic. It is not necessarily wrong for this reason: but it was overwhelmingly dramatic. It thus conceived nature as articulated in the way of a work of dramatic art, for the exemplification of general ideas converging to an end. Nature was differentiated so as to provide its proper end for each thing. There was the center of the universe as the end of motion for those things which are heavy, and the celestial spheres as the end of motion for those things whose natures lead them upwards. The celestial spheres were for things which are impassible and ingenerable, the lower regions for things impassible and generable. Nature was a drama in which each thing played its part.

It was only necessary for this cosmological drama to be given a moral twist to have the religion of ancient Greece made available for the mediaeval Christian mind. Santayana in *Three Philosophical Poets* needs only to quote a passage from Plato's *Phaedo* to show how it explains "the whole transition from antiquity to the middle age, from naturalism to supernaturalism, from Lucretius to Dante."[32] The transition involves merely a substitution of Moral Manicheanism for Naturalistic Pluralism. Nature was already composed of living beings. It is now only necessary to maintain that life is a conflict between sin and grace set in a natural environment itself the battle-ground between the forces of good and evil. Evil is identified with matter, spirit with the good, and natural forces are, accordingly, supernatural powers working virtuously or viciously. Santayana describes this ambience in the language of the theater, for he wishes to show also the sense in which the spirit of religion represents an exercise of the dramatic imagination.[33]

The Christians supplied *a dramatic action* for which that *stage* seemed admirably fitted, a story in which the whole human race or the single soul, passed successively through these higher and lower stages. There had been a fall, and there might be a salvation. . . . The material world was only a *scene*, a *stage-setting*, designed expressly to be appropriate for the *play;* and this play was the history of mankind, especially of Israel and of the Church. The persons and events of this history had a philosophic import; each *played some part* in a providential plan. Each illustrated creation, sin, and salvation in some degree, and on some particular level.

It may be, as Gide maintained, that the modern theater, in the limited sense in which he means it, is the locus of immorality (in the sense that it is the make-believe world of those passions which more conservative laws and morals forbid), but it cannot be denied that the dramatic imagination performs a role for religion as well as against it, and that the world-theater of Christianity to which Santayana refers is broader in scope than what may by chance take place at the *Marigny,* the *Chatelet* or the *Vieux Colombier.*

It is Santayana's peculiar virtue that he has appropriated the domain of the dramatic imagination for poetry, and above all for religion, without leaving them open to the charges of meaninglessness and triviality in which the positivistic mentality delights. The understanding has its own necessities, but it does not preempt the total area of meaningful experience. The intuitions which science cannot use remain the inspiration of poetry and religion. And "the impassioned soul," finding the conclusions of the understanding unsuitable to its purposes, must pass beyond it to something else.

From what quarter, then, will it draw the wider views, the deeper harmonies, which it craves? Only from the imagination. There is no other faculty left to invoke. The imagination, therefore, must furnish to religion and to metaphysics those large ideas tinctured with passion, those supersensible forms shrouded in awe, in which alone a mind of great sweep and vitality can find its congenial objects.[34]

The religious world is a system complete and consistent within itself, and if, as the *Divine Comedy* shows us, the domain of the Christian imagination is primarily the domain of moral experience, this is only to say that the same inspiration which is at work within the theater can create a work which is the drama—unraveling, climax, and denouement—of human destiny. It is a play which, in addition to being well constructed in itself, is allegorical in a fashion to engage the deepest interest and arouse the utmost tension in its participants. It is a drama which, its producers firmly believe, contains the moral autobiography of man.

8 IN THE last three sections I have tried to explore the multiple areas of operation of the dramatic imagination by selecting in three cases a principle of dramatic working. Thus the discussion has briefly centered on the role of "nemesis" in drama, of "opposition" in dialectic, and of "personification" in religion. The exploration has not been, nor could it be, systematic, but I hope it has been suggestive of the multiplicity and richness of the "dramatic" field. But in conclusion I want to turn from multiplicity to unity, from the many areas of "the dramatic" to the possible singleness of its experiential source. I want to ask and to consider in the briefest possible compass the question: *Is there a generically dramatic character of all experience upon which (as upon a solid although flexible support) the multiple areas of drama depend?*

The question is related to Aristotle's belief that man *instinctively* imitates and takes pleasure in the imitations of others, but it is also broader — less psychological than epistemological. It depends less upon the assertion of an impulse than upon a phenomenological analysis of the continuous flow of experience. It is true that something which links an Aristotelian and a phenomenological account has been contributed by Francis Fergusson.[35] He concludes his *The Idea of a Theater* with a section entitled "The Histrionic Sensibility: The Mimetic Perception of Action," and by "the histrionic sensibility" he means a form of perception which perceives and discriminates actions in such a way as to make the dramatic art possible. The dramatic art, he says, is based upon this form of perception as music is based upon the ear; it is a faculty of "make-believe" or pretending by means of which kittens play, teachers teach, and actors act. But to say that the histrionic sensibility is a basic or primitive virtue of the human mind is to point to a certain "pre-conceptual basis of the dramatic art." Fergusson appeals (quite rightly, I think) to Aristotle himself, and to his insight that we are aware of things and people "before predication," and he wants to borrow Aristotle's authority to indicate that the perception of action and the urge to imitate it define histrionic sensibility as primitive and direct awareness.

But almost any contemporary analysis of the perceptual process would also, I think, reveal an alternation of highs and lows, of oppositions and alterations, of those qualitative rhythms of experience which are also primitive, direct, and "before predication," and upon which the dramatic characteristics of existence depend. The analyses will differ as to which major concept is taken as of greatest critical importance, but in each will appear the same basic notions: "perception," "experience," and "time." In any case it will actually be what Merleau-Ponty calls it—*Phénomenologie de la perception,* and it is the kind of analysis which appears in Bergson's *Essai sur les donnés immédiates de la conscience (Time and Free Will),* Dewey's *Experience and Nature,* Heidegger's *Sein und Zeit,* as well as Merleau-Ponty's book of the above title. Bergson's analysis is centered about *"La Durée"* (duration), Dewey's about *"experience,"* Heidegger's about *"Zeitlichkeit"* (temporality) and Merleau-Ponty's about *"le corps"* and *"la temporalité,"* but they all have this in common: they call attention not to the abstract, universal, and objective aspects of experience which are the artificial constructions with which science deals, but rather to what Husserl has called the *Lebenswelt*—the ongoing continuity of "lived" experience, the "lived" body, "lived" time, and "lived" space.

The origins, I think, are Bergsonian, and they appear in his insistence that reality is to be reached not by any scientific analysis, but is, rather, given in the continuous process of becoming of our immediate experience which is grasped by intuition and by sympathetic insight. Variations in the intensity of our experiences are immediately qualitative and not to be apprehended in terms of a Newtonian time which flows equably, or the matrix of a homogeneous space. Bergson's chief *aperçu* is the distinction between a "time" which although homogeneous and measurable is yet but an artificial concept founded upon a spatial analogy, and a "duration" which is real, concrete, original and originating, memorable and dramatic.

But it is in Dewey's analysis of "experience" that the Bergsonian "duration" finds its fullest treatment. Dewey also distinguishes between the "gross, macroscopic, crude subject-matter in primary experience" and the "refined, derived objects of reflection," and he finds the latter dependent upon the former. Immediate qualitative differentiations, immediate enjoyments and sufferings are the primary data, and in terms of their outcomes, experience runs its course. "Empirically, things are poignant, tragic, beautiful, humorous, settled, disturbed, comfortable, annoying, barren, harsh, consoling, splendid, fearful; are such immediately and in their own right and behalf. If we take advantage of the word esthetic in a wider sense than that of application to the beautiful and ugly, esthetic quality, immediate, final or self-enclosed, indubitably characterizes natural situations as they empirically occur."[36] Thus, nature itself by its qualitative arrangement literally *has* "ends, terminals, arrests, enclosures," and in this "acknowledgment of nature as a scene of incessant beginnings and endings" we can, I think, discern the phenomenological source of that "direct awareness before predication" (as Fergusson called it) upon which the histrionic sensibility depends. If the tragic drama has its beginning, its middle, and its end, this is only because it is patterned upon an experience which has itself beginnings and endings, terminals, arrests, and enclosures.

The specialized meaning of drama is that it is "a composition arranged for enactment" (intended to portray life or character or to tell a story through action), and from this specialized meaning there are numerous popular extensions. It can therefore be applied to any series of real events invested with dramatic unity, or to any vivid gestures, or expressive movements, or unexpected conjunctions or intense oppositions or striking denouements. But the functioning of the dramatic imagination is itself grounded upon the inescapable rhythms of experience. Action-fatigue, hope-despair, waking-sleep, hunger-satiety, love-hate, curiosity-knowledge, desire-appeasement, emotion-relaxation, striving-contentment, anxiety-peace testify that there is a histrionic component of experience, and suggest that it is upon this component that the dramatic imagination feeds and builds its necessary structures.

Experience means "time," means "development," means "vivid contrast." It is inherently dramatic because it comes in blocks or quanta having incipience and finality, tensions and climaxes, beginnings and endings, recognitions and reversals. It is when one (as with Dewey) considers "experience" as a general, global concept, or (as with Heidegger and Merleau-Ponty) as an attitude of basic concern toward a world "lived from the inside" that one finds not only that it develops in time, but that it has an emotional and an episodic character which can only be described as dramatic. The dramatic poet merely adapts for his specific purposes those structures of lived experience which are common to us all.

Five / Forms of Literary Imagination: Poetry
& the Novel

OUR CONCLUSION in the last chapter was that there is a generically dramatic character of all experience upon which such various manifestations as actual theater, dialectic, and religious ritual depend. Or, in the language of Dewey:[1] "Contrast of lack and fullness, of struggle and achievement, of adjustment after consummated irregularity, form the drama in which action, feeling, and meaning are one." And again: "Because the actual world, that in which we live, is a combination of movement and culmination, of breaks and re-unions, the experience of a living creature is capable of esthetic actuality." The conclusion is suggestive, I think, not only as insight into the dramatic imagination, but for other uses of imagination as well, for it seems to declare a necessary relation between metaphysics and epistemology on the one hand, and literature or the plastic arts on the other. These latter are the undeniable loci of aesthetic quality, and if aesthetic quality derives from something generic to the ongoing experience of the human creature, may we not by a simple analysis of perceptual experience discover those categories which are presupposed by all of the arts? It is a line of inquiry which I think is promising, and it requires that we turn our attention from Bergson, Merleau-Ponty, Heidegger, and Dewey back to Charles Sanders Peirce.

Peirce, like Heidegger and Merleau-Ponty, has also provided us with a "phenomenology"—an investigation of the most universal or pervasive features of that "collective total of all that is in any way or in any sense present to the mind."[2] From such an investigation Peirce emerged with three "universal categories." By examining anything which is before the mind, by attending to any perception whatsoever, we shall discover three modes of existence in which things *are,* three forms of perception under which things *appear.* To these three modes of appearance or of perception Peirce assigned the neutral designation: *Firstness, Secondness, Thirdness.*

By *Firstness* Peirce means the immediate qualitative aspects of all our perceptual experience: the color of magenta, the odor of attar, the sound of a railway whistle, the taste of quinine. It refers to all in experience which is immediate, of the absolute present, novel, spontaneous, vivid. "What the world was to Adam on the day he opened his eyes to it, before he had drawn any distinctions, or had become conscious of his own experience—that is *first,* present, immediate, fresh, original, spontaneous, free, vivid, conscious, and evanescent. Only, remember that every description of it must be false to it."

If in Firstness is to be found the "feeling" character of the universe, in *Secondness* is to be found its "activity." Whenever we have the experience of tension, the sense of things confronting one another, of pushing against one another or causing one another, Secondness is the focus of our perception. It is the sense of the action and reaction of bodies, of movement in all its infinite variety, of dynamism in the world and the sense of strain and muscular effort in our own bodies. Naturally, it is impossible to isolate Secondness except through an artificial direction of attention or by a metaphor. But perhaps one comes closest to its essence by calling it the "oppositional" element in experience. For, wherever there is antagonistic juxtaposition, shock, surprise, sudden movement, gesticulation, and violence, our senses are in the presence of Secondness.

If Firstness lies in the qualities of things, and if Secondness lies in their oppositions, then *Thirdness* lies in their meaning. All items in experience have qualitative immediacy and interactive force. They also point to something beyond themselves, stand for something beyond their immediate presence, have the capacity to symbolize ideas or meanings which transcend their own local particularity. Thus whenever there is generality, whenever individual elements in experience symbolize classes, or permit generalizations, Thirdness is present.

Of course Firstness, Secondness, and Thirdness, as Peirce presents them, are not separable in actual fact. They are genuine *aspects* of a whole (as quality, movement, and meaning are genuine aspects of a painting or of a poem) and they can be separated only by acts of exclusive attention or abstraction. They are a map of experience, an account of what to look for. Here, for example, is a dark storm cloud in the summer sky. When we see it simply as a dense black ellipse before our eyes, we are attending to its Firstness. When we sense that it is really "out there" (as opposed to the region in which we are), or as blotting out the sun, or as pressing forcefully against the atmosphere, or as moving swiftly, driven by the wind, then we are attending to its Secondness. And when we look upon it as a *sign* of what's to come and mutter "So it's going to rain!," then its meaning is foremost in our consciousness, and we are attending to its Thirdness.

"We find," says Peirce, "the ideas of Firstness, Secondness, Thirdness, constant ingredients of our knowledge. It must then either be that they are continually given to us in the presentations of sense, or that it is the peculiar nature of the mind to mix them with our thoughts." But whichever epistemology we espouse leads to the same conclusion. Whether (as with Locke) these categories are *derived from* experience or (as with Kant) *imposed by the mind* upon experience, they are pervasive elements of our perception; just these three and no others.

What conclusions about aesthetics, and particularly about the literary imagination, can we draw from these findings? The answer, I think, is clear. The intrinsic conditions of "aesthetic" perception are the general conditions of any perception whatsoever, and in their phenomenological identification, no one has done better than Peirce. For, having inquired what are the peculiar characteristics revealed in perception, and having with him answered: Firstness, Secondness, and Thirdness, we may then say that any work of art must derive its meaning and its implications from this wider domain. The ultimate characteristic of any painting or sculpture, any work of literature or of the drama, is that its threefold function is *the presentation of qualities, the delineation of movements,* and *the expression of meanings.* The creative imagination in its productive activity will always be consciously or unconsciously directed to one or all of these three tasks.

But I want to narrow this emphasis upon the universal categories so that they apply only to the field of the literary imagination, and I want particularly to suggest their relevance for the field of contemporary poetry. For it seems to me that the poetic imagination, although it may address itself equally to the presentation of qualities, the delineation of movements, and the expression of meanings, yet cannot readily achieve excellence in all three, and that there will therefore be a narrowing of intent toward one in particular which is dictated by that mode of perception which uniquely defines the mentality of the poet. In this respect our three greatest contemporary poets, Wallace Stevens, Ezra Pound, and T. S. Eliot, may serve as illuminating examples.

Wallace Stevens is the "Gentleman of Qualities." His perception is sharp, but his mode of statement is gentle. His feelings are courteously disposed toward a world of secondary qualities (secondary in the sense which Berkeley would have understood—not unimportant, supremely important). He deals with surfaces, with the structure of appearance, and his aesthetic attitude is always elicited through the excitation of qualities themselves; sounds, tastes, vivid colors. His lyrics respond to the presentational immediacy of experience. Surely, he is *par excellence* a poet of Firstness.

Ezra Pound is the poet of movements and of oppositions. This is not always obvious in his early *Cantos*. But as one reads further, the dialectical design of the whole becomes increasingly apparent. Pound's poetic statements are anything but gentle. They are intensely muscular, and this muscularity, like the mediaeval prose of Abelard, is used as a kind of *Sic et Non* in Pound's poetic life. Even the apparent formlessness of his ragged phrases is deceptive, for what originally seem mere fragments ultimately reveal themselves as studied oppositions. The principle of contrariety rules Pound's poetic intent. He is the creator of an aggressive verse which is the objective correlative of an aggressive emotion. The tensions within his flat rhetoric are generated by the head-on collision of antagonistic moral forces. He is supremely the poet of Secondness.

T. S. Eliot is the poet of symbolic reference. He both illustrates the reflective elaboration of the materials of raw perception and also presents poetic "propositions" which then take their place in the structure of the religious life. His imagery is seasonal, occasional, and directly sensible of natural objects, but this imagery is used to illuminate a series of truths which lie beyond the sphere of perception. His poetic purpose seems to be to emphasize the "limited value in the knowledge derived from experience" and that "the purpose is beyond the end you figured."[3] This is only to say that his verse is reflective by temperament, concerned with meanings as to motive, transcendental in its intent. And therefore Eliot is the supreme poet of Thirdness in the contemporary world.

To a further brief examination of the way in which these three poets illustrate the Peircean categories I should now like to turn.

2 IN HIS little book *Symbolism* Whitehead presents a suggestion which is irresistibly reminiscent of the poetry of Wallace Stevens. "Presentational immediacy," Whitehead tells us,[4] "is the superficial product of complexity, of subtlety; it halts at the present, and indulges in a manageable self-enjoyment, derived from the immediacy of the show of things." Whitehead is speaking of perceptual experience, but he might well have been characterizing Stevens' poetry, for it is a "self-enjoyment" and it is constantly preoccupied with "the immediacy of the show of things." Stevens' verse depends upon a vivid enjoyment of immediate sense data, and it expresses loving concern with the decorative possibilities of the themes of sense. The consequence of such a poetic intent is that it makes the poem into a celebration of appearances construed as a complex manifold of surface qualities. Naturally, the enjoyment of appearance depends upon the whole intricate apparatus of sensation, and often for Stevens the content of the poem is nothing but the functioning of the sensory apparatus.

Here is the disclosure of what a taste may be:[5]

> Like Candide,
> Yeoman and grub, but with a fig in sight,
> And cream for the fig and silver for the cream,
> A blonde to tip the silver and to taste
> The rapey gouts.

And here the disclosure of taste is matched by the reflective elaboration of a universe of smell:

> Tilting up his nose
> He inhaled the rancid rosin, burly smells
> Of dampened lumber, emanations blown
> From warehouse doors, the gustiness of ropes
> Decays of sacks, and all the arrant stinks

> That helped him round his rude aesthetic out.
> He savored rankness like a sensualist.

Here from "The Idea of a Colony" is the portrayal of sound as sensory quality within the poetic content:

> The responsive man,
> Planting his pristine cores in Florida,
> Should prick thereof, not on the psaltery,
> But on the banjo's categorical gut,
> Tuck, tuck, while the flamingoes flapped his bays.

And here again is sound, presented, as in the foregoing, with the onomatopoeic strategy which animated so much of Stevens' verse. It is from "Cortege for Rosenbloom."

> To a chirr of gongs
> And a chitter of cries
> And the heavy thrum
> Of the endless tread
> That they tread;

But essentially the point of view of Stevens is the point of view of the man whose center is painting, and it is manifest in his acute sensitivity to the vocabulary of *color*. It is not only that Stevens has an exquisite sense of the emotional feel of colors, but also that he builds up a massive associative effort of color through the multiplication of clinging denotations; in this respect his inspiration is Chinese. Fenollosa noted that Chinese poetry always speaks with the vividness of painting, and he attributed this to the intrinsically metaphorical character of the Chinese ideogram.[6] Thus the Chinese language has a native pull toward concreteness. The scientific tradition has increasingly pushed English in the opposite direction. Platonically, we prod "red" ever further toward the abstract universal "redness," whereas for the Chinese "red" becomes the cumulative quality of cherry, rose, sunset, iron-rust, flamingo, ox-blood, and the like. It is as if Fenollosa were speaking not of Chinese poetry, but of the poetic method of Stevens. Here is what in "Holiday in Reality" Stevens does with yellow:

> It was something to see that their white was different,
> Sharp as white paint in the January sun;
>
> Something to feel that they needed another yellow,
> Less Aix than Stockholm, hardly a yellow at all,
>
> A vibrancy not to be taken for granted, from
> A sun in an almost colorless, cold heaven.

And in "Esthétique du Mal" here is the echo.

> The sun, in clownish yellow, but not a clown,
> Brings the day to perfection and then fails. . . .
>   . . . A big bird pecks at him
> For food. The big bird's boney appetite
> Is as insatiable as the sun's. The bird
> Rose from an imperfection of its own
> To feed on the yellow bloom of the yellow fruit
> Dropped down from turquoise leaves. In the landscape of
> The sun, its grossest appetite becomes less gross. . . .
>
> The sun is the country wherever he is. The bird
> In the brightest landscape downwardly revolves
> Disdaining each astringent ripening,
> Evading the point of redness, not content
> To repose in an hour or season or long era
> Of the country colors crowding against it. . . .

The "sun in clownish yellow" dominates the poem, as it dominates the landscape which is the poem's stage, and the yellow of bloom and fruit, of glitter and brightness cast their glow here as they do over the harvest fields of Arles on the canvases of Van Gogh. And we are reminded of Picasso's picture of which he said: "I go for a walk in the forest of Fontainebleau. I get 'green' indigestion. I must get rid of this sensation into a picture. Green rules it. A painter paints to unload himself of feelings and visions."[7] Almost it is as if Stevens were saying: "I get yellow indigestion and make the poem. And yellow rules it."

What is more initially abstract than the common name for a quality like yellow? But if each of its uses is grounded in

sensory particularity: the yellow of Aix, the yellow of Stock-
holm, the clownish yellow of the sun, the yellow bloom,
the yellow fruit, the yellow bird; then the work becomes
richer from line to line and from poem to poem. So that within the context of Stevens' poetry experienced as a corporate
body, the abstract yellow grows into a luminosity of metaphorical accretion which through its compounding finally
simulates the immediacy of the direct sensory experience of
real yellow objects. This is a part of the Stevens magic, and
it is how the poem gives to color a permanent residence in
the mind.

But this is not all. For there are times when an actual image of considerable abstractness somehow adds to the concreteness of a color experience already granted massiveness by
the array of particulars. We have spoken of yellow. Here is
what Stevens can do with white. (It is from "The Auroras of
Autumn," the title poem of one of his later volumes.)

> Farewell to an idea. . . . A cabin stands,
> Deserted, on a beach. It is white,
> As by a custom or according to
>
> An ancestral theme or as a consequence
> Of an infinite course. The flowers against the wall
> Are white, a little dried, a kind of mark
>
> Reminding, trying to remind, of a white
> That was different, something else, last year
> Or before, not the white of an aging afternoon,
>
> Whether fresher or duller, whether of winter cloud
> Or of winter sky, from horizon to horizon.
> The wind is blowing the sand across the floor.
>
> Here, being visible is being white,
> Is being of the solid of white, the accomplishment
> Of an extremist in an exercise. . . .

This poem, like the previous one, is a poem of landscape.
It is a scene, very pictorial in suggestion, capable of being the
subject of a painting. The details are elaborated in terms of
the perception of white, and the emotional suggestiveness

comes through the variations in formation, modulation, and degradation of white. White is a color of great brightness and purity, but by that very fact is dramatically capable of dinginess and dirtiness. The degenerations of white may symbolize fading, dessication, decay. The cabin is bleached white by weather, the flowers are dried into whiteness, the aging afternoon is white, the winter cloud, sky, horizon a degenerate white. The careless sand blowing across the floor is also white. But it is only at the last moment that these atoms of the naturalistic imagination are pulled taut by an unmistakable reference to abstraction.

Here, as usually with Stevens, the landscape of nature is analogized to painterly working. The given in experience is set against the compositional tendency of the artisan, the *being* of nature against *the being made* of art. The solidity of white—"the accomplishment of an extremist in an exercise" —is irresistibly suggestive of Mondrian or of Malevitch. Not exactly landscapists, to be sure, but extremists in the accomplishment of their exercise, and passionate for white.

I have tried to illustrate by poems devoted to taste, smell, sound, and color the sense in which Stevens' poetic intent is grounded in a devotion to the immediacies of perception. But the lessons of Stevens' verse are reinforced by the insistence of his prose. This is in the direction of limiting the reflective powers of the mind to the messages of sense. The creation of the poet is a representation, but it must be submissive to the text we do not write—the text presented in sensation. "What our eyes behold may well be the text of life but one's meditations on the text and the disclosures of these meditations are no less a part of the structure of reality. . . . What the eye beholds may be the text of life. It is, nevertheless, a text that we do not write. The eye does not beget in resemblance. It sees."[8]

This "seeing" often approaches in its vividness to a kind of ultimate vision where (as Santayana also noted) poetry can become an invitation to metaphysics, or metaphysics a phase of poetry. And like that which Santayana so often employs, Stevens' imagery here is the neo-Platonic one of light. "Poetry

is the scholar's art. The acute intelligence of the imagination . . . its power to possess the moment it perceives—if we
were speaking of light itself, and thinking of the relationship
between objects and light, no further demonstration would
be necessary. Like light, it adds nothing except itself."[9]

But this acute intelligence of the imagination is *firstness*,
the power to possess the moment of perception in its immediacy. There is no gaunt world of reason here, nor the paleness
of reflection at a decent distance from the central perception.
The pleasure of the poet as imaginative man, says Stevens,[10]
is "the pleasure of powers that create a truth that cannot be
arrived at by the reason alone, a truth that the poet recognizes
by sensation. *The morality of the poet's radiant and productive atmosphere is the morality of the right sensation.*"

3   *The Cantos* of Ezra Pound are written in
ten languages. There are passages in Lat-
in, Greek, French, German, Italian, Spanish, and Provençal.
There are occasional phrases transliterated from the Hebrew.
There are innumerable Chinese ideograms. There are nota-
tions in Arabic. There is a subtle typographical calligraphy.
The man presents his dream in the image, the metric, and
the look of the page. Nor is that all. Presupposed is the entire
"Penelope web of European awareness." He has gone through
the Sordello manuscript in the Ambrosian in Milan. He has
appropriated the African anthropology of Frobenius. He has
drawn upon Père Lacharme's Latin translation of the *Chi-
King*. He is on intimate terms with Victor Bérard's Homeric
geography. He knows the Greek manuscript of Gemistho Ple-
thon in the Laurenziana in Florence. He has examined the
manuscript of Miquel de la Tour in the Bibliothèque Na-
tionale at Paris. To what end?

There is no doubt, I think, that Pound's work has a central
subject, and that this subject is moral. *The Cantos* are about

integrity. They assert that integrity is the right guide óf men and states. They assert this in two demonstrations, one direct, the other indirect. The direct demonstration exhibits the life of perfect integrity according to the canon of Confucius. Its culmination is in Canto XIII and in Canto LIII. The indirect demonstration exhibits the absolute lack of integrity: the idea of usury and its consequences within society. Its culmination comes in Cantos XLV, XLVI, and LI.[11]

The key to Pound's achievement in *The Cantos* lies in their moral intent. And the key to Pound as a poetic voice lies in the recognition that ethical concern is the ruling form of his perception. For Wallace Stevens reality is to be *enjoyed.* In this aesthetic response to the world is the source of his interest in presentational immediacy. For T. S. Eliot reality is to be *transcended.* In this essentially religious response to the world is the source of his use of symbolic reference. But for Pound reality is perpetually to be *judged,* to be subjected to the instruments of moral choice. And in this ethical response to the world he brings to bear all the devices of his poetic equipment: vigorous insistence, strain, muscular effort, polarity, shock, sudden change, antagonistic juxtaposition, and the whole paraphernalia of moral struggle as it may appear within the texture of the verse.

The voice of Stevens is well modulated and suave. The voice of Eliot is quiet and meditative. But Pound thunders with the accents of a Dante inveighing against Florence, or of·a Jeremiah crying out against the iniquities of his people.

> The ant's a centaur in his dragon world.
> Pull down thy vanity, it is not man
> Made courage, or made order, or made grace,
>   Pull down thy vanity, I say pull down.
>
>   .   .   .
>
> Thou art a beaten dog beneath the hail,
> A swollen magpie in a fitful sun,
> Half black, half white

Nor knowst'ou wing from tail
Pull down thy vanity
   How mean thy hates
Fostered in falsity,
   Pull down thy vanity,
Rathe to destroy, niggard in charity,
Pull down thy vanity,
   I say pull down.
                    (Canto LXXXI)

In the *Cantos* Pound's affirmative presentations of the moral life seem to me less insistent than his negative demonstrations. The atmosphere of the *Analects* and the *Ta Hio* is there (as well as overtones of Homer and Greek lyric perception), but they are a quiet contrast to the thunderings of the aroused moralist. In fact, one is sometimes tempted to read the negative demonstration as the whole story, to find *The Cantos* little more than a jewel-studded attack upon usury and the usurious history of Western civilization. Cantos XIV and XV are the culmination of this enterprise, constructed in conscious imitation of Dante's *Inferno* ("the sacharescent lying in glucose, the pompous in cotton wool"). Pound's hell contains the politicians, the profiteers, the financiers,

And the betrayers of language
   . . . . and the press gang
And those who had lied for hire;
the perverts, the perverters of language,
   the perverts, who have set money-lust
Before the pleasures of the senses;
                    (Canto XIV)

the bigots, the vice-crusaders, the English, the liars, the slum-owners, the panders to authority, the obscurers of texts with philology, the orators, the preachers, the monopolists, the obstructors of knowledge, the obstructors of distribution, the pompous, the respecters, the Fabians, the conservatives, the back-scratchers, the litigious, the news-owners, and the whole lot *nulla fidentia inter eos.* It is a heterogeneous group given unity by a common treasonableness to natural society, and the hell which they inhabit is, as secularized *Inferno,* perhaps the most potent instrument of Pound's negative demonstration.

Very early Pound said: "I believe in technique as the test of a man's sincerity."[12] And he also said: "There are only two passions in art; there are only love and hate."[13] The polarity of love and hate rules the form of Pound's perception, and the technical devices which are the test of his sincerity also reinforce this dynamic form. Two devices in particular are worthy of note here: the enthronement of verb forms in the syntactical structure of the verse, and the contrast and shock of juxtaposed segments of material within the body of the narrative. For the first we have the widespread and conscious rendering of activity through the music of the verb and the participle.

> And the running form, naked, Blake,
> Shouting, whirling his arms, the swift limbs,
> Howling against the evil,
>   his eyes rolling,
> Whirling like flaming cart-wheels,
>   and his head held backward to gaze on the evil
> As he ran from it,
>   to be hid by the steel mountain,
> And when he showed again from the north side:
>   his eyes blazing toward hell mouth. . . .
>   (Canto XVI)

But also the constant shock and contrast of juxtaposed segments of material provides a constant poetic demonstration, a metaphor perhaps, of the dialectic of values within the universe. For, minutely, within almost any canto is to be found *the contrast of values.* Canto VII, for example (a great dialectical canto), presents the double polarity of time and existence, past *versus* present, life *versus* death.

"Beer-bottle on the statue's pediment!
"That, Fritz, is the era, today against the past,
"Contemporary." And the passion endures.
Against their action, aromas. Rooms against chronicles.
.   .   .

And all that day
Nicea moved before me
And the cold grey air troubled her not
For all her naked beauty, bit not the tropic skin. . . .
.   .   .

And all that day, another day:
    Thin husks I had known as men,
Dry casques of departed locusts
    speaking a shell of speech. . . .

And to the beer-bottle against the statue, Nicea in her naked
beauty against the empty locust shells, add such polarities as
that of form and content, the stubborn and the delicate, the
reasonable and the mystic, good and evil in Israel, distinction
against vulgarity, and even a polar invective relative to the
American Constitution.

These fragments you have shelved (shored).
    "Slut!" "Bitch!" Truth and Calliope
Slanging each other sous les lauriers:
                                        (Canto VIII)

And the old man went on there
    beating his mule with an asphodel.
                                        (Canto XXI)

Taught and not taught. Kung and Eleusis
    to catechumen alone.
                                        (Canto LIII)

    to redeem Zion with justice
sd/Isaiah. Not out on interest said David rex
                the prime s.o.b.
                                        (Canto LXXIV)

> in contending for certain values
> (Janequin per esempio, and Orazio Vechii or Bronzino)
> Greek rascality against Hagoromo
> Kamasaka vs/vulgarity

(Canto LXXIX)

> God bless the Constitution
> and *save* it
> "the value thereof"
> that is the crux of the matter
> and god damn the perverters

(Canto LXXIX)

Pound's poetry sometimes gives a sense of fragmentation because it does not provide an obvious commentary as a bond of linkage between discrete blocks of perception. But this is not technical carelessness. It is deliberate method. A beer-bottle on the pediment of the monument to a war hero; beating a mule with an asphodel; the juxtaposition of these incongruous images without further comment provides a comment nevertheless, and that comment is deeply ironic. And irony is a kind of wry muscularity in the intellect. But it is more than that. Irony is a criticism of life. Any active cognition of disparity and incongruity is a critical commentary upon the nature of the world. To be acutely aware of the contrast between fact and value, the fake and the fine, the cheap and the beautiful, Kung and Herr Krupp, modern hypocrisy and Homeric truth, Ch'ing Ming and contemporary advertising, *neschek* and *ethos*, a concentration camp near Pisa and the Tempio Malatestiano, St. Trophime and the Albert Memorial, John Adams and Franz Joseph, is to be a moralist. And to present these contrasts within the texture of an epic poem is to orchestrate values according to an ironic method.

Pound's use of ironic contrast shows his sense of mockery of the fitness of things. It sees the good as mocked by the evil, the beautiful by the ugly, and it not only exists at the level of phrase and phrase, image and image, but also regulates the

order in which the Cantos appear, and the way they are juxtaposed to one another as total entities. Canto XIII, the Confucian canto, is followed by Canto XIV, the Hell canto. The
anecdotes and the wisdom of the moral sage are mocked by
the account of profiteers, betrayers, and perverters which follows. So the moralizing expresses itself in the oppositions of a
technical contrast.

The intelligence which has been working behind *The Cantos* is unusual—in its range, in its command of technique,
and in its muscularity. It is an intelligence which has not
only devoted itself to a rehabilitation of the tradition, but
which through the mode of its perception, its reading of the
universe in terms of polarity and moral struggle, has again
enthroned the ethical way of life in the heart of the body of
poetry.

4   *The Hollow Men* cuts the poetry of T. S.
     Eliot in two. Behind it lies the ironic and
despairing consideration of modern culture, three or four of
the finest lyrics in the English language and *The Waste Land*.
Beyond it lie *Ash Wednesday*, prelude and announcement of
the new dispensation; *The Rock*, which elaborates the new
wisdom in the old language; and *Four Quartets*, Eliot's masterpiece and the crown and consummation of his poetic life.

Eliot's poetic achievement is not a product of the naturalistic, but of the religious imagination, and to understand it
we must employ not a metaphor from natural life, but a metaphor from religion. The heart of Eliot's poetic development
hinges upon a crisis of religious feeling, a moment of conversion or of confirmation which cuts life in two. All that preceded this moment was prelude; all that follows it is consequence. Before was an emptiness which stemmed from an
imperfect faith; what follows has a new quality—the consequence of fullness of faith at the moment of renewal. The

essence of Eliot's early poetry is disgust and emptiness moving toward mysticism. The essence of his later poetry is the quiet and meditative exploration of the mystical vision itself. But between the two, and key to Eliot's poetic development, is the transforming illumination of the moment of religious rebirth.

Eliot's first poems inhabit a metropolitan landscape of great dreariness and a moral atmosphere of ennui, meaninglessness, and indecision. The landscapes are the restless glimpses of Spengler's late city man, the teeming but at the same time desolate byways of the mindless urban proletariat. They are the landscapes peopled by those who are both traditionless and insecure, and for that very reason perhaps possess a special talent for óbedience and for failure. So it is with Prufrock and with others. But for the real excursions into symbolic reference we must turn to *The Waste Land, Ash Wednesday,* and *Four Quartets.*

The Waste Land is a veritable storehouse of tradition. It echoes Ezekiel and Ecclesiastes, Baudelaire and Verlaine, Ovid and Dante, the Buddha and St. Augustine, Webster and Middleton, Marvel and Shakespeare. But these references are always a reaching out to that body of tradition within which the poem seeks to incorporate itself, like a Christian soul seeking an ultimate reconciliation with the source of its being. Similarly, the employment of the symbolic mode of perception involves the reaching out of any sign to a meaning which lies above and beyond itself. It is inherent in the very employment of symbolism that its consequences are transcendental, and this is why the intention of all of Eliot's later verse seems to be to somehow pass beyond the words themselves to the states of belief and illumination to which they point. This is not merely an inference from Eliot's practice; it is a matter of his explicit acknowledgment. Just before beginning *Four Quartets* Eliot spoke of a "poetry so transparent that in reading it we are intent on what the poem points at and not what is in the poetry; this seems to me the thing to try for. To get *beyond* poetry as Beethoven in his later works strove to get beyond music."[14] "To get beyond the poem" is to recognize it as a symbolic mechanism, but to attend not to the symbol *quâ* symbol, but to that which it symbolizes. It is to concentrate neither upon qualities nor upon tensions, but upon meanings.

When in *The Waste Land* Eliot asks[15]

> What are the roots that clutch, what branches grow
> Out of this stony rubbish? Son of man,
> You cannot say, or guess, for you know only
> A heap of broken images, where the sun beats,
> And the dead tree gives no shelter, the cricket no relief,
> And the dry stone no sound of water. . . .

this also seems an imagery of natural qualities. But it is clear that the heap of broken images, the dead tree, the dry stone mean allegorically more than themselves; mean an actual drought in the land of the poem, but mean also a spiritual drought within the modern psyche where Christian revelation haunts the scene but at such distance that the dead tree of the Cross provides no shelter. Metaphor is but an intermittent symbolism. But from Dante Eliot has learned the continuous symbolism of allegory.[16]

The Waste Land and *The Hollow Men* are Eliot's "dark night of the soul" (as *"Champ de Blé aux Corbeaux"* is Van Gogh's, or the final strains of the "Coriolan Overture" are Beethoven's), and the next movement can only be a movement upward. That movement toward recovery is fully expressed in *Ash Wednesday*, which registers his emergence from despair into an ambience of grace. It is a deeply religious poem, the first in which Eliot explores the imagery and the urgent sincerities of the religious life, and with it is fixed the theme and the incentive for the pursuance of his later verse.

Ash Wednesday is a renunciatory and a penitential poem. It is a preparation not for happiness but for quietness. It is humility slowly and difficulty working toward peace. It uses for its purposes the ritual language of the Christian Church, and it is dominated by a Lady (reminiscent of Dante's Beatrice), lovely and bright, who "honors the Virgin in meditation." The Lady, like Beatrice, is an image of purity, set in sharp contrast to the fiddles and the flutes of the senses. In the fourth episode of *Ash Wednesday* she reappears:[17]

> Who walked between the violet and the violet
> Who walked between
> The various ranks of varied green
> Going in white and blue, in Mary's colour,
> Talking of trivial things
> In ignorance and in knowledge of eternal dolour
> Who moved among the others as they walked,
> Who then made strong the fountains and made
> > fresh the springs

and the poet asks her to be mindful of him (*Sovegna Vos*) as Arnaut Daniel had asked in the same words (*Purgatorio* XXVI) of Dante. Through her the higher dream is restored. The fountain springs up. The time is redeemed.

It is instructive to notice this passage, for the reliance upon adjectives already noted in Wallace Stevens is here a perfect exemplification of Eliot's symbolism. The adjective in Stevens is a device of presentational immediacy, used for the pictorial representation of surface quality. But the adjective in Eliot is used allegorically, for the elucidation of meanings which transcend surface appearances. The violet is the violet of penance. The green is the green of hope. The white is the white of purity. The blue is the blue of Heaven. Even the sensory vividness of color is used in the service of symbolic reference.

Four Quartets,[18] unlike *The Waste Land* or *Ash Wednesday*, is reminiscent of the philosophy of Heracleitus. For it is ruled by a method which consists in the reflective presentation of opposites, but in such a way that the mind is not permitted to dwell upon the tension of their permanent opposition, but is rather brought to the gentle acceptance of the paradox of their identification.

What we call the beginning is often the end
And to make an end is to make a beginning.
The end is where we start from.

(Little Gidding V)

Man's curiosity searches past and future
And clings to that dimension. But to apprehend
The point of intersection of the timeless
With time, is an occupation for the saint. . . .

(The Dry Salvages V)

But the faith and the love and the hope are all in
the waiting.
Wait without thought, for you are not ready for thought:
So the darkness shall be the light, and the stillness
the dancing.

(East Coker III)

The message of *Four Quartets* is a mystical one, not merely
because it echoes the language of St. John of the Cross and
Julian of Norwich, but because it relies upon a logic (implicit in Heracleitus) which has always been standard strategy
for the expression of the mystical vision. *It is a logic which
first seems to oppose, but then identifies the significant terms
of discourse.* This mystical method is announced in the quiet
meditative passage with which *Burnt Norton* begins: a reflection upon the identities implicit in past, present, and future
and the paradoxical intersection of time and eternity. And it
is brought to its height a moment later where, through the
basic metaphor of the motionless center of all movement
(which is the quiet of the dance) the oppositions of existence
are asserted, denied, and reconciled in the same long breath.

At the still point of the turning world. Neither flesh nor fleshless;
Neither from nor towards; at the still point where the dance is,
But neither arrest nor movement. And do not call it fixity,
Where past and future are gathered. Neither movement from nor
toward,
Neither ascent nor decline. Except for the point, the still point,
There would be no dance, and there is only the dance.

I can only say, *there* we have been; but I cannot say where.
And I cannot say how, how long, for that is to place it in time.
The inner freedom from the practical desire,
The release from action and suffering, release from the inner
And the outer compulsion, yet surrounded
By a grace of sense, a white light still and moving. . . .

(Burnt Norton II)

It is important, I think, to pause for a moment and to notice what such a passage tells us of Eliot's poetic method. *The
Waste Land* indicated that Eliot's was a poetry of symbolic
reference, that his interest in language is primarily as a vehicle for the communication of meanings which transcend the
particularity of the natural images which he employs. *Ash
Wednesday* showed that Eliot was a Christian poet whose
sensibility was centered in the poetic equivalence of the emotions of renunciation, penitence, reverence, and humility.
Four Quartets forsakes neither Eliot's symbolic bent nor his
Christianity, but enriches them with the resources of a mystical logic.

Eliot's images are drenched in the logic of mysticism. And
in this he differs profoundly both from Wallace Stevens and
from Ezra Pound. The universe of Stevens reflects a Platonism in which the items of experience disclose myriad and
interesting resemblances. The universe of Pound reflects an
ultimate Manicheanism where all things may be grouped in
polar oppositions and where there is no escape from antagonistic tensions. But the universe of Eliot reflects an ultimate
monism—a world of images which point beyond themselves,
which are at first seen as contrasts, but which upon deeper
consideration turn out to be identities.

These are profound metaphysical differences, but they are
due less to a structure of beliefs systematically held than to
an intrinsic difference in the type of imagination illustrated
in three separate forms of poetic perception. It would not be
beyond the truth to say, as I believe, that Stevens, Pound,
and Eliot are adherent to different forms of imagination and

that this commits them to different epistemologies, different methods of knowing the truth which entail a considerable difference in actual poetic practice. Stevens exploits simile, Pound juxtaposition, Eliot statements equating opposites. The poetic logic of Stevens is a logic of analogy. The poetic logic of Pound is a logic of disjunction. The poetic logic of Eliot is a logic of identity.

5   LET ME summarize what I think we have learned about the forms of the poetic imagination through our consideration of Stevens, Pound, and Eliot.

Wallace Stevens is a poet of aesthetic awareness; this commits him to an interest in immediately presented qualities. But this interest has a double consequence. On the one hand it means that his technique for the faithful representation of qualities is patterned after the pictorial arts, and that the linguistic resource which he exploits to the fullest is the adjective. Here poetry is assimilated to landscape. But on the other hand, in any poetry of immediate sensory perception there must be a natural duality of reference; toward the qualitative vividness of the object and toward the qualitative vividness of feeling which the object evokes—delight in the thing, and delight in seeing the thing. It is the latter which is the most significant for Stevens' poetic practice. For if, as his principle asserts, "all things exhibit resemblance," then the crux of the poetic enterprise is the exhibition of resemblance, and the poetic content must be molded according to a logic of analogy. Of course, the resemblances which Stevens details are not a mere consequence of any poetic employment of metaphor. His is a kind of poetic Platonism; a reading of metaphor into the structure of the universe. But the poetry which results from this natural Platonism depends for its effectiveness upon the employment of an analogical method.

Ezra Pound, on the other hand, is a poet of ethical awareness; this makes him peculiarly sensitive to the tensions, the
polarities, and the oppositions of experience. But this interest too, has a double consequence. On the one hand it leads
him to explore the principle of polarity where its relevance
to human life is greatest, that is to say, at the moral level,
where the oppositions between right and wrong, the reason-
ably human and the perverse, loyalty and perfidy, integrity
and corruption have their natural application. Pound's concern for conduct and his passion for moral judgment are
founded upon a conviction that the clue to the universe lies
in the antinomies of value. Nor is this without consequences
for the structure of his verse. Since the form of Pound's perception implies sensitivity to the oppositional element in all
experience, it is not surprising that the logic which governs
his creativity should be a logic of disjunction, a general view
of the world which leads him to say: "Experience must always choose between two possibilities. It must be one or the
other. It cannot be both." If the essential quality of an imagination is of this character, what kind of poetry must it write?
Surely if it sees the world as a strain between the valuable and
the evil, as an active struggle without surcease, then the symbolic manifestation of this struggle will appear in the muscularity of the verse. Adjectives are the portrait-painters of the
world. In the participle and the verb lie the dynamism of
life. The test of Pound's sincerity is the congruence between
his moral presuppositions and his technical accomplishment.
For his verse enthrones the verb in its syntactical center and
it offers the contrast and the shock of juxtaposed segments of
material within the body of the poetic narrative.

T. S. Eliot is a poet of religious awareness; this makes
him particularly concerned with the transcendental meanings
which objects and events in the natural world may carry. But
this also has a double consequence. On the one hand it leads
him to utilize symbolic method, to press his symbolism as far
as possible for the creation of a poetic world instinct with the

Divine presence. His later subject matter is Christian belief in all its mystery, and the relationship of inner states of human consciousness to this central mystery. But a symbolism so used strays from the occasionalism of metaphor, and in the thickness and density of its employment approaches the mediaeval practice of sustained allegory. I say "approaches" because Eliot's symbolism never reaches the level of abstraction which we associate with mediaevalism, but there is at least a sufficient strain in this direction to make the comparison with Dante not wholly inappropriate.

But it is also true that the religious subject matter of the later poetry recapitulates a poetic method which has been implicit even in Eliot's earlier verse. The Heracleitean strategy by means of which ambiguities of contradiction symbolize an ultimate unity (in which all oppositions are mystically reconciled) has implications for poetic method. It points in the direction of a symbolic usage which blurs the outlines of fixed meaning, which enriches the denotation of words so that images merge into one another and opposite qualities are symbolically equated. Thus Eliot's form and his content cooperate in the presentation of a monistic view of the world. The chief resource of Stevens is the adjective. The chief resource of Pound is the verb. The chief resource of Eliot is the substantive which draws meanings to itself like a magnet and which is expanded by a syntactical form which predicates of it a series of opposite qualities.

If the foregoing treatment of Stevens, Pound, and Eliot rings true, then it should be clear not only that they are three of the most brilliant and significant poets of the modern world, but that considering them together suggests something about the relationship between poetic experience and the imagination. It suggests that if poets are "philosophical," this is perhaps due less to doctrinal content than to that form of perception and general attitude toward experience which is implicit in their work. It suggests also a certain phenomenology of the poetic experience—a range of imaginative possibilities in which a poet may concentrate upon the presentation of the qualitative immediacies of experience, upon the dynamic interactions implicit in experience, or upon the symbolic meanings which experience proposes. And it suggests further (although much more lightly and tentatively) that one to whom qualitative immediacy is primary will be peculiarly sensitive to the merely aesthetic possibilities of poetic transformation, just as one who is impressed by dynamic interaction will exploit the ethical, and one who is peculiarly drawn to symbolic meanings will tend toward the sacramental and the religious.

Firstness, Secondness, and Thirdness, therefore, although they originate in a metaphysical attempt to construct a phenomenology for all experience whatsoever, are finally more than mere categories of interest to the epistemologist. For they are also the determinants of types of literary imagination. Loosely and experimentally applied, they may illuminate (as in the case of Stevens, Pound, and Eliot) certain pervasive qualities of the poetic experience. And when such an application is made, it appears that there is a certain relatedness, a *zusammenhang* of various aspects often expressed separately. Presentational immediacy, causal efficacy, and symbolic reference seem to combine structurally in different wholes a factor of perception, an area of life concern, a poetic form, a grammatical element, and a logical approach.

Wallace Stevens is the great poet of Firstness in the modern world. Dominated by an interest in sensory quality, his mode of perception is aesthetic, and he writes a lyric poetry in which the adjective is central and which is governed by a logic of analogy. Ezra Pound is the great poet of Secondness in the modern world. Dominated by an interest in oppositions, his mode of perception is primarily ethical, and he writes an epic in which the verb is central and which is governed by a logic of disjunction. T. S. Eliot is the great poet of Thirdness in the modern world. Dominated by an interest in the symbolizing function of language, his mode of perception is religious and he writes a form of verse in which the substantive is central and which is governed by a logic of identity. Poetry, it seems, is philosophical in that the forms of its practice reflect distinctions which lie at the heart of the experience of human knowing. The dramatic imagination is based upon qualities which are precipitated by the natural flow of human experience. But the resources of the poetic art also depend upon a phenomenology of the imagination.

6 CAN THE same be said for the art of the novel? I think so, although here the forms are so Protean that it would be risky to attempt to contain them within the molds of a Peircean epistemology. If, indeed, there is a certain epistemic structure in the natural flow of human experience, the reflection of this structure should appear in the novel as in the poem or the drama. But the tripartite division of quality, movement, and meaning which covers so admirably the major intent of Stevens, Pound, and Eliot is now less satisfactory. For our inquiry here must shift from content to form, from the subject matter of the work of art to the point of view of the artist. Here too there will be epistemic categories, but they will be the more familiar ones of internality and externality, inward looking and outward looking, subjectivity and objectivity.

In a sense this corresponds to what we all feel. If I say that Hemingway was a disciple of John Locke (understanding, of course, that he may not even have been aware of the work of the British empiricist), whereas Proust was a Cartesian, the statement may seem pretentious, but the idea which underlies it is simple. For *The Sun Also Rises* is a straightforward, even naive presentation of *life as sensation*, whereas *A la Recherche du Temps Perdu* is an attempt to reduce all experience (however cumbersomely) to the level of clear and distinct ideas. Naturally the novelist does not define or explain; he *presents,* but the presentation may be strictly an expression of the sub-conscious and unformulated epistemology to which the novel-ist adheres. Like Locke (and in the spirit of Wallace Stevens, whose words we borrow), Hemingway might also have pro-claimed "the morality of the novelist's radiant and productive atmosphere is the morality of the right sensation"; like Des-cartes, the aesthetic foundation upon which the wonderful work of Proust is constructed is the epistemic motto *"Cogito ergo sum."*

There is, indeed, implicit in the novelistic form a meta-physics and an epistemology, although this occurs less as ma-terial included within the body of the narrative than in the *modus operandi*, the point of view. If we compare the for-mal accomplishment of a Madame de la Fayette, a Balzac, a Thomas Mann, then we must be persuaded of the truth of Erich Auerbach's thesis that in *the form of a story* lies a peculiar representation of reality, and we can understand Sar-tre's insistence that divergent philosophies lie concealed in the majestic flow of fictional time. "A fictional technique," says Sartre,[19] "always relates back to the novelist's meta-physics. The critic's task is to define the latter before evaluat-ing the former." But like every rationalist, Sartre has put the cart before the horse. The metaphysics *cannot* be defined *be-fore* the technique is evaluated, because for the novel the definition of the metaphysics can be only *an inference from the technique.* I should like to show this by a brief considera-tion of the techniques (and therefore the metaphysics) of Dostoyevsky and Tolstoy, and I will begin at the humble level of gastronomy: with the oysters of Stepan Arkadyevitch and Pyotr Stepanovitch's beefsteak.

Early in *Anna Karenina* (Part I, Chapter X) Levin is car-ried off by Stepan Arkadyevitch Oblonsky for dinner at a famous Moscow restaurant, the "England." After the usual appetizer of fish and vodka, the waiter confers with them and announces that fresh oysters have arrived (Flensburg, not Ostend) and then, although Levin half seriously announces that he would just as soon have cabbage soup and porridge, Stepan Arkadyevitch ceremoniously orders an elaborate dinner: three dozen oysters, clear soup with vegetables, turbot with thick sauce, roast beef, capons, sweets. The waiter rehearses the whole menu to himself according to the bill of fare (*"Soupe printanière, turbot, sauce Beaumarchais, poulard à l'estragon, macédoine de fruits . . . etc."*) and then comes the question of wines: Champagne (*Cachet blanc*) with the oysters, for table wine "the classic Chablis." A final choice of Parmesan cheese completes the ceremony.

And the Tatar ran off with flying coat-tails, and in five minutes darted in with a dish of opened oysters on mother-of-pearl shells, and a bottle between his fingers.

Stepan Arkadyevitch crushed the starchy napkin, tucked it into his waistcoat, and settling his arms comfortably, started on the oysters.

"Not bad," he said, stripping the oysters from the pearly shell with a silver fork, and swallowing them one after another. "Not bad," he repeated, turning his dewy, brilliant eyes from Levin to the Tatar.

Levin ate the oysters indeed, though white bread and cheese would have pleased him better. But he was admiring Oblonsky. Even the Tatar, uncorking the bottle and pouring the sparkling wine into the delicate glasses, glanced at Stepan Arkadyevitch, and settled his white cravat with a perceptible smile of satisfaction.[20]

The scene is characteristically Tolstoy, for although it is used to contrast the rough and simple and unpretentious Levin with the good-natured and sophisticated and epicurean Oblonsky ("But that's just the aim of civilization," Oblonsky says during the course of dinner, "to make everything a source of enjoyment"), the complicated richness of this aspect of life is made superbly manifest. The dinner is not assumed, it is detailed, so that the life of the senses receives documentation through a loving attention to the *objects* through which it is manifest. The oysters in their mother-of-pearl shells, the silver fork, the starchy napkin, the delicate glasses, the sparkling wine—all are given; and they provide a backdrop of externality, of *things* and their opulence *interesting in themselves* against which the comfortable dialectic of character can work. But in Dostoyevsky all is different.

Late in *The Possessed* (Part III, Chapter IV, Sec. II), just before the murder of Shatov, occurs a curious scene between Pyotr Stepanovitch Verhovensky, leader of the conspirators, and Liputin, one of his accomplices. Pyotr is, as usual, overbearing and high-handed, and Liputin hates him for it. Shatov's murder is on the mind of both as they trudge along the narrow street of the town, Pyotr walking in the middle of the narrow planking which passes for sidewalk and covers the mud, Liputin choking with resentment one step behind him.

Suddenly Pyotr Stepanovitch halted in one of the principal thoroughfares and went into a restaurant.

"What are you doing?" cried Liputin, boiling over. "This is a restaurant."

"I want a beefsteak."

"Upon my word! It is always full of people."

"What if it is?" . . .

Pyotr Stepanovitch went to a room apart. Liputin sat in an easy chair on one side, angry and resentful, and watched him eating. Half an hour and more passed. Pyotr Stepanovitch did not hurry himself; he ate with relish, rang the bell, asked for a different kind of mustard, then for beer, without saying a word to Liputin. He was pondering deeply. He was capable of doing two things at once —eating with relish and pondering deeply. Liputin loathed him so intensely at last that he could not tear himself away. It was like a nervous obsession. He counted every morsel of beefsteak that Pyotr Stepanovitch put into his mouth; he loathed him for the way he opened it, for the way he chewed, for the way he smacked his lips over the fat morsels, he loathed the steak itself. At last things began to swim before his eyes; he began to feel slightly giddy; he felt hot and cold run down his spine by turns.[21]

How differently function the oysters of Stepan Arkadyevitch Oblonsky and the beefsteak of Pyotr Stepanovitch Verhovensky! There is food and drink here in Dostoyevsky to be sure; the beefsteak and the mustard and the beer, but they do not work as objects, but as the *symbols* or tokens or correlatives of the interior state. Pyotr Stepanovitch, Dostoyevsky tells us, is "capable of doing two things at once—eating with relish and pondering deeply," and since in this case the pondering deeply is a rehearsal of Shatov's murder, the eating with relish while planning murder becomes the expression of callousness, calculation, and cruelty. The intrinsic innocence of a beefsteak and a glass of beer is transformed into images of nausea and disgust reflected in Liputin's loathing. Each morsel of steak is a register of guilt and complicity, and when Verhovensky smacks his lips over the fat morsels, it is as if he is smacking his lips over a corpse. Incarnation is here also symbolically at work, and it is the obscenity of the meaning and an obscure consciousness of his own implication in Verhovensky's voracious cannibalism as well as impatience and resentment and anger which drive Liputin toward nausea so that he feels giddy and things begin to swim before his eyes.

Oblonsky's oysters are interesting in themselves and as the furniture of life; Verhovensky's beefsteak is but an icon of the murderous devouring, simultaneously occupying the mind and the teeth. This contrast between the two "restaurant scenes" in Tolstoy and Dostoyevsky is characteristic of the two men and of the two uses of the novelistic imagination which they respectively exemplify. Tolstoy is an objectivist, even an Aristotelian. For him the world consists of a plurality of primary substances, solid, resistant, characterizable by adjectives. Dostoyevsky is dominated by the subjectivist principle; he suggests more what might have been produced by the interval in modern philosophy from Berkeley to Kant, a world of flux where violent acts are prepared in the grotesque theater of the mind. Characters for Tolstoy are what they *are* and what they *have;* for Dostoyevsky they are what they *do,* but chiefly what they *think.* Dostoyevsky's novelistic imagination always crystalizes around a nucleus of violent action: murder, rape, suicide, or bloody accident. Tolstoy operates within a solid world of objects—a universe fitted out like a St. Petersburg drawing-room with its necessary accessories of silken drapes, crystal chandeliers, thick Chinese carpets, and insubstantial French furniture. Time in Dostoyevsky moves swiftly, and although there are long interludes of breathtaking dialectic, there are moments when no speech is swift enough and we have the sudden substitution of the dramatic gesture like the stunning blow in the face which Shatov gives to Stavrogin, Sonya's kneeling before Raskolnikov, Father Zossima bowing to the earth before Mitya, Prince Myshkin's sudden epileptic fits. Time in Tolstoy unrolls slowly like the budding of the seasons and the stately transformations of nature, and the inner metamorphoses are finely registered in the bodies which house them (objects also); in the loss of vivacity in the step and sparkle in the eye, or the appearance of heaviness in a middle-aged body and wrinkles on a forehead hitherto smooth and unwrinkled.

In general Dostoyevsky's characters live in a purely interior world of moral and religious significance, full of anguish and decisions, horrified contemplation and philosophical problems. They do not eat or dress, relax in the parks or pay money for bread and cheese. The commonplaces of existence are presupposed, but there is no "romance of the quotidian." But in Tolstoy the commonplace is the frame of life; whether the landowner doing his daily accounts, the urban nobility with its endless dinners and card-playing, or the domestic routines of instructing the servants and caring for the children. And this is why the contrast in the novelistic imagination illustrated by the two restaurant scenes could be duplicated for almost any aspect of life whatsoever.

7 CONSIDER, for example, the matter of dress. Again early in *Anna Karenina* (Part I, Chapter XXII) occurs the famous scene at the ball where for the first time Kitty realizes that Vronsky is attracted to Anna

and not to herself. Korsunsky takes Kitty's arm, they look for Anna, and suddenly she appears.[22]

Anna was not in lilac, as Kitty had so urgently wished, but in a black, low-cut, velvet gown showing her full throat and shoulders, that looked as though carved in old ivory, and her rounded arms, with tiny, slender wrists. The whole gown was trimmed with Venetian guipure. On her head, among her black hair—her own, with no false additions—was a little wreath of pansies, and a bouquet of the same in the black ribbon of her sash among white lace. Her coiffure was not striking. All that was noticeable was the little wilful tendrils of her curly hair that would always break free about her neck and temples. Round her well-cut, strong neck was a thread of pearls.

Tolstoy's description is, again, loving in its detail, like a portrait by Sargent; all objects are united in the whole and each is characterized by its appropriate adjective. Each detail contributes to the massiveness of the effect. Anna at this moment is not what she feels, but what she appears, simple, natural, and elegant, and if there is also gaiety and eagerness, those are qualities like grace and precision rather than agencies of movement or decision. As in the case of Stepan Arkadyevitch's dinner with its glow of silver and crystal, what is presented here is the sensual lure of *the object*. If the key word for the dinner is "opulence" or "richness," here it is clearly "fascination." A moment later this is made abundantly clear by Tolstoy himself.[23]

Some supernatural force drew Kitty's eyes to Anna's face. She was fascinating in her simple black dress, fascinating were her round arms with their bracelets, fascinating was her firm neck with its thread of pearls, fascinating the straying curls of her loose hair, fascinating the graceful, light movements of her little feet and hands, fascinating was that lovely face in its eagerness, but there was something terrible and cruel in her fascination.

Dostoyevsky's novelistic imagination is ruled by quite another intent. Toward the end of *The Possessed*, after the conclusion of the ill-starred fête and the outbreak of the fire, Lizaveta Nikolaevna, also a strikingly beautiful woman, stands in the large ballroom of Skvoreshniki.[24]

At daybreak, soon after five in the morning, Liza was standing at the farthest window on the right looking intently at the fading glow. She was alone in the room. She was wearing the dress she had worn the day before at the matinee—a very smart light green dress covered with lace, but crushed and put on carelessly and with haste. Suddenly noticing that some of the hooks were undone in front she blushed, hurriedly set it right, snatched up from a chair the red shawl she had flung down when she came in the day before, and put it round her neck. Some locks of her luxuriant hair had come loose and showed below the shawl on her right shoulder.

Here too there is a dress and its description, but its details are sketched with the barest economy, almost with an impatience indicating that for the dress itself Dostoyevsky has no concern whatsoever. His interest is not with the object, but with the interior state which is revealed by the object. That the dress is light green and covered with lace is of no particular interest, but that it is crushed and with the hooks undone in front is of the greatest importance. Like the luxuriant hair come loose, it indicates the carelessness and haste, the inattentiveness to things which symbolizes the desperate and uneasy state within. Anna has dressed with care, whereas Lizaveta was too perturbed to be really conscious of what she was doing, and the contrast reveals the essential characteristics of Tolstoy and Dostoyevsky as novelists. Tolstoy always dresses his characters and his situations with objectivity and with care. Dostoyevsky, with an eye chiefly on the interior struggle, either takes his objects for granted, assumes them as shadowy background, or forgets them altogether.

Objectivity (as in Tolstoy) and subjectivity (as in Dostoyevsky) are, then, two possibilities for technical accomplishment which exemplify two types of unconscious philosophy expressing themselves as modes of literary imagination. One cannot really simplify the distinction by saying, for example, that Tolstoy, like Balzac, is a sociologist in literature, whereas Dostoyevsky, like Richardson, is a psychologist. The two concepts of "mind" or "self" on the one hand, and "society" on the other, are polar, not disjunctive. The novel is always concerned with movement, with the minute unfolding of plot and character, but as a matter of technique this can be done with primary reference either to the elaborate matrix of social organization or to the inner convolutions of the human brain and heart. In the one case (as for example that of the slow maturation of Pierre Bezhukov in *War and Peace*) all of the deepest problems of the self are projected outward, are given their meaning and virtue through an account of what happens outside the self in the "objective" region of society. In the other (as for example for Shatov or Kirillov in *The Possessed*) just the reverse is true, and all of the deepest problems of society are caught up in the interior monologue, in the tortured dialectic of the soul.

In a sense this difference is a matter of philosophic commitment which goes back to ancient dualisms between things and ideas, body and mind, materialism and idealism, Aristotle's world of primary substances and Berkeley's subjectivist principles. For whether one takes as point of primary reference the furniture of the world or the encapsulated area of mind has implications for the novelist. In Tolstoy and Dostoyevsky the contrast is dramatized by the attitude toward objects—contempt in Dostoyevsky and basic respect in Tolstoy. And this difference in attitude can be seen reflected, I think, in the life experiences of the two men. In Tolstoy is much of the commitment to place, the traditional anchorage of the old landed aristocracy; in Dostoyevsky is much of the wandering, the restless homelessness of the urban proletariat. Dostoyevsky's rootlessness is registered in the gambling rooms of Wiesbaden, the boulevards of Paris, and the house in Florence just opposite the Pitti where most of *The Idiot* was written. Tolstoy's life is meaningless apart from the rolling fields and ancestral memories of Yasnaya Polyana. When Dostoyevsky in his *Winter Notes on Summer Impressions* describes his European wandering, he sounds like some ill-natured and dyspeptic tourist. The Cologne cathedral impresses him as a lace paperweight five hundred feet tall. In London he sees only the monstrous buildings and the painted women in the Haymarket, and the Parisian bourgeoisie fills him with contempt. But Tolstoy's books and his diaries are filled with the solace of the countryside near Moscow and his writing is full of the deep satisfactions of the soil and of the life of nature. Nor is this respective "restlessness" and "rootedness" irrelevant to that other dualism with which we are concerned. For there is a sense in which the attitude toward place is but a metaphor embodying the basic metaphysics. The "rootedness" of things hangs (as Whitehead has said) upon the fact that they possess "simple location" in space. The "restlessness" of ideas lies in the limitless way in which they rove the corridors of time.

About a hundred pages into *Anna Karenina* (Part I, Chapter XXVI) is the section in which Konstantin Levin, having been rejected by Kitty, leaves Moscow in the morning, and toward evening reaches the country estate which is his home. And slowly the confusion, dissatisfaction, and shame of the Moscow visit give way to relaxation and tranquillity. In the evening he retires to his study.

The study was slowly lit up as the candle was brought in. The familiar details came out: the stag's horns, the bookshelves, the looking glass, the stove with its ventilator, which had long wanted mending, his father's sofa, a large table, on the table an open book, a broken ash-tray, a manuscript-book with his handwriting. As he saw all this, there came over him for an instant a doubt of the possibility of arranging the new life, of which he had been dreaming on the road. All these traces of his life seemed to clutch him, and to say to him: "No, you're not going to get away from us, and you're not going to be different, but you're going to be the same as you've always been. . . ."[25]

It is the tranquillity of the man again in the presence of

familiar and much loved *objects*, and it is irresistibly reminiscent of those pictures of Tolstoy's own study at Yasnaya
Polyana, also littered with objects: the great leather sofa, the
reproductions of Raphael on the walls (among them the Sis-
tine Madonna), the endless photographs of family and friends,
the scattered books, papers, and magazines, the little tables
and the lamps. I have never seen a picture of Dostoyevsky's
study, but from that characteristic contempt for objects which
is implicit in almost every chapter of *The Brothers Karamazov* and *The Possessed*, I should expect it to be as bare,
scrubbed, and "objectless" as Shatov's room, or the Berlin
quarters of Bertolt Brecht.

8   OF THE division in the novelistic imagination between the method of objectivity
and the method of subjectivity, it is difficult to say whether
it stems from the givens of temperament or the accidents of
the sociological situation. But as traditions they go back at
least as far as Homer and St. Augustine. Erich Auerbach begins his fine work on "The Representation of Reality in
Western Literature" with a treatment of Homer's *Odyssey* in
which he shows beyond dispute the scrupulously externalized
narration which is a Homeric hallmark.[26] The essential procedure of Homer is to supply a present which "fills both
the stage and the reader's mind completely," and Auerbach
quotes with approval Schiller's statement that what Homer
gives us is "simply the quiet existence and operation of *things*
in accordance with their natures." This means that the
method of Homer is that of the clear intaglio of the school
of Pisanello rather than the *chiaroscuro* of Rembrandt; the
presentation of reality as a foreground rather than in depth,
as open outline rather than as dramatic focus shading into
darkness. Thus even the Homeric epithets are traceable to
a need "for an externalization of phenomena perceptible to

the senses," and the basic impulse of the Homeric style can be seen as the effort "to represent phenomena in a fully externalized form, visible and palpable in all their parts, and completely fixed in their spatial and temporal relations."[27] It is eminently clear from this account how one tradition for the modern novel, that of objectivity, takes its rise from a purely externalized impulse, and how, for example, it is so easily possible to make the usual comparisons between *Anna Karenina* or *War and Peace* and the Homeric epic.

With the externalized style of Homer, Auerbach wishes to contrast the more psychologized perspective of the Old Testament (he chooses for examination the passage on the sacrifice of Isaac in Genesis 22:1), but here the analysis is much less satisfactory. For if we wish to establish the roots of the tradition of the novel of subjectivity, we must turn from the ancient world to the beginnings of the modern; from the Greeks to Christianity. The important text here is not the Old Testament but the *Confessions* of St. Augustine.

Spengler is, I think, right in saying that while the spirit of the classical culture lies close to the spatiality of objects, it has little affinity with the temporality of the inner life. Selfhood as such, cut off from the matrix of civil society, is hardly a category for Greek thought. Autobiography as a literary form simply does not appear among the Greeks, and it is from the basic spirit of autobiography that the tradition of the psychological novel takes its origin. It is not until the establishment of Christian eschatology with its emphasis upon sin and repentance, the inward searchings of the individual soul in its quest for salvation, and the confessional act which is the culmination of this search, that inwardness becomes a climate of opinion and that confession, autobiography, and interior monologue alike become established as experiences upon which much later the modern novel can draw. It is not irrelevant to remember that Goethe viewed his literary works as "fragments of one great confession" and that Dostoyevsky's last great projected work (of which *The Brothers Karamazov* was only a part) was to be entitled "The Life of a Great Sinner." If there is an analogy between Homer and Tolstoy, surely there is a similar one between St. Augustine and Dostoyevsky.

The legacy of St. Augustine lies not merely in the subjectivism of Dostoyevsky, where the dialectic of sin and saintliness, love and hate, passionate simplicity and the cruelest cynicism dominates the interior states. It lies also in the technical accomplishment of the modern novel, in the work of Joyce, Proust, and Virginia Woolf. For here we find that objective facts (narrated by a kind of fictional master of the event *"wie es eigentlich gewesen ist"*—with the pretense, that is, of objectivity and factuality) have been supplanted by the appearances of things in the consciousness of characters in the work. The single viewpoint of a Cervantes or a Fielding has become obsolete; the center of narrative focus shifts from character to character, not only compromising our assurance of the objective reality of objects and events, but also undermining our subjective confidence in the structure of a single series of formal relations. In fact, the possibility of an inconstant shift back and forth between objectivity and subjectivity constitutes a kind of absurdity. It was this vacillation and the curious atmosphere which it produces which Sartre found so moving in the novels of John Dos Passos.[28]

We are neither mechanical objects nor possessed souls, but something worse; we are free. We exist either entirely *within* or entirely *without*. Dos Passos' man is a hybrid creature, an interior-exterior being. We go on living with him and within him, with his vacillating, individual consciousness, when suddenly it wavers, weakens, and is diluted in the collective consciousness. We follow it up to that point and suddenly, before we notice, we are on the outside. The man behind the looking-glass is a strange, contemptible, fascinating creature. Dos Passos knows how to use this constant shifting to fine effect. . . .

But this (unless one speaks of the novels of Camus and Sartre) is a special case. The general rule is that of the unconfined flow of consciousness and its seemingly formless play with the surfaces of experience as they appear. The result of such a technique is to render the freedom of consciousness in random (and therefore practically purposeless) terms. This is not true of Dostoyevsky, where the interior emotions of sin and anguish, passion and despair, however exhausting, are structured by the tissue of religious problems which they illuminate, and the issues of moral choice to which they lead or from which they stem. Even if within the mind there is a hideous disorder, it is at least in contrast to an order which lies outside and above. But the very *playfulness* of internal revery as it occurs in the subjective modern novel, the continuous rumination of consciousness in its natural and purposeless freedom, calls into question any objective structure of the world. The stream of consciousness, however stimulated, is a contingent stream; even in Proust, where the sense of unity is greatly heightened by the single perspective of the ego of Marcel, the narrator, the operation of that memory out of which the entire novelistic reality is generated is dependent upon the fortuitous recurrence of the memory-stimulating sensations.

In short, the philosophic consequence of the subjective novel with its shifting narrative viewpoint (now centered in one consciousness, now in another) is a disintegration of the continuity of external events. This has produced what Auerbach calls[29] "a transfer of confidence" from those great exterior turning points and blows of fate which produced the narrative crises and the great tragic actions of the past to the random fragments of experience, hit upon by chance or occurring by accident, through whose proliferation the whole of a life may gain point and context (as the whole of *A la Recherche du Temps Perdu* grows out of a morsel of cake dipped into a cup of steaming tea). The consequence is philosophic because it presents the essence of experience under the aspects of randomness and contingency. This shows us that the modern subjective novel is not outside the main-

stream of contemporary culture, but one of its basic manifestations. The "absurdity" in Camus' novels and the "radical
contingency" in Sartre's have been fed by the techniques of
Joyce and Virginia Woolf.

But I want to present a new possibility for the novelistic
imagination, a new synthesis which combines a brutal objectivity with an interiorized narrative viewpoint. What this
amounts to will become clearer if we contrast the two view-
points at their most extreme. For this purpose one can do no
better than to juxtapose a passage from Joyce with one from
Robbe-Grillet. The first is taken from the final section of
Ulysses.[30]

a quarter after what an unearthly hour I suppose they're just getting up in China now combing out their pigtails for the day well
soon have the nuns ringing the angelus they've nobody coming in
to spoil their sleep except an odd priest or two for his night office
the alarmclock next door at cockshout clattering the brains out of
itself let me see if I can doze off 1 2 3 4 5 what kind of flowers are
those they invented like the stars the wallpaper in Lombard street
was much nicer the apron he gave me was like that something only
I wore it twice better lower this lamp and try again so as I can get
up early I'll go to Lambes there beside Findlaters and get them to
send us some flowers to put about the place in case he brings him
home tomorrow today I mean no no Fridays an unlucky day first
I want to do the place up someway the dust grows in it I think
while I'm asleep then we can have music and cigarettes I can ac-
company him first I must clean the keys of the piano with milk
whatll I wear shall I wear a white rose or those fairy cakes in Lip-
tons I love the smell of a rich big shop at 7½ d. a lb. . . .

The second is from "The Dressmaker's Dummy" by Alain
Robbe-Grillet.[31]

The coffee pot is on the table.
It is a round table with four legs, covered with an oil-cloth
checkered red and grey on a neutral background—a yellowish-
white that was once ivory perhaps, or just white. In the middle of
the table is a porcelain tile instead of the usual table mat: the de-

sign on the tile is completely covered, or at least made unrecogniz-
able, by the coffee pot that is standing on it.

The coffee pot is made of brown earthenware. It is in the form
of a sphere surmounted by a cylindrical percolator and a mushroom-shaped lid. The spout is an S with flattened sides, slightly
more rounded at the base. The handle has more or less the shape
of an ear, or rather of the outer rim of an ear. Even so, it would be
a deformed ear—too round and without enough lobe; more or less
an ear shaped like a pot handle. The spout, the handle, and the
mushroom-shaped lid are cream color. The rest of the pot is a
bright, shiny, even shade of brown.

There is nothing else on the table except the oilcloth, the tile
and the coffee pot.

There is perhaps in all literature no more extreme contrast
than this between the section of Molly Bloom's nocturnal
soliloquy and Robbe-Grillet's flat description of the coffee
pot on the table. In the former there are, of course objects:
pigtails, nuns, alarm clocks, wall-paper, flowers, dust, cigarettes, milk, a piano, and a white rose, but their *reality*, and
above all, their matrix of connectedness lies within a mind.
In the latter the table, the porcelain tile, the oil cloth and
the coffee pot are (as in any naturalistic still-life) a "family"
of objects; their relations are external and their qualities in-
here in their natures with the simplicity of any primary substances simply located in space and time. If we need any
demonstration of Cartesian dualism, it lies in the juxtaposition of passages like this. But if we raise the issue of literary
merit, our doubts and our uneasiness will be directed not
toward Joyce but toward Robbe-Grillet. Since Lessing, we
have been persuaded that a medium like literature, based on
the serial presentation of images in time, is intrinsically inappropriate for the presentation of objects simultaneously
coexisting in space. A literature of description is unworthy
precisely because such objects are better handled by the language of science, and the dilemma is clearly statable: If co-
existences in space are to be treated wholistically, then they

must be dealt with by the plastic arts, and if they are to be treated analytically, then they are natural material for science but not for literature. But if we consult Robbe-Grillet, he will deny our argument, and he will do so on grounds no less philosophical than Lessing's.

Quoting a sentence of another of the "new objectivists," Nathalie Sarraute: "The novel passes for a minor art only because of its obstinate attachment to exhausted techniques," Robbe-Grillet passes to the philosophical justification of the objectivist method. Objectivity is the total impersonality of observation, and if we adopt this as a novelistic method, it is in the face of our real estrangement from things. Objects are not either comprehensible or reassuring, but as Sartre might say "the irreducibly other," and this recalcitrance, this ultimate impermeability, as it were, must be dealt with in its own terms. By failing to do so, both radical subjectivists like Proust and existentialists like Sartre and Camus fail to do justice to reality. "But the world is neither significant nor absurd. It *is*, quite simply. That, in any case, is the most remarkable thing about it. . . . Around us, defying the mob of our animistic or protective adjectives, the things *are there*. Their surfaces are clear and smooth, *intact*, neither dubiously glittering, nor transparent. All our literature has not yet succeeded in penetrating their smallest corner, in softening their slightest curve."[32]

The pragmatist sees objects as tools for human appropriation and use, the idealist sees them as extensions of the human mind, gaining significance and content from the secondary and tertiary qualities imported into them, but the new objectivism owes much to a phenomenological method which asks only that objects declare themselves by their presence, that they show themselves to be *recalcitrantly there*. And the result in terms of novelistic technique is a kind of literary positivism, a denial of the distinction between appearance and reality, a resolute attempt to confine oneself to the structure of appearance, and to enlist in this enterprise only sight and the language of a stoic descriptivism. Robbe-Grillet writes:[33]

It is therefore the whole literary language that has to change, that is changing already. We witness from day to day the growing repugnance that people of greater awareness feel for words of a visceral, analogical, incantory character. On the other hand, the visual or descriptive adjective—the word that contents itself with measuring, locating, limiting, defining—indicates a difficult but most likely direction for the novel of the future.

It is clear, I think, that this is the most extreme Cartesianism of all, and that it results from taking infinitely more seriously than Sartre himself the Sartrian distinction between being-in-itself and being-for-itself, consciousness and things, selves and objects. And it places beyond the pale every attempt to humanize objects, to employ an analogical vocabulary, to exploit that form of anthropomorphism which consists in endowing mere things with the qualities of human emotion. In these terms Robbe-Grillet can criticize the metaphysical presuppositions of the novels of both Sartre and Camus. Even Camus' spare and "cleansed" style cannot dispense with objects "burdened with a flagrantly obvious human significance" and his famed *absurdity* "turns out to be a form of tragic Humanism. It is not a recognition of the separation between man and objects. It is a lovers' quarrel between them, which leads to a crime of passion. The world is accused of complicity in murder."[34] And the *nausea*, that visceral suffering so celebrated in the work of Sartre, turns out to be little more than a sort of morbid solidarity of man and nature ("All the objects surrounding me," says Roquentin, "are made of the same matter as myself, a sort of rotten suffering.")

Robbe-Grillet's aspirations for the novel presuppose a metaphysics which is at variance with every romanticism of the speculative intellect. It is aimed at once against Wordsworth's "living nature," Whitehead's panpsychism, and Bergson's intuitive penetration of objects. Indeed, the repudiation of the method of intuition and the espousal of that of analysis gives to Robbe-Grillet's technical suggestions the character of a purposively inverted Bergsonianism.

To describe things, in point of fact, requires that we place ourselves deliberately outside, in front of them. We must neither appropriate them to ourselves, nor transfer anything to them. Admitted at the outset as *not* being man, they remain always out of reach and are not, in the end, to be either accepted in a natural alliance or redeemed by suffering. To limit oneself to description is obviously to challenge all other modes of approach to objects. It entails calling sympathy anti-realistic, deeming tragedy productive of madness, and relegating understanding to the exclusive realm of science.[35]

This blatant positivism is also a pattern of the novelistic imagination.

Six / Appearance & Reality, Illusion—the Meta-physical Imagination

ℝ ROBBE-GRILLET'S aspirations for the novel, as we have just seen, presuppose a point of view which is the literary equivalent of the imperatives of traditional positivism in philosophy. He asks the novelist for objectivity, for a total impersonality of observation, to confine himself to the structure of appearance. And like every positivist, he is devoted to the abolition of our illusions: in this particular case to what he calls "the dismissal of the old myth of *depth*." "We know," he says, "that the whole literature of the novel was based on this myth, and on it alone. The traditional role of the writer consisted in excavating nature, in burrowing deeper and deeper to reach some ever more intimate strata, in finally bringing to light some fragment of a disconcerting secret."[1] And he adds with his new methodological passion: *"Profundity* has functioned like a trap. . . ."

We must admit, I think, that in his description of the nature of the traditional novel, particularly as it has recently flourished in France, M. Robbe-Grillet is correct. Inevitably so. For the language of "depth," of "excavating" nature, of "burrowing" deeper and deeper, and of "bringing to light" the disconcerting secrets, is the language of the search to penetrate appearances and hinges upon that distinction between "appearance" and "reality" which is one of the cornerstones

of the metaphysical imagination. Certainly it is a distinction
without which the work of Proust and Sartre, Robbe-Grillet's
two older compatriots, cannot be understood. Sartre himself
offers an obvious confirmation. "The real novelist," he says,
"is stirred by things that offer resistance; he is excited by
doors because they must be opened, by envelopes because
they must be unsealed." And Samuel Beckett, writing about
the work of Proust, uses a language almost identical with that
of Robbe-Grillet. "The work of art," he tells us, is "neither
created nor chosen, but discovered, uncovered, excavated,
pre-existing within the artist, a law of his nature."[2]

But if Sartre in his novels and short stories is interested in
penetrating the seemingly opaque façades of bad faith, and
if Proust's explorations of the many facets of Bergsonian time
demand a contrast between the superficiality of the *"haute
monde"* and the deepest strata of memory and desire, these
are only expressions in literature of an impulse which begins
at the humblest level of human experience, although it flowers subsequently in the most sustained products of the metaphysical imagination. To this initial impulse, no one has
called attention better than Gide as he tells us of his childhood and of the images and visions by which it was haunted.[3]

The vague, ill-defined belief that something else exists along-
side the acknowledged, above-board reality of everyday life, in-
habited me for many years; and I am not sure that even today I
have not still some remnants of it left. It had nothing in common
with tales of fairies, ghouls, or witches, nor even with Hoffman's
or Hans Andersen's stories. No, I think it was more *a kind of unskilful desire to give life more thickness*—a desire that later on
religion was better able to satisfy: and also *a sort of propensity to
imagine a clandestine side to things.*

This "unskilful desire to give life more thickness," and perhaps also the more suspect "propensity to imagine a clandestine side to things," has ruled the domain of metaphysics
since the days when Parmenides asserted *The One* against
the flux of sensation, and Plato lost himself in visions of an

"intelligible world" above and behind the shifting scenery of the world of mere appearance.

For in truth Robbe-Grillet's presumptuous dismissal of the old "myth of depth," however it may momentarily give a specious originality to the modern novel, is yet an act of treason committed against the metaphysical imagination. As an act of the understanding it would be meaningful and right, for it contributes to the purity of science by that sort of expurgation of mythical elements to which Santayana has called attention. But as a principle directed *to* the imagination it is a contradiction in terms. The myth of depth enthrones within the nature of events just that intrinsic purposiveness and dramatic quality which is the hallmark of imaginative functioning. Science, as William James long ago pointed out, has utterly repudiated emotion as a qualification of the "things which are." It catalogues its elements and records its functional covariations and its relative frequencies, indifferent to the role which they play in the human drama and careless of the teleological implications which might be imputed to them. Thus the "Nature" which science defines in an abstract symbolism and describes wherever possible in a mathematical language "has no one distinguishable tendency with which it is possible to feel a sympathy."

Nor is this surprising if (in following Kant) we recognize that the understanding, for the extraordinary success which it achieves in rigorous description and accurate prediction, must employ the mathematical and mechanistic modes of conception which science demands. Those contemporary models of causal "explanation" derived from Hume, and enlarged and purified by the schools of Carnap, Reichenbach, and Russell, must of necessity reject both the theory of an "order of nature" which expresses the relational character of the real events which jointly constitute the existences to be found in nature, and the theory (implicit in Plato, and surely held by Newton) that if physics deals with the flux, behind the flux lie certain necessities which control it. For Plato a dialectical physics of appearances gives intimations of the permanences behind, and for Newton the discernment of a cosmological pattern suggests the rationality of a God beyond. But where (as with Bacon and Hume and modern science alike) the aim is that solidity of concentration which must finally permit sequential regularity to be detected, the emphasis is upon the sequential stream itself, and scientific "experience" is flattened into the succession of phenomena cut off from either animistic base or metaphysical superstructure. Here Gide's desire to give experience more "thickness" and to imagine a "clandestine" side to things earns only resentment and impatience, for now the distinction between "appearance" and "reality" has collapsed. The only realities *are* the appearances. This *phenomenalism* is at once the natural metaphysic of the understanding, and the inevitable climate of positivistic science.

It is true that the early Russell is concerned about the relation of appearance to reality, but his characteristic strategy is to redefine the issue in the only way in which it might make scientific sense—as the relation of the "physical object" to those "sense-data" immediately perceived for which it might be said to be causally responsible[4]—a far cry indeed from the originally metaphysical formulations of Plato and of Kant. Even Sartre in the first few pages of *Being and Nothingness* paradoxically denies that there is any being-behind-the-appearance; on the contrary, phenomenal being is nothing but the well connected series of its manifestations, the object shows itself only as the structure of the appearances, and is, in fact, a "center of opacity" for consciousness. It is as if we had here another of those "meetings of the philosophical extremes" to which Bosanquet of an earlier generation called attention—in this case that of positivism and existentialism.

Phenomenalism boldly asserts that there are no things-in-themselves, but only things in immediate relation to our experience, and it therefore reaffirms the ancient dogma of Protagoras (against the counterclaim of Plato's *Theatetus*) that *sensation as such* is reality, and that the immediate appearance of the qualities of things in perception is knowledge. But in the same fashion in which Kant prophesied that from reason itself would arise questions which reason itself would be unable to answer, from the initial assurance of phenomenalism arises the uneasy feeling that all is not well. The authentic phenomenalism of positivistic science leaves no room for a realm of self-existences outside the sensory continuum, and yet so scientifically oriented a philosopher as C. D. Broad (who attempted the construction of a theory of sense-data or "sensa" not unlike Russell's own) must in all candor add a dimension of extraterritoriality to the sensationalist domain. "The belief," he says,[5]

that our sensa are appearances of something more permanent and complex than themselves seems to be primitive, and to arise inevitably in us with the sensing of the sensa. It is not reached by inference, and could not logically be justified by inference. On the other hand, there is no possibility of either refuting it logically, or of getting rid of it, or—so far as I can see—of co-ordinating the facts without it.

If, as Broad suggests, our primitive belief in the existence of a world of relatively permanent independent things is extremely vague, this may well be because the metaphysical imagination contributes even to the analysis of the physical world a penumbra of insistent meanings which the understanding mistrusts, but which it is yet unable wholly to eliminate.

The scientific chain of meaning which is the product of the understanding has no room for the distinction between "appearance" and "reality" or for that "illusion" which is a secondary concept consequent upon the assumption of this particular metaphysical stance. If there is a dualism presupposed by the understanding, it is that between the continuum of true, probable, and false propositions on one level, and the evidence according to which their assertion or denial constitutes rational belief. And when the correspondence between propositional assertion and evidence breaks down, this is not "illusion"; it is "error." But the distinction of "appearance and reality" *is* a part of the furniture of the humanistic complex. It is a characteristic product of the teleological imagination, and one of the traditional resources (perhaps even the cornerstone) of all classical metaphysics. To its further examination I should now like to turn.

2   IN THE early pages of Plato's *Timaeus* Critias, one of the participants, tells a story which he has learned from his own grandfather. Solon, wisest of the Greeks and of revered memory, was once traveling in Egypt and, cognizant of the great age of the history and traditions of that country, he attempted to tell the Egyptian priests of the ancient legends and traditions of his native Greece. Whereupon one of the priests, "a prodigiously old man," said, "O Solon, Solon, you Greeks are always children; there is not such a thing as an old Greek." On hearing this Solon asked, "What mean you by this saying?" The priest replied, "You are young in spirit, every one of you. For therein you possess not a single belief that is ancient and derived from old tradition, nor yet one science that in hoary with age."[6]

It is impossible, I think, not to feel this youthfulness and vitality of early Greek thought. The Greeks are speculatively bold because they are close to the first emergence of European rationality, but for this reason also their thought takes its origins in a twilight zone where (as Aristotle so finely intimated in his *Metaphysics*) philosophic "wonder" has not yet emerged from religious "awe," and therefore metaphysics and cosmology are close to the age of myth, the age of gods and heroes. Therefore also, it is impossible, I think, to read the fragmentary utterances of the great pre-Socratics, those often dark and hieratic sayings of the Ionians, Pythagoreans, and others, without feeling the essential closeness of cosmology— that first production of the metaphysical imagination—and myth. Empedocles discovers the fourfold root of all things— the divine elements—but calls attention too to the process ("mixture" and "separation") in which they participate guided by the principles of "Love" and "Strife." He is a physicist, if not a Milesian, but his physics is close to a human teleology, and his images of process are drawn from such mythical terms as "marriage" and "warfare."

Heracleitus too, a lover of the hermetic and the enigmatic, exploits the "hidden" (again Gide's "clandestine" side to things) which is finally to flower in a sense of the distinction between appearance and reality. "Nature," he says, "loves to hide" (Fr. 123) and "The hidden harmony is better than the manifest" (Fr. 54). And the insistence of his physical theory is that even above the "process" or "flux" of nature (the discovery for which he is famous) there is a *logos*—a principle of order—which arranges the measured progress of "the upward and the downward paths." Heracleitus has been often identified as a precursor of the metaphysics of Bergson and Whitehead, and it is true that his account of physical change carries with it a certain mistrust of the accuracy of perceptual experience. If nothing is really "solid" or at rest, we cannot really know objects, since in close perception they dissolve. But if the senses are untrustworthy, the *logos* is apprehended by the mind "looking within." Thus even in this philosopher of the flux is to be found an almost Parmenidean opposition of perception and thought which celebrates on the level of epistemology a dualism usually expressed in more metaphysical terms. But of course it is in Parmenides above all that the One Eternal Immobility is the bedrock of metaphysical existence.

In Plato's *Sophist* (246a-c) is celebrated that eternal "Battle of Gods and Giants" by which he means to contrast the "materialism" of Ionian science and the "idealism" of Eleatic

metaphysics. "One party," he says, "is trying to drag everything down to earth out of heaven and the unseen, literally
grasping rocks and trees in their hands: for they lay hold
upon every stock and stone and strenuously affirm that real
existence belongs only to that which can be handled and offers resistance to the touch. They define reality as the same
thing as body, and as soon as one of the opposite party asserts
that anything without a body is real, they are utterly con-
temptuous and will not listen to another word." On the other
hand, "their adversaries are very wary in defending their position somewhere in the heights of the unseen, maintaining
with all their force that true reality consists in certain intelligible and bodiless Forms. In the clash of argument they
shatter and pulverise those bodies which their opponents
wield, and what those others allege to be true reality they
call, not real being, but a sort of moving process of becoming."[7]

But it is extremely doubtful whether Plato in his Parmenidean zeal has not disproportionately overemphasized the common-sense materialism of the Ionians. Since the sixth century
B.C. Greek cosmology had been neatly divided between the
Milesian science from the east and the Eleatic and Pythagorean metaphysics from the west, but what is interesting is
that the crucial distinction between appearance and reality
holds as much for Milesian science as for the metaphysics of
the Italians. The Ionians also seek "the real nature of things"
in some ultimate kind of matter, but even in the atomism
which in Leucippus and Democritus is their final outcome,
this ultimate material may be inaccessible to the senses and
hence a qualification of reality rather than appearance. The
Parmenideans sought reality not in tangible body but in supersensible things, and the Pythagoreans found reality not in
matter but in the relations of number which lie behind; both
discredit appearance in favor of the "thickness" which lies
beyond. Already, therefore, in this primitive age of cosmology
we find the two forms of dualism to which we have already

called attention; the scientific version of Broad and Russell, which at least distinguishes two conceptual levels of scientific existence, and the more esoteric version of Plato and Hegel, inspired by the intransigent insistence of Parmenides upon the supersensible.

Parmenides (according to the tradition and the few inconclusive fragments assembled by Diels) wrote a poem in hexameter verse addressed to his pupil Zeno which, apart from its Prologue, was divided into the Way of Truth and the Way of Opinion; the first investigating the supersensible Being which *is* and the second the illusory Non-being upon which the senses fasten. But the *locus classicus* for the distinction between appearance and reality as it infuses the entire metaphysical tradition is the famous allegory of the cave which opens Book VII of Plato's *Republic*. The men confined in the underground cavern know only the realm of the senses, and the shadows of the statues thrown by the flickering fire upon the walls of the cave are those "images" of the senses in the presence of which our lives are spent. But those who escape from the cave into the sunlight above survey the landscape of reality, contemplating the forms of things by the illumination cast by the supreme form of the good.

The distinction between appearance and reality, between the cave of sensation and the real universe of ideas, haunts Plato's later dialogues. The construction of the universe which is the subject of the discourse of Timaeus hinges upon it. "Now first of all we must, in my judgment, make the following distinction. What is that which is Existent always and has no Becoming? And what is that which is Becoming always and never is Existent? Now the one of these is apprehensible by thought with the aid of reasoning, since it is ever uniformly existent; whereas the other is an object of opinion with the aid of unreasoning sensation, since it becomes and perishes and is never really existent."[8] Thus we have in Platonic language the proportion which at once expresses the deepest insight of Parmenides and analogizes metaphysics and epistemology in a single statement: *as Being is to Becoming, so is Truth to Belief*. And a close attention to the *Theaetetus* and the *Sophist* will show that what the *Republic* presents as an allegory and the *Timaeus* as the presupposition of a dialectical physics, these dialogues between them exhaust in a continuous examination which disposes of a popular but inconvenient epistemology before expounding what is to Plato an adequate metaphysics.

The *Theaetetus* early makes an equation of "appearing" and "perceiving,"[9] and this identification of the Heracleitean universe of sensory flux and the domain of appearance prepares us perfectly for the Parmenidean proposition implicitly asserted by the later *Sophist*. The Sophist, whose nature this dialogue is attempting to define, may be a creator, but if so, like the artist, he is a mere imitator of actual things, a maker of images or semblances, a creator of illusions. Like the semblance-makers of the *Republic* (human artists) and the image-maker of the *Timaeus* (the Demiurge or divine artisan) his identification too requires the cutting off of a world of true Being from a world of semblance and illusion. And so the *Sophist* too is dominated by the distinction between reality or "the real" (*to on*) and appearance or "the semblance" (*eidolon*). When subsequently (*Sophist* 247e) the Eleatic stranger proceeds to give his "suggestion" as to the nature of the real ("I suggest that anything has real being, that is so constituted as to possess any sort of power either to affect anything else or to be affected, in however small a degree. . . . I am proposing as a mark to distinguish real things, that they are nothing but power."), the word *dynamis*, translated "power," suggests not only the exterior and sensible aspect of bodies, but equally their internal and mysterious nature, the hidden reality which they encompass.

The mature thought of Plato (and indeed, of Aristotle also) is never far from the influence of early Greek cosmological ideas, impregnated as these are by the atmosphere of the mythical imagination, and if, therefore, the term "reality" is central to Greek philosophy,[10] it is only because the distinction between appearance and reality, originating in the imagination rather than the understanding, is a resource which no philosophy considerate of metaphysics can possibly ignore.

3 IF THE distinction between appearance and reality is a product of the metaphysical imagination, it is in the pre-Socratics and in Plato that its expression reaches its highest point, for here the emphasis of Parmenides and Plato alike is upon the realm of reality which is above and behind the senses. But we have also noted in passing that there is a second form of the distinction, implicit in the Milesians, and appealed to both by Russell and by Broad, which assimilates the problem to that of the levels of scientific knowledge, and which at the same time attempts to remain true to that "phenomenalism" which we have identified as the natural metaphysics of the understanding.

The point is of some interest, for it suggests that if the understanding is in constant danger of subversion by mythical and imaginative elements, the converse is no less true, and there are distinctions which originate in the imagination which the understanding is constantly attempting to subvert to uses which are its own. This can be interestingly demonstrated, I think, if we note how the distinction between appearance and reality appears at the end of a long period of scientific accomplishment in the philosophy of Kant, and if we recognize in addition how Kant's treatment of metaphysics (dominated by the standpoint of the understanding) is rescued by Schopenhauer (a true if less profound philosopher of the arts and of the imagination) and restored to that level of metaphysical concern upon which it had been left by Plato over two millennia before.

Perhaps the only lyrical passage which appears within that literary waste land called the *Critique of Pure Reason* occurs at the end of the Transcendental Analytic—at the beginning of the chapter entitled "The Ground of the Distinction of All Objects in General Into Phenomena and Noumena," which was intended as an introduction to the Transcendental Dialectic by making a schematic transition to it from what had gone before. "We have now," says Kant,[11]

not merely explored the territory of pure understanding, and carefully surveyed every part of it, but have also measured its extent and assigned to everything in it its rightful place. This domain is an island, enclosed by nature itself within unalterable limits. It is the land of truth—enchanting name!—surrounded by a wide and stormy ocean, the native home of illusion, where many a fog bank and many a swiftly melting iceberg give the deceptive appearance of further shores, deluding the adventurous seafarer ever anew with empty hopes, and engaging him in enterprises which he can never abandon and yet is unable to carry to completion. Before we venture on this sea, to explore it in all directions and to obtain assurance whether there be any ground for such hopes, it will be well to begin by casting a glance upon the map of the land which we are about to leave, and to enquire, first, whether we cannot in any case be satisfied with what it contains—are not, indeed, under compulsion to be satisfied, inasmuch as there may be no other territory upon which we can settle; and, secondly, by what title we possess even this domain, and can consider ourselves as secured against all opposing claims.

The realm of the understanding (science) is a tight little island, dedicated to the truth about phenomena, but hedged about with fog banks and the stormy sea of the imagination, where illusion beguiles the hopeful traveler in search of metaphysical knowledge· and ultimate reality—those "things-in-themselves" or noumena which loom like icebergs in the troubled water, giving promise of solidity from a distance, but dissolving into nothingness as we approach.

Kant's metaphor is instructive, particularly if we note that it is precisely the opposite of that presented by Plato in the allegory of the cave. Each appeals to the distinction between

appearance and reality, phenomena and noumena, but with a
striking reversal of intent. Kant's tight little island of scientific security is the blindness of Plato's cave. Plato's pure realm
of Being, dazzlingly illuminated by the sun, is Kant's stormy
sea of fog and illusion. The distinction remains, but its moral
has been reversed, and in the two accounts the invidiously
defined "illusion" has radically shifted its abode. What has
been responsible for this profound metaphysical displacement?

The new flowering of the subjectivist principle in Descartes and Hume has prepared us for a shift in the statement
of philosophical problems, so that if Parmenides and Plato
deal always with reality in terms of "things," we are not surprised to find in Kant that metaphysics has turned into epistemology, and that the ancient concern with things has here
transformed itself into an interest in the process and the pre-
conditions governing "how things are known." But it was,
of course, the growth of modern science, and particularly the
new mathematical physics discovered and invented by Gali-
leo, Descartes, and Newton which called out for philosophic
rationalization, and which Descartes himself as well as Locke
and Leibniz, Berkeley and Hume, transformed into material
which philosophers could use to explain the process of acquiring knowledge precisely because its foundations and its predictive accomplishments seemed so unquestionably secure.
Kant is, therefore, only the last and the greatest of those who
take the mathematico-observational sciences for granted in
constructing his brilliant schematization of the human mind.

The conclusion of the first two parts of the *Critique of
Pure Reason* is that everything which the understanding
contributes to knowledge, although *not borrowed from* experience, is yet available solely for *use in the ordering of
experience*. The understanding can employ its various principles and concepts only in an "empirical," never in a "transcendental" manner; always with an application to the structure of appearances, never in an application to the domain of

"things-in-themselves." Appearances, in so far as they are thought of as objects, require the unity of the categories, and they constitute that phenomenal world which is the subject matter of science. But the "intelligible world" consisting ideally of those "objects" which might be given to the understanding, but outside of the normal agencies of sensation, cannot be under any circumstances even a possible object amenable to scientific treatment. Noumena (by which we would mean things *insofar as they are not objects of our sensible intuition*) are thus, in the absence of any faculty of intellectual or non-sensible intuition, impossible to establish. But here Kant leaves a curious and strikingly significant loophole. The noumenon cannot be presented as determinate knowledge of anything positive, but an adequate epistemology is forced to posit it as a *negative* concept, and moreover as a necessary concept if we are to prevent sensible intuition from being extended beyond its proper limit. Denying that "intellectual intuition" which Plato or Parmenides might have invoked as the guarantor of our knowledge of "the Real," for Kant "the concept of a noumenon is thus a merely *limiting concept*, the function of which is to curb the pretensions of sensibility; and it is therefore only for negative employment."[12]

This treatment of the distinction between appearance and reality denies the theoretical validity of metaphysics and affirms only the theoretical validity of science, and it brings the opposition of noumena and phenomena into line with that general intermediate dualism which asserts the native phenomenalism of the understanding at the same time as it retains the prior furniture of the metaphysical imagination on the hollow pretense of its "regulative" rather than its "constitutive" use. Reason has indeed principles of its own, but regarded as objective, they are one and all "dialectical," and can have no validity save as regulative principles for its employment in experience with a view to making experience itself systematically coherent. In the last few pages of the

Critique of Pure Reason, in that rewarding and often neglected "Transcendental Doctrine of Method," Kant summed
it all up.[13]

The concepts of reason are, as we have said, mere ideas, and
have no object that can be met with in any experience. None the
less they do not on this account signify objects that having been
invented are thereupon assumed to be possible. They are thought
only problematically, in order that upon them (as heuristic fictions), we may base regulative principles of the systematic employment of the understanding in the field of experience. Save in this
connection they are merely thought-entities *(Gedankendinge)* the
possibility of which is not demonstrable, and which therefore do
not allow of being employed, in the character of hypotheses, in
explanation of the actual appearances.

Here are celebrated the solemn funeral rites of the metaphysical imagination. Here is that final subversion which the
scientific logic of the understanding works upon the tradition of Parmenides and Plato. The concepts of pure reason,
whether of Platonic forms, Aristotelian essences, a Thomistic
first cause, or a Newtonian God, are mere ideas, with no content to be met with in any experience. As objects of thought
they may be employed "problematically," that is, as limitations upon the aspirations of science; as definitions of that
terra prohibita upon which the scientific enterprise may not
legitimately encroach. They are merely "thought-entities,"
figments of the mind, "heuristic fictions," "as-if constructs"
(as Vaihinger was soon to label them) without either existential dignity or status in reality. It is true that when in the
Preface to the Second Edition of the *Critique* Kant summarized his results, he admitted that "when all progress in the
field of the supersensible has been denied to speculative reason, it is still open to us to enquire whether in the *practical
knowledge* of reason, data may not be found . . . to enable us,
in accordance with the wish of metaphysics . . . *though only
from a practical point of view,* to pass beyond the limits of
all possible experience." This is the equivalent of his fa-

mous: "I have therefore found it necessary to deny *knowledge*, in order to make room for *faith*." But from such makeshifts the Platonic metaphysician will derive cold comfort indeed. From his point of view here is the prophetic foretaste of the wintry blasts of Russell, Reichenbach, and Carnap, which is to usher in the heralded Ice Age of the metaphysical imagination.

4 WHEN WE say that Schopenhauer rescued Kant's treatment of metaphysics, and restored it to its Platonic eminence, we do not mean either that he denied the master from whom he had learned so much or that in his criticisms of him (good-natured as compared with his treatment of Fichte and Hegel) he completely understood the destruction which Kant had wrought.[14] The first book of *The World as Will and Idea* is almost a literal restatement of the first two parts of the *Critique of Pure Reason:* Schopenhauer's "principle of sufficient reason" is simply a capsule formulation of all that Kant had laboriously drawn out concerning space, time, and causality in describing the presuppositions of the scientific understanding. But whereas Kant went on in the Transcendental Dialectic to deny that metaphysics has any theoretical validity whatsoever, the second and third books of *The World as Will and Idea* reinstate metaphysics by the precise devices (though with not quite the same consequences) as may be found in Plato and Parmenides. Again Robbe-Grillet's "myth of depth" reappears. Once more the distinction between appearance and reality asserts itself as the essence of the metaphysical imagination.

In his treatment of "the world as idea" Schopenhauer drew from Kant the proper inference: that from the standpoint of the understanding "the aim and ideal of all natural science is at bottom a consistent materialism."[15] He continues:

The recognition here of the obvious impossibility of such a system establishes another truth which will appear in the course of our exposition, the truth that all science properly so called, by which I understand systematic knowledge under the guidance of the principle of sufficient reason, can never reach its final goal, nor give a complete and adequate explanation: for it is not concerned with the inmost nature of the world, it cannot get beyond the idea; indeed, it really teaches nothing more than the relation of one idea to another.

But this distinction between the "idea" or "appearance" or "image" (*Vorstellung*) and "the inmost nature of the world" (*ihr innerstes Wesen*) is a return to Plato. Goethe, surely no positivist, and, indeed, fighting with all the resources of his imagination the abstractions of that same Newtonian physics upon which Kant in fact based his system, yet was able to observe:

> *Natur hat weder Kern*
> *Noch Schale*
> *Alles ist sie mit einemmale.*

(Nature has neither kernel nor shell—she is everything at once.)

But Schopenhauer uses the identical metaphor to reassert the metaphysical dualism. "The objective world, the world as idea, is not the only side of the world, but merely its outward side; and it has an entirely different side—the side of its inmost nature—its kernel—the thing-in-itself." It is true, of course, that the outcome of the Platonic dualism is a realm of forms, static and eternal, known by some intellectual intuition (akin to dialectic) which Plato names, though he does not further specify, whereas for Schopenhauer the higher realm, less "knowable" perhaps than Plato's, is constituted by a "force" of nature; dynamic, restless, endlessly striving; not merely the form of order in which things participate, but that *will* which is the active agency that drives them in its frenzy.

And such a conception must, above all, reveal the epistemic limitations of science.

Kant's forms of sensibility and understanding (which Schopenhauer assimilates to "the principle of sufficient reason") lose their efficacy just here where all scientific endeavor must stop because its explanatory powers do not extend beyond an empirical employment. Here philosophy must pick things up and treat them after its own method, which clearly is distinct from the method of science. About this Schopenhauer is insistent. The most complete causal explanation of the whole of nature can never be more than an enumeration of forces which cannot be really explained. For we can never arrive at the real nature of things from without. However brilliant our technical apparatus, however rigorous our investigations, we can never grasp anything but "images" and "names." The understanding which determines the position of phenomena in space and time according to a law whose special content is derived from experience, but whose universality of form and necessity is, at the same time, independent of experience, affords us no insight about their inner nature. For the causal model (with its presupposition of constant uniformity) permits us to isolate laws of nature at the very moment when it must remain ignorant of, or when it even, in its positivistic pride, attempts to abolish the *forces* of nature. But these forces—the inner nature of phenomena, their strange and unknown further side—their secret—these, for the most complex, as for the simplest phenomena, are simply will.

It would be misleading to say merely that Schopenhauer's "will" is less "knowable" than the Platonic world of forms. It is less cognitively available, but precisely because our knowledge of it is more immediate. It is intuitively known as the Cartesian or Bergsonian self is known; by no means a problematic quantity, or something arrived at analytically and by inference, but fully and immediately comprehended, as the childhood we have never outgrown, or the lifetime friend whose habitual responses we recognize as the supporting cli-

mate of our own existence. Schopenhauer uses a metaphor
which is slightly different, but it too expresses the supporting
and enveloping character and a Parmenidean oneness. As
the magic lantern, he says,[16] "shows many different pictures,
which are all made visible by one and the same light, so in
all the multifarious phenomena which fill the world together
or throng after each other as events, only *one will* manifests
itself, of which everything is the visibility, the objectivity,
and which remains unmoved in the midst of this change; it
alone is thing-in-itself; all objects are manifestations, or to
speak the language of Kant, phenomena." To this "One" is
attributable the origin of all natural teleology, the unmistakable analogy of all the productions of nature; that "family
resemblance" on the basis of which we may regard them as
variations on the same ungiven theme. So likewise is revealed
that harmony, that essential connectedness of all the parts of
the cosmos which Kant in his Third Critique considered as
a regulative and not a constitutive principle of our reflections
about the world.

We already have seen in Chapter 3 that from this work
of Kant's we may learn much about the teleological imagination, but Schopenhauer reinforces with a metaphysical bold-
ness what Kant could only assert with a faintheartedness nur-
tured by the skepticism of Hume. Kant's timid treatment of
teleology in the *Critique of Judgment* is simply the extension of his unwillingness in the *Critique of Pure Reason* to
grant validity to metaphysics. But when Schopenhauer interprets the Kantian thing-in-itself no longer procedurally, but
with substantive authenticity, then the teleological principle
is reinstated as a consequence of the metaphysics, and purposiveness is reintroduced as constitutive of the world.

The philosophy of Schopenhauer is indeed an abandonment of Kant and a return to Plato, but with a reversal of
the dualistic insistence by which Plato accommodates the
Heracleitean insight to the master-wisdom of Parmenides.
For now the grades of objectification of the will, the classes

of phenomena, the appearances, become the static Platonic ideas, and it is the inner nature of things, the transcendent reality of will, which exhibits eternal becoming, the restless and the endless mobility of the Heracleitean flux.

Schopenhauer himself would have denied that his philosophy was the abandonment of Kant and the return to Plato. In the face of all the evidence, what he wished to believe was that in his concept of the will as "the thing-in-itself" and its objectification at various levels as the "ideas" was joined the Kantian *Ding-an-sich* and the Platonic *ontos on*. For him these "two greatest philosophers of the West" have a single message: *that the visible world can be explained only as the manifestation of a borrowed reality which it appropriates from what lies behind*. This is true for Plato, but it is false for Kant, and if Schopenhauer wished to find in them an identity of aim and a like conception of the universe, it was at the cost of systematic distortion of the Kantian materials in order to "bring Kant's mode of expression nearer the Platonic."[17]

For in the end Kant *is* the philosopher of the understanding, of that natural science which imposes laws upon phenomena, while Plato is a philosopher of the humanistic complex and of the imagination, perpetually demonstrating the analogies of discourse to the creative act, and utilizing the resources of myth for the adumbration of a wisdom which is beyond analysis. Perhaps Schopenhauer dimly recognized this opposition which he seemed unwilling to acknowledge overtly. It almost seems so when a few pages later in Book III of *The World as Will and Idea* he contrasts science with art. Science is that which, proceeding according to "the principle of sufficient reason," takes as its theme the laws, connections, and relations of phenomena.

But what kind of knowledge is concerned with that which is outside and independent of all relations, that which alone is really essential to the world, the true content of its phenomena, that which is subject to no change, and therefore is known with equal truth for all time, in a word, the *Ideas*, which are the direct and adequate objectivity of the thing-in-itself, the will? We answer, *Art,* the work of genius. It repeats or reproduces the eternal Ideas grasped through pure contemplation, the essential and abiding in all the phenomena of the world; and according to what the material is in which it reproduces, it is sculpture or painting, poetry or music. Its one source is the knowledge of Ideas; its one aim the communication of this knowledge. . . . We may, therefore, accurately define it [art] as the *way of viewing things independent of the principle of sufficient reason,* in opposition to the way of viewing them which proceeds in accordance with that principle, and which is the method of experience and of science.[18]

The first, says Schopenhauer, is Plato's way, the second is Aristotle's—and, he should rightfully have added, that of Kant. In choosing as his own preference the first over the second, Schopenhauer at once reaffirms the distinction between appearance and reality, and in full awareness joins his fortunes not with science, but with the imagination.

Schopenhauer's return to the crucial strategy of distinguishing between appearance and reality means a restoration of the metaphysical imagination, and is perhaps as responsible as is Hegel himself for the revival which is to spring to life in nineteenth-century absolute idealism, and to flower luxuriantly in the work of F. H. Bradley. For the very title of his "metaphysical essay" *Appearance and Reality* suggests what he might have learned equally from Plato or from Schopenhauer, that "we may agree, perhaps *to understand by metaphysics* an attempt to know reality against mere appearance."[19] And if, in Bradley, this leads to an Hegelian attempt to comprehend the universe "not simply piecemeal or by fragments, but somehow as a whole," this too has been stimulated by that organicism of the imagination which Kant's theory of purposiveness and Schopenhauer's theory of art has prepared. Bradley, I think, is right that metaphysics is akin to poetry, art, and religion, and that with them it shares the delight in *chiaroscuro*, the excitement of half-light and shadow. "When," he says, "the sense of mystery and enchantment no longer draws the mind to wander aimlessly and to love it knows not what; when, in short, twilight has no charm —than metaphysics will be worthless."[20] But he knows too that this time will never come. For metaphysics takes its start on a dependable side of human nature; in a willing commitment to Robbe-Grillet's "myth of depth" and in Gide's eternally childlike desire to give a greater "thickness" to the outer crust of experience which we inhabit. "All of us, I presume," says Bradley (in a tone which especially reminds us of Gide), "more or less, are led beyond the region of ordinary facts. Some in one way and some in others, we seem to touch and have communion with what is beyond the visible world. In various manners we find something higher, which both supports and humbles, both chastens and transports us."[21] And this is why there will always be a metaphysics. The positivistic mentality will make its eternal protest, and the metaphysical temperament will continue unheeding, if itself unheeded. For, to paraphrase the famous dictum of Pascal: The imagination has its own need for "understanding," which the scientific understanding does not know.

5   THE metaphysical distinction between appearance and reality is attended inevitably by a value preference for the latter and a sometimes ambiguous unwillingness to be content with the former. Plato's prisoners in the cave, freed from their fetters, and compelled to stand up and walk around, note the fire and the images and the resultant shadows on the wall as a single phenomenon, and at last understand that what they had seen before was "all a cheat and an illusion." Schopenhauer, speaking about the world of appearance, appeals to the ancient wisdom of the Hindu philosophers, and quotes from the Vedas and the

Puranas: "It is Maya, the veil of deception, which blinds the eyes of mortals, and makes them behold a world of which they cannot say either that it is or that it is not: for it is like a dream: it is like the sunshine on the sand which the traveller takes from afar for water, or the stray piece of rope he mistakes for a snake."[21a]

But the obsession of the imagination with the distinction between appearance and reality shows itself not only in metaphysics, but also in poetry. Whether indeed all is "a cheat and an illusion," whether the most solid furniture of our social world is not like "the sunshine on the sand which the traveller takes from afar for water, or the stray piece of rope he mistakes for a snake" is a literary, no less than a philosophical problem. C. M. Bowra, for example, uses this very criterion to define the achievement of the romantic age:[22] "In it," he says, "five major poets, Blake, Coleridge, Wordsworth, Shelley, and Keats, despite many differences, agree on one vital point: that the creative imagination is closely connected with a peculiar insight into an unseen order behind visible things. This belief gave a special character to their work and determined their main contributions to the theory and practice of poetry." And what Bowra finds true of romantic poetry, Lionel Trilling generalizes for the novel and, indeed, for literature *en gros.* "All literature," he says,[23] "tends to be concerned with the question of reality—I mean quite simply the old opposition between reality and appearance, between what really is and what merely seems." Blindness to the facts, resistance to the clear claims of reality, seduction by mere appearance until the very existence of reality becomes problematic—these are the very stuff of the permanent authenticity of Oedipus, Lear, Gloucester, and Othello. And by this recognition Trilling is led back to the great archetype of them all. "It has been said that all philosophy is a footnote to Plato. It can be said that all prose fiction is a variation on the theme of *Don Quixote.* Cervantes sets for the novel the problem of appearance and reality: the shifting and conflict of social classes becomes the field of the problem of knowledge, of how we know, and of how reliable our knowledge is which at that very moment of history is vexing the philosophers and scientists."

Trilling, we must remember, is primarily a moralist if not a sociologist of literature, and so we shall find it necessary to go beyond his rather exclusive preoccupation with manners, money, and social class as the indices of reality. For social reality they may indeed be decisive, but *Don Quixote* is infinitely more than a social novel, and if it mirrors "the shifting and conflict of social classes" in Cervantes' time, it also mirrors much more—the fine frenzy of the dislocated mind and the permanent knight-errantry of the unquiet heart.

The very cause of Don Quixote's madness, as Cervantes sets it for us, is bizarre, and yet we accept it as only an extreme case of the natural inversion of fact and fiction which is a possible consequence of the literary experience. If Don Quixote has filled his imagination with the stuff of a romantic literature, with battles, challenges, and wounds, with knightly encounters, enchantments, and the artificialities of courtly love, and as a result has come to believe that all these happenings are true, we accept the displacement because the intrinsic character of the literary experience suggests the latent irony of a contrast between delusion and reality, appearance and fact.

The Knight-Errant of La Mancha is a prodigy because he has the power to concentrate the entire content of life and the total significance of his world of illusion into the single wish with which he confronts reality. And the density of his act of concentration is what makes his universe. When the gelder of pigs approaches the inn blowing several blasts on his horn, Don Quixote is confirmed in his belief that the inn is indeed a famous castle, and at once the wretched codfish given him by the host becomes trout, the black and moldy bread white bread of the finest, the wenches noble ladies, and

the sly innkeeper the castellan. It is a transformation sustained
by the power of imagination, and it is irresistibly comic because the distance between the Don's hermetically sealed and
logical universe and the insistent though thwarted claims of
reality is an absurd distance. But the point of Don Quixote's
life lies at the intersection of an infinite dream and a finite
reality, and it is this intersection that generates the absurd.
As Don Quixote journeys through the Spanish landscape with
its realistic detail, his very movements drip with absurdity,
and the tension of his life proceeds from the incompatibility
between the inward dream and the Spanish landscape.

Don Quixote is not, perhaps, so hermetically sealed within
his obsession as to be completely unaware of the irony of his
position. He does from time to time sense the contrast between his vision and Sancho Panza's view of the world. But
he always closes the gap with the further resources of imagination; he smooths over the discrepancies and buttresses up
his vision by the supplementary myth of "an enchantment."
At the conclusion of the windmill episode, as he lies with the
breath knocked out of him on the ground, Sancho rides up.

"O my goodness!" cried Sancho. "Didn't I tell your worship to
look what you were doing, for they were only windmills? Nobody
could mistake them, unless he had windmills on the brain."

"Silence, friend Sancho," replied Don Quixote. "Matters of war
are more subject than most to continual change. What is more, I
think—and that is the truth—that the same sage Friston who
robbed me of my room and my books has turned those giants into
windmills, to cheat me of the glory of conquering them. Such is
the enmity he bears me, but in the end his black arts shall avail
him little against the goodness of my sword."

But the point of Cervantes' tale is not the enchantment
without, but the "enchantment" within; the brilliant madness
of the Don which, as Erich Auerbach says, "in its bright
equanimity illumines everything that crosses his path and
leaves it in a state of gay confusion." For this inner "enchantment," if it implies little that is tragic, yet fills the quotidian

with adventure, and manages (wholly without ostentation) to suggest the problematic and the bizarre. Such results, Cervantes suggests, can come from the power of imaginative literature. Upon the return of Don Quixote from his first unfortunate adventure, those classic representatives of sobriety, the niece, the housekeeper, the curate, and the barber, filled with dismay, begin their censorious scrutiny of Don Quixote's library which has caused all the trouble. Having rooted out the books on chivalry, they come to those of poetry.[24]

> "Those, I take it," replied the curate, "are not romances but poetry. . . . These do not deserve to be burned like the others, for they are not harmful like the books of chivalry; they are works of imagination such as may be read without detriment."
>
> "Ah, but Senor!" exclaimed the niece, "your Grace should send them to be burned along with the rest; for I shouldn't wonder at all if my uncle, after he has been cured of this chivalry sickness, reading one of these books, should take it into his head to become a shepherd and go wandering through the woods and meadows singing and piping, or, what is worse, become a poet, which they say is an incurable disease and one that is very catching."
>
> "The young lady is right," said the curate. "It would be just as well to remove this stumbling block and temptation out of our friend's way. . . ."

The episode is glancing and light, but the niece has an earthy intuition which has escaped the curate. No work of imagination can be read without detriment, for it may lead to that commitment to illusion which counsels rashness of behavior—even poetry. What, asks Miguel de Unamuno, has Don Quixote bequeathed to culture? "I answer: Quixotism, and that is no little thing! It is a whole method, a whole epistemology, a whole esthetic, a whole logic, a whole ethic— above all, a whole religion—that is to say, a whole hope in what is rationally absurd."[25]

Here again the imagination and the scientific understanding are in eternal opposition. Don Quixote stands for the madness of poetry, for the hermetically sealed universe of illusion, for structured fantasy uncontaminated by criticism. And in this lies his power. For as Unamuno (like Santayana) insists further, the world desires illusion *(mundus vult decipi)* —"either the illusion antecedent to reason, which is poetry, or the illusion subsequent to reason, which is religion."

Cervantes says it implicitly. After his final adventure, Don Quixote returns home and falls ill. In the doctor's opinion melancholy and depression are putting an end to his life. It is first thought that this is due to Don Quixote's consciousness of failure, to his sorrow over his humiliation and his disappointment at not having been able to accomplish the disenchantment and liberation of Dulcinea. But it turns out otherwise. Don Quixote is dying not out of illusion, but out of sanity. He speaks, and it is clear that he is on his deathbed.[26]

"My mind now is clear, unencumbered by those misty shadows of ignorance that were cast over it by my bitter and continual reading of those hateful books of chivalry. I see through all the nonsense and fraud contained in them, and my only regret is that my disillusionment has come so late, leaving me no time to make any sort of amends."

. . . Amazed at his words, they gazed at one another in some perplexity, yet they could not but believe him. One of the signs that led them to think he was dying was this quick return from madness to sanity and all the additional things he had to say, so well reasoned and well put and so becoming in a Christian that none of them could any longer doubt that he was in full possession of his faculties. . . .

It is of the essence of this inner "enchantment" that only at the end has Don Quixote's consciousness turned to the distinction of appearance and reality as it bears upon subjectivity, as it conditions the self. Formerly it has been projected entirely outward, upon the external world. And this suggests that in Cervantes are to be found intimations of a metaphysic akin to Plato's.

On the surface this may not seem to be the case, for Cervantes is always attracted by the colorful and the sensory, the vivid flow of feeling and action in a landscape warmly Spanish. In Don Quixote's clashes with reality, there is never any overt suggestion that reality is without justification in being precisely what it is. It is always right and he is always wrong, and after his brief encounters, the windmills turn as before, the noble ladies return to their ancient profession, the castellan again becomes a thieving innkeeper. But the cumulative effect is insidious. The movements which the Don makes are all absurd, and yet slowly and magically he gains the rewards of our love and sympathy, so that as he loses the chivalric goals one by one, his life produces a constant increment of affection. And by this fact Cervantes has as much reversed the customary relations of the sensory and the supersensory as did Plato. For despite Lionel Trilling, Cervantes' purpose is *not* social, but *metaphysical,* and even if an essential realism is the heart of his novelistic technique, still, it is not this perception with which we are finally left. Don Quixote is one of the paradoxes of the metaphysical imagination. For those who remain in Plato's cave he is the epitome of absurdity, grotesquerie, and foolishness. But for those who have escaped, he personifies the absoluteness of *the Ideal.*

6 IN THOMAS MANN'S remarkable short story "Felix Krull" the narrator relates how as a boy of fourteen his father takes him to a performance in the theater at Wiesbaden to see the actor Mueller-Rosé. On the stage Mueller-Rosé appears as a glamorous young attaché in evening dress, top hat, and white kid gloves; immaculate, graceful, and charming. But when his father takes the boy backstage after the performance to meet the famous actor, he is an aging man sitting at a grubby dressing table before a dusty mirror, his lined faced hideous with half-washed-off grease paint, wearing a wig, his naked shoulders covered

with red-rimmed suppurating pimples, and young Felix, who before the footlights had been breathless and enraptured at the theatrical illusion, can now scarcely repress a shudder of disgust at the loathsome reality. Felix thinks: "So this then—this pimpled and smeary individual is the charmer at whom the indistinguished masses were just now gazing up blissful-eyed! This repulsive worm is the reality of the glorious butter-fly in whom all those deluded onlookers thought to see real-ized all their own secret dreams of beauty, grace, and perfec-tion!" Mann has expressed all of the ironic contrast implicit in the very nature of theater. The proscenium arch is the portal into an illusory world. This is axiomatic, and except to an adolescent, no occasion for surprise.

Cocteau expresses it more equivocally. In the dedication to *La Machine infernale* he says: "I have often repeated that a thing ought not both *to be* and *to seem*. This motto, how-ever, loses its applicability when we come to the theater and feel that somewhat dubious enchantment where *seeming* holds sway as in those deceptively real paintings on Italian ceilings." He continues with a reference to the art of Christian Bérard, those stage sets in which we have "a truth in itself"—a truth which disdains reality. Elsewhere he goes beyond the contrast of "being and seeming" which is implicit in the very structure of theater to the curious duplicity of all dramatic art. *"Les choses que je conte,"* he says *"sont des mensonges vraies"*—the things which I relate are truthful lies—and in so doing he turns from the formal ambiguity of theater to the truth-claims of its content. For it can easily be that the problem of appearance and reality overflows the set conditions of the histrionic art to appear redundantly in its actual sub-ject-matter. Here the classic case is that of Pirandello.

Pirandello's problem is the precise obverse of Cervantes'. While in *Don Quixote* the perplexities of appearance and reality are projected outward as oppositions of action in the external world, in the drama of Pirandello they appear as a consequence of the ambiguous disguises of the self. The problem of the structure of appearance in *Don Quixote* is literally a problem of what occurs in space. The sense involved is vision, and the absurdity results because the eye sees not what is intersubjectively verifiable, but according to a deformation produced by a conceptual bias. Here thought is not the consequence of perception, but its cause. Whereas in the plays of Pirandello it is not the external world that is problematic, but the self, and all of the deformations reveal themselves in time, which, as Kant quite rightly pointed out, is the medium of intuition and the form of the inner sense.

In the 1925 Preface to *Six Characters in Search of an Author* Pirandello explained both the meaning of that play and the philosophical themes which have been his constant preoccupation:[27]

> And here is the universal meaning at first vainly sought in the six characters, now that, going on stage of their own accord, they succeed in finding it within themselves in the excitement of the desperate struggle which each wages against the other and all wage against the Manager and the actors, who do not understand them.
>
> Without wanting to, without knowing it, in the strife of their bedevilled souls, each of them, defending himself against the accusations of the others, expresses as his own living passion and torment the passion and torment which for so many years have been the pangs of my spirit: the deceit of mutual understanding irremediably founded on the empty abstraction of the words, the multiple personality of everyone corresponding to the possibilities of being to be found in each of us, and finally the inherent tragic conflict between life (which is always moving and changing) and form (which fixes it, immutable).

Understanding *and* deceit, central self *and* multiple personality, permanence *and* change in desire, purpose, and character: these are the central ambiguities whose presentation makes his plays. And just as the Spanish landscape in *Don Quixote* becomes equivocal through the brilliant obsession of the Don, so here the clarity of psychological reality is compromised by the perplexities of multiple presentation.

In *It Is So If You Think So (Cose e, se vi pare!)* the better
people of a small Italian provincial town try desperately to
unravel the tangled skein of relationships which hold between
three new arrivals in their midst: Signora Frola, Ponza, her
son-in-law, and Signora Ponza, his wife. Laudisi, one of the
older inhabitants (who speaks for Pirandello) constantly
insists that there is no certain truth in these matters.[28]

LAUDISI. . . . you see me? And you are absolutely sure about me,
are you not? Well now, Madam, I beg of you; do not tell your husband, nor my sister, nor my niece, nor Signora Cini here, what you
think of me; because, if you were to do that, they would all tell
you that you are completely wrong. But you see, you are really
right; because I am really what you take me to be; though, my
dear madam, that does not prevent me from also being really what
your husband, my sister, my niece, and Signora Cini take me to be
—because they also are absolutely right!

SIGNORA SIRELLI. In other words you are a different person for
each of us.

LAUDISI. Of course I'm a different person! And you, madam,
pretty as you are, aren't you a different person, too?

SIGNORA SIRELLI (hastily). No siree! I assure you, as far as I'm
concerned, I'm the same always, yesterday, today, and forever!

LAUDISI. Ah, but so am I, from my point of view, believe me!
And, I would say that you are all mistaken unless you see me as I
see myself; but that would be an inexcusable presumption on my
part—as it would be on yours, my dear madam!

SIRELLI. And what has all this rigmarole got to do with it, may
I ask?

LAUDISI. What has it got to do with it? Why . . . I find all you
people here at your wits' ends trying to find out who and what
other people are; just as though other people had to be this, or
that, and nothing else.

Needless to say, Laudisi does not restrain them, and the
stories told them respectively by Signora Frola and Ponza are so
excessive and so contradictory that the town concludes that
one of them must be mad. Only, the question remains: Which

one? In desperation they search for confirming documents, marriage licenses, birth certificates, etc., etc.

SIRELLI. You mean to say you wouldn't give in if we stuck that certificate under your nose tomorrow or the next day? Would you still deny . . .

LAUDISI. Deny? . . . Why . . . why . . . I'm not denying anything! In fact, I'm very careful not to be denying anything. You're the people who are looking up the records to be able to affirm or deny something. Personally, I don't give a rap for the documents; for the truth in my eyes is not in them but in the mind, and into their minds I can penetrate only through what they say to me of themselves.

SIRELLI. Very well—She says he's mad and he says she's mad. Now one of them must be mad. You can't get away from that. Well which is it, she or he? . . .

LAUDISI. . . . Well which one? You can't tell, can you? Neither can anybody else. And it is not because those documents you are looking for have been destroyed in an accident—a fire, an earthquake—what you will; but because those people have concealed those documents in themselves, in their own souls. Can't you understand that? She has created for him, or he for her, a world of fancy which has all the earmarks of reality itself. And in this fictitious reality they get along perfectly well, and in full accord with each other; and this world of fancy, this reality of theirs, no document can possibly destroy because the air they breathe is of that world. For them it is something they can see with their eyes, hear with their ears, and touch with their fingers. Oh, I grant you— if you could get a death certificate or a marriage certificate or something of the kind, you might be able to satisfy that stupid curiosity of yours. Unfortunately, you can't get it. And the result is that you are in the extraordinary fix of having before you, on the one hand, a world of fancy, and on the other, a world of reality, and you, for the life of you, are not able to distinguish one from the other.[29]

It Is So If You Think So is still one of Pirandello's most "objective" plays, for it shows the townspeople trying to penetrate the mystery from outside, and it takes the network of human relationships, therefore, as susceptible to the resolution of the status of objects in space. But most of the Pirandello plays are the reverse. They show the agonies of a tortured selfhood as it wrestles with the truth about itself, anguished as much by the ambiguity and impermanence it discovers as by any confrontation with an evil will or despicable intentions. Ersilia Drei in *Naked* tries through the power of a lie to create the myth of a selfhood of which she is herself completely unsure. Henry IV plays for half a lifetime the masquerade of mediaeval pageantry in a twilight zone neither madness nor sanity, deceiving those about him, but in the end deceiving no one more than himself. The Father and Step-Daughter of *Six Characters in Search of an Author* furiously debate their respective natures within the matrix of a fantasy in which at the same time they do not exist and live forever.

But Pirandello goes much further than the mere mixing of the categories of philosophy and dramatic action. Like Brecht's "theater of action," Artaud's "theater of cruelty," or Cocteau's "theater of the streets," Pirandello's approach to drama is revolutionary and iconoclastic, for it breaks the conventions at precisely that point where they themselves constitute an inadequate metaphysics. Felix Krull may be stunned by the contrast between Mueller-Rosé before the footlights and in his dressing room, but to say that the proscenium arch is the portal into an illusory world is to consecrate the dualism of appearance and reality in a theatrical convention. A decent distance, a modest reticence separates fact and fiction, illusion and reality, but Pirandello's whole point is the untenability of this insistent dualism of the understanding ("It's only make-believe, it's only pretense" cry the "real" actors at the end of *Six Characters in Search of an Author* to reassure themselves against the unbearable horror, and the "unreal character," the Father, replies with a terrible cry: "Pretense? Reality, sir, reality!").

Thus, in *Six Characters in Search of an Author* the "real-

ism" of the unadorned back stage atmosphere is made the
backdrop of a tragedy of literary characters, as if embodied
Platonic ideas had somehow come to dance before an audience
of particulars, and in *Each in His Own Way (Ciascuno a suo
modo)* the characters of the "comedy" on the stage and the
"real" people appearing in the theater lobby provide an overheard commentary upon one another's reality, so that the
equivocal relation between Delia Morello and Michaele
Rocco in the play is made uncanny and outrageous by the
appearance in a box of Delia Moreno and Baron Nuti, their
real-life counterparts and sources. But Pirandello's "theater
within a theater" is not a technical adventure in the sense in
which the expressionist theater of pre-Hitler Germany was
daring and "experimental," but rather a performance in the
sense in which Dadaist art functioned to make a statement
rather than to ask a question. The Pirandello method utilizes
a technique of theatrical shock, not for its own sake but to
enforce a peculiar sense of life—a sense of life created by a
metaphysical imagination in which the tenuous cobwebs of
illusion are found to be realities and the massive foundations
of reality are found to be illusions.

7 INEVITABLY the enterprises of Cervantes
and Pirandello lead to the problem of
truth—not so much to the problem of its determination and
its nature as to the problem of its value and its ultimate significance. And here we have an eternal dialectic represented
in many fields and in many areas, but always returning to its
sources in the dualism of the understanding and the imagination.

Kant saw clearly that the question of truth or illusion is
not dependent upon *the object* in so far as it is perceived,
but upon *the judgment about it* in so far as it is thought.[30]
This means that truth and error lie always in a judgment

which considers the object under the categories and principles imposed by the understanding. Conformity with the laws of the understanding is, thus, the formal element in all truth, as its material element is the data derived from sense perception. Kant thought that this same sense perception *(Sinnlichkeit*—"sensibility") as it influences the operations of the understanding was the cause of *error*. But something quite different is the cause of *illusion*. For if there is an "empirical" source of error, there is a "transcendental" source of illusion, and by this Kant means a use of the mind *beyond the requirements of science,* beyond the limits of sense experience, and toward the satisfaction of quite other "cognitive" needs. To be sure, Kant did not here recognize this source of illusion as "the imagination" (although in his *Critique of Judgment* he suggests as much), but his treatment fits in well with our theory. For *the natural and inevitable illusion* of which he speaks rests on subjective principles and springs from a subjective need. And if this is further analyzed, it will be found to consist of just those dramatic and teleological qualities which we have found in the imagination.

The language of science requires a vocabulary relevant to the formalizing of knowledge, to the truth and falsity of propositions, to the congruence of evidence and assertoric weight, to the achievement of rational belief. Truth is the end, falsity is the danger, and attention to the *procedures* by which propositions are formulated and asserted yields the crucial concept of *error* (whether this be in the form of perceptual mistakes in the process of observation and experiment or formal mistakes in the inference of propositions or the calculus of statistical probabilities). But the language of the imagination, whether employed in metaphysics or in poetry, is a language of events, devoted to sensuous quality, and concerned with the crucial distinction between appearance and reality. If there is a "natural metaphysics" underlying science it is, as we have seen, phenomenalism—the collapsing of this polarity of the imagination so that only "the appearances" are "the reality," and any search for the realities behind is thought of as "romantic" or "metaphysical" or "illusory." But the distinction between appearance and reality *is* the cornerstone of metaphysical concern, and in writers like Cocteau and Mann, Cervantes and Pirandello, it is the focus of fictional or dramatic interest.

It is the purpose of the scientific enterprise to achieve an ever more adequate approximation to the truth and to be ever on guard against the encroachment of error; but however much poetry and metaphysics may strive toward "reality," their motive power lies in the imagination, and makes them hospitable to the values of illusion. In the writing of John Stuart Mill, a firm believer in the saving grace of science, there is one surprising and little-known passage which makes the point. "Those," he says,[31] "who think themselves called upon, in the name of truth, to make war against illusions, do not perceive the distinction between an illusion and a delusion. A delusion is an erroneous opinion—it is believing a thing which is not. An illusion, on the contrary, is an affair solely of feeling, and may exist completely severed from delusion. It consists in extracting from a conception known not to be true, but which is better than the truth, the same benefit to the feelings which would be derived from it if it were a reality."

Mill's language is, perhaps, over-simple, for "illusion" and "delusion" do not quite function as the contraries which he wishes to make them, but in noticing that an illusion is "an affair of feeling" and that it may be even "better than the truth," he is at least showing a sensitivity to imaginative values which his underlying commitment to science does not permit him to formulate with the complex accuracy which the facts demand. But this is hardly surprising, since within the quaint dualism of "illusion" and "reality" not even poets are prepared to make a united stand. Wallace Stevens (speaking personally, to be sure) claims fealty to "the clear sovereign that is reality."[32]

> On a few words of what is real in the world
> I nourish myself. I defend myself against
> Whatever remains. . . .

And he implies that this "reality," whether tradition, the inmost self, "the enormous harnesses and writhing wheels of this world's business," or the wide expanses of "mountainous rock and sea" looms given, enormous and actual, needing no rhetoric to bring it into being.

But Yeats, generalizing, sees it differently:[33]

> Civilisation is hooped together, brought
> Under a rule, under the semblance of peace
> By manifold illusion; but man's life is thought,
> And he, despite his terror, cannot cease
> Ravening through century after century,
> Ravening, raging, and uprooting that he may come
> Into the desolation of reality. . . .

In seeing that civilization is rendered unified and peaceful through illusion and that the "ravening" of thought leads only into the "desolation" of reality, Yeats is in fact suggesting the counterclaim of the poetic imagination against the preferences of the positivistic mentality, and shows himself, therefore, on the side of Santayana against Carnap, Vico against Auguste Comte, Otto Rank against Sigmund Freud. For the dialectic of truth and illusion permeates many areas, among them the philosophy of symbolic forms, the eighteenth- and nineteenth-century readings of the course of Western history, and the basic presuppositions of contemporary psychotherapy.

Giambattista Vico published his *Scienza nuova* (in its third and definitive edition) in 1744. In it he distinguished three historical ages of the world: the age of gods, the age of heroes, and the age of men. In harmony with this threefold division of historical epochs was an axiom of the threefold stages of human mentality. "Men," says Vico,[34] "at first feel without observing, then they observe with a troubled and agitated spirit, finally they reflect with a clear mind. This axiom is the principle of the poetic sentences, which are formed with senses of passions and affections, in contrast with philosophic sentences which are formed by reflection and reasoning. . . ." The age of gods is the period when religion is strongest, when the discursive intellect is yet unborn, when the poetic and creative impulse is at its zenith, and to this first stage Vico gives the name of Poetic Wisdom. But the age of Poetic Wisdom is also the age of metaphor and allegory—what Cassirer (who owes more to Vico than he has ever explicitly acknowledged) calls the age of the mythical consciousness—and the poetry which it produces is founded upon the illusion of anthropomorphism and personification. Upon this insight Vico founded one of his axioms of interpretation:[35] "The most sublime labor of poetry is to give sense and passion to insensate things; and it is characteristic of children to take inanimate things in their hands and talk to them in play as if they were living persons. This philologico-philosophical axiom proves to us that in the world's childhood men were by nature sublime poets." Naturally, it is for this period of Poetic Wisdom, of the childhood of man, that Vico reserves his most fervent admiration.

Almost exactly one hundred years after the *Scienza nuova,* Auguste Comte published his *Cours de philosophie positive,* and this too contained a threefold scheme of development. Each of our leading conceptions, says Comte, each branch of our knowledge passes through three different theoretical stages: the Theological or fictitious, the Metaphysical or abstract, and the Scientific or positive. In the first men find causal agency in supernatural beings, in the second in abstract forces, in the third the search for causes is abandoned for the study of the laws of phenomena—their invariable relations of succession and resemblance. Reasoning and observation are the means to this knowledge, and its systematic product is Science. But Comte goes further. The development of the individual recapitulates the evolution of the race. Every child is a theologian (that is to say, a poet), every youth a metaphysician, every full-grown man a scientist. The moral of Comte's classification is clear, and it is the precise opposite of Vico's: from poetry to science means from muddle-headedness to clarity, from foolish infancy to the rugged maturity of the human mind. For, as Comte (and the positivism which he classically introduced into the mainstream of Western philosophy) is the representative of the claims of the scientific understanding, so Vico, in a vocabulary at once recondite, incoherent, and visionary is the protagonist of the language of metaphor and the poetic imagination.

As Vico stands to Auguste Comte, so Otto Rank stands to Freud. It is a commonplace that Freud saw himself as a pioneer of empirical science, as one who believes firmly in "the facts," in objectivity, in a chastity of mind which refuses to let belief go beyond the limits of strict evidence. Thus his brief but brilliant treatise on religion is entitled *The Future of An Illusion,* and he finds the profession of religious faith "patently infantile" and completely "incongruous with reality." The language is revealing, for the aim of Freudian therapy is to seek the *truth,* to get the patient to face *the realities* about himself, and in leaving behind his infantile fixations and childish dependencies to achieve emotional *maturity.*

But Otto Rank, in his slow evolution away from his master, sees it differently. The hallmark of neurosis is a tormenting self-consciousness (not unlike the anguish of Pirandello's characters), and the only "trueness" in terms of actual psychic reality is to be found in emotion, not in thought (as in Mill's "illusion," which is an affair wholly of "feeling" and which is therefore "better than the truth"). Thus Rank insists:[36] " . . . our seeking the truth in human motives for acting and thinking is destructive. With the truth, one cannot live. To be able to live one needs illusions, not only outer illusions such as art, religion, philosophy, science and love afford, but inner illusions which first condition the outer. The more a man can take reality as truth, appearance as essence, the sounder, the better adjusted, the happier will he be. At the moment when we begin to search after truth we destroy reality and our relation to it. . . ."

What Yeats has found to hold for man's restless exploration into historical time, Rank discovers in the personal search for the authentic self. Man's life, like that of civilization, is held together "by manifold illusion," and when the ravening search for truth in either sphere outruns its bounds, we are brought painfully "into the desolation of reality."

8 FROM Robbe-Grillet's dismissal of the old "myth of depth" to the theory of illusion behind Rank's psychotherapy, we have traveled a winding path. And yet it has, too, its own inner consistency. For in each case we have seen an illustration of the "logic" of the imagination—its peculiar vocabulary, its mode of functioning, its sinuous strategy vis-à-vis the scientific understanding. In particular we have been concerned with the metaphysical imagination, and the distinction between appearance and reality which it celebrates. This has led us to its philosophic *locus classious,* Plato and the pre-Socratics, then to Kant, an ambiguous figure whose *Critique of Pure Reason* abandons Plato's claims in order to assert those of the understanding, and finally to Schopenhauer, who in the truest sense is an abandonment of Kant and a return to Plato. But another facet of the interest in appearance and reality is the concern with illusion, and here we left the trail of philosophy to follow that of literature.

It was a natural leap. For even those most conscious of the rigor of philosophic thought know the need for their reconciliation. It is this need that underlies alike the metaphysical novel and the theater of ideas—the marvelous natural gaiety of *Don Quixote* and the gloomy ironies of Pirandello. The reconciliation, when it occurs, happens because literature imitates life and surpasses it, because the fictional is at once an intellectual reconstruction of experience which mirrors all the opacity and ambiguity of existence and at the same time imaginatively oversteps it, since, as Simone de Beauvoir has said, its mission is *"dépasser sur le plan imaginaire les limites toujours trop étroites de l'expérience réellement vécue"*—to surmount on the map of the imagination the always too narrowly circumscribed limits of experience actually had.

Metaphysics, and particularly the metaphysics of the imagination, is not just a system which one constructs like a physical theory or a mathematical demonstration. It is the expression of a self in its confrontation with the world. And therefore it can be expressed equally in the Platonic dialogue, the Schopenhauerean treatise, the Cervantean novel, and the Pirandello play. The imagination can attempt to uncover the mystery of existence in a philosophic treatise or evoke it concretely in the theater, and each will be an adventure in metaphysical vision. The scientific understanding, naturally, functions otherwise, and it would be as absurd to write a Kantian novel as it would to attempt a Carnapian play. Even in the case of literary naturalism, the forced objectivity of Zola or Robbe-Grillet, the imaginative effort, it might be argued, although genuine, is bound to fail, for it borrows and imports into the domain of imagination techniques and a perspective more native to the alien realm of the scientific understanding.

The theater, as we have seen from Mann and Cocteau and Pirandello, is the native home of illusion, but the hospitality to illusion *per se*, the willingness to entertain its phantoms as salutary and as life-giving convictions, is not restricted to the drama. Yeats and Vico and Rank, each in his own way, restate this preference for the imagination. But the major assertions come from philosophy. In Chapter 2, I have already traced the development of this aspect of imagination from

Kant to Cassirer, and here in closing I want to refer briefly
once again to those two who might be called *the* philosophers
of the imagination *par excellence*—Nietzsche and Santayana.

Nietzche's early *Die Geburt der Tragoedie* (1873) is a brilliant apology for art against science, the necessities of the
imagination as reflected in the tragic spirit against the ex-
cesses of the critical intelligence, the healing powers of illusion against the wounding impact of "truth." Nietzsche asks:
What meaning did the tragic myth have for the ancient
Greeks? and he answers in two ways. Since the horrors of
brute existence can be justified only in aesthetic terms, art,
rather than science or ethics, constitutes the essential metaphysical activity of man. In a universe of manifold suffering,
only illusion is capable of giving metaphysical solace, and the
Apollonian impulse with its commitment to dreams, to the
immediate apprehension of form, to those beautiful *images*
which are the fruit of our inner world of fantasy, is a basic
source of those arts which alone make life possible and worth
living. For all art, as well as life itself, depends on appearances, the laws of optics, illusion, on the inevitability of "perspectives" and the necessity of "error."[37] And if we are
tempted by the scenes from Homer (this most "dreaming"
of all Greeks), we must realize that the shining fantasy of the
Olympian gods is only a dream of beauty precipitated out of
an original hierarchy of terror perceived and given expression
by the Dionysian spirit. Tragedy combines them both, the
image and the ecstasy, but in the sculptor and the epic poet
the pure contemplation of images reaches its apogee.

It would be a mistake to interpret Nietzsche's view of art
as "merely contemplative." He knows also that "understanding" (the bloodless intervention of the mind) kills action,
that the truth once seen, we are invaded by nausea and the
ghastly absurdity of existence, that in order to act we require
the veil of illusion. In the end this leads him from his original
polarity of the Apollonian and the Dionysian ingredients in

tragedy to a greater opposition between the Socratic and the Tragic spirit. Greek tragedy, Nietzsche believed, perished in consequence of an insoluble conflict between its original mythic impulse and the new rationalism of Socrates and Euripides, and this new Socratism with its lack of mystical sympathy, its corrosive influence upon instinctual life, its *logic,* becomes in time the garments of the theoretical man—the mantle of the scientific spirit. Here Nietzsche has turned from an historian of the art forms of ancient Greece into a critic of the whole of Western civilization. Socratic man—the Western scientist—is preoccupied in laying bare the workings of nature and of separating true knowledge from myth and illusion, and in doing so he has forgotten the lesson of the Greeks—the inevitability of tragic resignation and the need for art. In the subversion of Aeschylean art by Socratism is prefigured the conquest of imagination by the scientific understanding.

Santayana has learned well this lesson from Nietzsche. It pervades his treatment of religion and poetry, his preference for Platonic essences, his own poems, and his various soliloquies upon the theme of science and the imagination. But it is concentrated, summed up, essentialized in the brief "Lovers of Illusion," the fifth of his celebrated *Dialogues in Limbo*. It is a Platonic dialogue with a Nietzschean moral, and although the minor figures of Alcibiades, Aristippus, and The Stranger appear, it is really Democritus the protagonist of science and Dionysius of Syracuse, the philosopher of imagination, whose opposition carries the burden of the argument.

Democritus, the father of atomic theory, naturally asserts that science is better than illusion. He has a rational preference for things actual and material over things dreamed and invented. He professes to ignore moral distinctions so as "to describe reality without fondness or displeasure." He is secretly convinced that to perceive facts is a blessed privilege and to create imaginary beauties a disgraceful self-delusion, and when pushed to justify this conviction, falls back upon the pragmatic criterion. Young and old agree in finding it irksome to see things as they are. The will to illusion is pervasive. But still, the souls of animals must be watchful; they cannot live on mere hope, "and dreams are fatal to them when, action being necessary, true perception is indispensable. Thus a creature endowed with locomotion lies under a mighty compulsion to discover the truth."

But Dionysius will not have it so. He thinks the imagination does not betray nature, because nature itself is only an excuse for the imagination. Fancy, he says,[38] "is not a falsification of nature, because nothing in nature is worth noting, or even possible to note, save for the fancy which overlays it. I have known many a masquerade in my time, royal splendour, love, friendship, philosophy, treachery, and exile; but in all I have loved only the image. . . ." And he scorns science precisely because its lack of emotion, its objectivity, denies the very quality which distinguishes the human person from the lens of a microscope: ". . . there is nothing worth having in kingship but what a penniless dreamer may enjoy in conceiving it, and . . . the illusion in love, in wisdom, and in enthusiasm is the true and only virtue in them. To have a clean and scentless intellect, my noble Democritus, that should merely report things as they are, would be almost like not existing; so clear and transparent a medium would hardly be a soul."

Like Plato, his master in the real world, Dionysius believes that if it is possible to behold absolute truth face to face, it must be in an inward vision, and, thus, from this dialogue, it can be inferred of Santayana himself what in his last speech Democritus says of another: "He honors reality only for illusion's sake, and studies in nature only pageants and perspectives, and the frail enchantments which are the food of love. . . ."

Seven / Destiny, Fortune & Fate

IN THE fourth chapter of the first volume of *The Decline of the West*, Oswald Spengler presents an antithesis which, although it is for him the solution to the problem of world history, may be for us an important clue toward a further understanding of the functioning of the imagination. He calls it "the opposition of the *Destiny Idea* and the *Causality Principle*," and he uses it to provide the demarcation between the two important perspectives which he terms respectively "the world-as-history" and "the world-as-nature."

In every higher language there is a series of words like "destiny," "luck," "fortune," "doom," and "fate" over which there lies, as it were, a veil. No rational analysis, no merely scientific consideration can ever exhaust what we feel when we let ourselves sink into the meaning of these words. For they are not concepts of the scientific understanding by which we describe and correlate the impersonal succession of natural events, but rather symbols imaginatively constructed, intuitively grasped, and urgently felt. Spengler, to be sure, does not invoke our concept of the imagination, but when he says:[1] "The Destiny-idea demands life-experience and not scientific experience, the power of seeing and not that of calculating, depth and not intellect," the "power of seeing" and the "depth" to which he refers are undoubtedly the contribution of what we have called the teleological imagination.

"There is," Spengler continues, "an *organic logic,* an instinctive, dream-sure logic of all existence as opposed to the *logic of the inorganic,* the logic of understanding and of things understood—a logic of direction as against a logic of extension—and no systematist, no Aristotle or Kant, has known how to deal with it. They are on their own ground when they tell us about judgment, perception, awareness, and recollection, but as to what is in the words hope, happiness, despair, repentance, devotion, and consolation they are silent." It is an interesting juxtaposition of terms, and although not identical with, it is at least analogous in its intention to the similar juxtaposition which we have presented in Chapter II. It demands little perception to see in Spengler's first series what we have called the language of the understanding, and in his second the language of the imagination. And when finally he concludes:[2] "We bring out that which is in the causal by means of a physical or an epistemological system, through numbers, by reasoned classification; but the idea of destiny can be imparted only by the artist working through media like portraiture, tragedy and music," our assurance is complete. For the physical system with its variables, numerical coefficients, and rational classifications requires those linguistic elements which we have distinguished as "the scientific chain of meaning," while the artist in plastic and literature (and above all in the form of the tragic drama) utilizes that special terminology of the imagination which I have called "the humanistic complex."

Spengler's reference to Kant in the quotation above as "a systematist," as the proponent of a mechanistic logic, rings a bell, for it redirects our attention back to that very passage from the *Critique of Pure Reason* with which we first began. Let me recall it. When Kant showed how the ideas or concepts with which we customarily operate are derived either from our experience, or from the nature of human reason, he added: "But there are also usurpatory concepts; such as *fortune, fate,* which, although allowed to circulate by almost universal indulgence, are yet from time to time challenged by the question: *quid juris.* This demand for a deduction involves us in considerable perplexity, no clear legal title, sufficient to justify their employment, being obtainable either from experience or from reason." The two concepts which Kant used were not chosen at random, for "fortune" and "fate" have a long history which stretches back to the time of the Babylonians and early Greeks, and from those days to this they have been a stumbling block and an embarrassment to the truly scientific mentality. Kant himself, as we have seen in the last chapter, perhaps even more than David Hume, is the philosopher who most clearly appreciates the nature of modern science, and he therefore found it necessary to outline a structure for the scientific understanding which should make sense out of the "Nature" which is the object at once of mathematical and observational treatment. It was this necessity which led him (in the section of the First Critique on the "Postulates of Empirical Thought") to deny the applicability of the notions of "fortune" and "fate" to the understanding of natural phenomena. "The proposition," he says,[3] "that nothing happens through blind chance *(in mundo non datur casus)* is therefore an *a priori* law of nature. So also is the proposition that no necessity in nature is blind, but always a conditioned and therefore intelligible necessity *(non datur fatum).* Both are laws through which the play of alterations is rendered subject to a *nature of things. . . ."* The operations of that faculty of understanding through which science is made possible allow of no concepts which shall do violence to the intelligible order of nature. And this "order of nature"—really for Kant an order in the sequence and linkage of our perceptions of nature—means a continuous, mechanical (and therefore *intelligible*) linkage of appearances in which the vagaries of "fortune" and the essentially mysterious operations of "fate" can have no legitimate place.

Modern science has of necessity followed the Kantian restriction, although it has found the chain of causal connections emphasized by both Kant and Hume too primitive for a science in an advanced stage of development. The original Aristotelian notion of efficient causality (which might be called causality as *production*), involving as it does the more elementary notion of the active agency of one substance upon another, has been supplanted in modern physical theory by the notion of causality as *description* and *prediction*; that is, as a functional relation between measures expressed in a series of differential equations. It is true that the Kantian idea is not completely revoked, since a grasp of physical events still requires some notion of regularity of sequence and high probability for recurrences, but even the model of "the causal stream" has been largely supplanted by the functional concept which merely requires invariance in the representation of physical laws. In this context causality becomes equivalent to the methodological principle that the aim of an advanced science is to express the covariance of events in lawlike statements, which are essentially formulae enabling us to make accurate predictions.[4] Thus the Kantian formulation is not altogether outmoded. The old law of causality has undergone important modifications but in effect what has always been called "the uniformity of nature" remains as the principle of the permanence of scientific law.

Spengler is, I think, therefore right that between the Destiny Idea and the Causality Principle there is an irreconcilable opposition which defines the regions of operation of the scientific understanding and the mythical imagination, and that to be able to see the world as a system of causal connections is not only a "late," but a highly sophisticated conception. *Real* history in the Spenglerian sense is "heavy with fate, but free of laws." To put it this way is, as we shall see in a moment, to suggest a fateful dialectic which the mythological consciousness has bequeathed to the study of history. Of course, in one sense, destiny and causality are related, for in calling the great tragedians of ancient Athens "the pilgrim fathers of the scientific imagination" Whitehead has simply indicated that the *knowledge* of cause and effect may be founded on the *unmistakable intuition* of destiny. But to say (with Spengler) that destiny as an idea is incapable of being *cognized* or *described* or *defined,* but only capable of being *lived* and therefore *inwardly felt,* is only once again to call attention to that characteristic expurgation of imaginative elements through which science becomes possible. *Fortune* and *fate* are the mythic and imaginative equivalents of *chance* and *causality,* but in the latter two every vestige of subjectivity, emotion, human reference, teleology, and drama has been systematically eliminated. To the first of the imaginative conceptions, that of *fortune,* I should now like to turn.

2 WHAT, AFTER all, is "Fortune"? It is *causation viewed as an ethical, or, at least, as a humanly relevant power.* It is a mysterious external accidentality controlling the human world. It is (as with Aristotle) an indefinite efficient cause. It is the paradoxical and mystic residuum which remains after the power of nature, man's free will, and divine intervention have been taken away. It is the perplexing cause of effects which are rare and purposeful. Or, more generally, it is the outcome of all causes affecting a human life considered from the viewpoint of personal advantage or disadvantage.[5] The Greeks distinguished between a *Chance (Automaton)* which appears in Nature and a *Fortune (Tyche)* which sometimes appears to govern human life, but the distinction is not always well maintained, and there is a penumbra of indistinct meanings: chance, spontaneity, luck, and fortune, which cluster about a central mythic intuition. Even the Romans, to whom "Fortuna" is a goddess to be reckoned with, yet in their hardy way make no consistent attempt to refine what was clearly a cosmological puzzle to the more subtle Greeks. In any case Fortune is a fickle deity, turning now one way and now another, and

the Greeks themselves, beginning with the concept (*Tyche*) as a neutral power, soon distinguish its extremes as "luck" (*Eutychia*) and "misfortune" (*Atychia*).

It is clear that the concept of "chance" has scientific relevance. When the understanding constructs a logic of probable inference it may utilize the notion of an antecedent mathematical probability for a class of events and for the possible occurrence of alternative, independent, and mutually exclusive events. In the field of literature and the drama, its imaginative correlative "fortune" has certain utilities for plot construction and the enlistment of our ironic interest. That Desdemona loses her handkerchief is an act of misfortune which permits us to say that it is "by fortune" as much as by craft that Iago persuades Othello of her guilt. And when in *Romeo and Juliet* Friar Lawrence's letter miscarries, it is this "mischance" which permits the final tragedy. And equally in the case of the fortunate. Thus Bassanio in *The Merchant of Venice* impatiently puts aside Portia's interruption with "But let me to my fortune and the caskets" and then, fortunate indeed, chooses the leaden one which signifies his happiness and success. Thus (as Aristotle has told us) in the Polyidus version of *Iphigenia in Tauris* Orestes, about to be sacrificed, remarks "by chance," "So it was not my sister only, but I too, who was doomed to be sacrificed." And by that remark he is saved.

For the tragic drama the notion of "fate" is far more important than that of "fortune." This, I think, is because it is the more global notion, more indicative of totality, whereas dramatic "fortune" seems too closely tied to the immediacies of "incident" and "episode." But where the concept of "fortune" *is* more nearly globally relevant is in the case of the continuous account of the life-span, in the biography, in the wealth and heterogeneity of the historical narrative. And it is just here in the theory and practice of history that the question of the status of "fortune" arises to suggest the opposition between a scientific and an imaginative historiography. This

opposition becomes an interesting dialectic in the examples
of Plutarch, Burckhardt, and Machiavelli.

Half Greek, half Roman in his inspiration, Plutarch of
Chaeroneia (*circa* 50-125 A.D.) represents a high point in the
historical application of the concept of "fortune," and thus
a demonstration of how this construct of the imagination
may be used not merely as a device of the "likely story" which
infuses all Platonic history, but as a technique of historical explanation indistinguishable from historical judgment. Among
the contents of Plutarch's *Moralia*[6] are two treatises of a philo-
sophical-historical nature, the first "On the Fortune of the
Romans" (*De Fortuna Romanorum* or, since Plutarch wrote
in Greek, *Peri Tes Romaion Tyches*), the second "On the
Fortune or thē Virtue of Alexander" (*De Alexandri Magni
Fortuna aut Virtute* or *Peri Tes Alexandroi Tyches E Aretes*).
Both contain the same essential message: although human
motivation and character in the form of wisdom and virtue
have their place, it was really Fortune which produced the
successes of Alexander and the hegemony of Rome. But the
classic demonstration comes in the *Parallel Lives*, in the Life
of Timoleon of Corinth,[7] which was written expressly to
paint the portrait of "the fortunate man" of antiquity. When
Syracuse sends an embassy to Corinth to ask for the loan of
a commander against the Carthaginians, Plutarch narrates the
event as follows:[8] "And while they were seeking for a commander, and the magistrates were writing down the names of
those in the city who were eager for the honour and proposing them for election, one of the common people rose to his
feet and nominated Timoleon the son of Timodemus, although he no longer took part in public business, and had no
expectation or purpose of doing so; but some god, as it would
seem, put it into the man's mind to nominate him, such was
the kindliness of Fortune that shone forth at once upon his
election, and such the grace that attended his subsequent
actions and adorned his virtues."

This sets the tone of the entire narrative. Time after time

Timoleon's victories on the battle field or political successes
are explained by Plutarch with the words "by some freak of
fortune" or "this unexpected good fortune" or "though the
misfortune of Dionysius seemed extraordinary, none the less
did the good fortune of Timoleon have something marvelous
about it." And at one point Plutarch even analyzes the personified Fortune as follows: "Some of the bystanders . . . wondered, too, at the dexterity of Fortune, seeing how she makes
some things lead up to others, brings all things together from
afar, weaves together incidents which seem to be most divergent and to have nothing in common with one another, and
so makes use of their reciprocal beginnings and endings."
But the climax comes in the attitude of Timoleon himself:
". . . all his successes were ascribed by him to fortune . . .
moreover in his house he built a shrine for sacrifice to Auto-
matia, or Chance, and the house itself he consecrated to man's
sacred genius."

In his reliance upon fortune as a principle of historical explanation Plutarch, like Herodotus, exhibits the mythical consciousness among historians. In the first chapter of his *History
of the Peloponnesian War* Thucydides, apparently criticizing
Herodotus, demands factual truth in history. Many centuries
later a similar criticism of Plutarch is made implicitly by
Jacob Burckhardt in *Force and Freedom*. In the famous chapter "On Fortune and Misfortune in History" Burckhardt
says that although "we are wont to regard our personal fate
under the two categories 'fortunate' and 'unfortunate,'" we
should feel real misgivings when we without hesitation attempt to transfer these categories to history.[9] For judgments
of fortune and misfortune (e.g. that it was fortunate that the
Greeks conquered Persia and that in the eighth century Europe held Islam at bay; unfortunate that Athens was defeated
by Sparta in the Peloponnesian war and that the German
Emperors were defeated in their struggle with the Papacy)
are optical illusions, no matter how decked out with analogies
and metaphors, and in the end they are the deadly enemies
of true historical insight.

It would perhaps be going too far to find in Burckhardt the animating spirit of a positivistic historiography—he is too cultivated, too mindful of artistic and literary influences to be so classed—but in the end his vision of history comes closer to the vision of the scientific understanding than to that of the mythical imagination. He attributes our judgments of fortune and misfortune in history to impatience, personal taste, political sympathies, egoism, and the like, as a philosopher of science might find the barriers to true science in our prejudices, our emotions, and our ridiculous tendency to construct a teleology based upon our personal needs and present welfare. And so, finally, although there is in Burckhardt more than a touch of Stoic resignation, he counsels us that we must always be on our guard against taking *our* historical perspective for the decrees of history. The ideal situation is to shake off our individuality so as to be able to contemplate history with impersonality and detachment— with the objectivity and personal unconcern of the scientist. For ultimately the motivation of the historian should not be that of the ethicist or the literary artist with his mind fixed upon fortune and misfortune. Instead he should spend his life in the quest for pure knowledge and in the search for truth.

Plutarch's reliance upon "fortune" and Burckhardt's mistrust of its place in historical explanation represent opposite evaluations. But there is another position in this matter which is somehow intermediate in scope as it is in historical situation. It is the paradoxical position of Machiavelli.

Machiavelli's *The Prince*, like Aristotle's *Politics*, is one of those early treatises on political theory which attempts to assimilate the conventions of men to the regularities of nature, that is to say, to see politics as a science where the law of causality holds, and where there is inherent necessity in political events as there is in the series of natural change. Machiavelli's treatise, of course, more than Aristotle's, is a species of "diplomatic literature," concerned with negotiation and threats in the game of political power, and for this very reason perhaps Machiavelli is led to a curious mystique of events which compromises the purity of his scientific intentions. The problem of diplomacy is that of a cool assessment of a political situation, the motives and resources of the opposition, the advantages and limitations of alternative policies, and, above all, of shrewdness in predicting the logic of events and foreseeing a political outcome. But just at this last point, where causality operates in a predictive capacity, Machiavelli falls back upon the resources of the mythical consciousness, and half deserts the scientific understanding for the literary imagination. I am referring to the famous Chapter 25 of *The Prince:* "What Fortune Can Effect in Human Affairs, and How to Withstand Her."

To the opinion that the affairs of the world are so governed by "Fortune" that no man can truly direct them—an opinion not uncongenial to Plutarch at certain points—Machiavelli replies with a half-assent expressed in a remarkable metaphor:[10]

Nevertheless, not to extinguish our free will, I hold it to be true that fortune is the arbiter of one half of our actions, but that she still leaves us to direct the other half, or perhaps a little less.

I compare her to one of those raging rivers, which when in flood overflows the plains, sweeping away trees and buildings, bearing away the soil from place to place; everything flies before it, all yield to its violence, without being able in any way to withstand it; and yet, though its nature be such, it does not follow therefore that men, when the weather becomes fair, shall not make provision, both with defenses and barriers, in such a manner that, rising again, the waters may pass away by canal, and their force be neither so unrestrained nor so dangerous. So it happens with fortune, who shows her power where valour has not prepared to resist her, and thither she turns her forces where she knows that barriers and defenses have not been raised to constrain her.

By "fortune" princes may be happy today and ruined tomorrow, less because of change of character or disposition than because they do not direct their actions "according to

the spirit of the times." But this is political mysticism, indeed, for it means that human success is defined as congruence with the course of fortune, and that, apart from maxims
of extreme generality, there is no coming to terms with a factor in political events which is recalcitrant to formalization
and hence to prediction. Machiavelli's last rhetorical figure
both presents such a maxim and shows how close he is to the
language of the mythical imagination:[11] "For my part I consider it better to be adventurous than cautious, because fortune is a woman, and if you wish to keep her under it is
necessary to beat and ill-use her; and it is seen that she allows
herself to be mastered by the adventurous rather than by
those who go to work more coldly. She is, therefore, always,
woman-like, a lover of young men, because they are less cautious, more violent, and with more audacity command her."

Machiavelli's "Fortune" is a woman, as is Plutarch's, and
both are opposed to the stern impersonality of Burckhardt.
In Plutarch the question of how much in history is due to
virtue and how much to fortune is raised, but the argument
goes implicitly in favor of the latter. In Machiavelli fortune
and free will divide the power in a fashion which makes real
predictability impossible. But to appeal to fortune at all is
to leave the realm of science and to enter that of the imagination.

3 PERHAPS IN no work of world literature is
the concept of *fate* so consistently presupposed, so explicitly appealed to, so constantly cited, as in
Aeschylus' *Oresteia*.[12] The citations in the *Agamemnon* are
numerous, in *The Libation Bearers* hardly less so, and if *The
Eumenides* seems a falling off, it is only because by this time
the "destiny" has become so much a presupposition that more
explicit reference would seem redundant. Throughout, the
Chorus is the bearer of Destiny's burden. From its first prophecy in *Agamemnon*

Danaans and Trojans
they have it alike. It goes as it goes
now. The end will be destiny.
You cannot burn flesh or pour ungents,
not innocent cool tears,
that will soften the gods' stiff anger

to the last reconciling choral procession of *The Eumenides*

There shall be peace forever between these people
of Pallas and their guests. Zeus the all seeing
met with Destiny to confirm it. . . .

the same mythic message is proclaimed. Clytemnestra, laying
for Agamemnon the fatal carpet, vows "with the gods' aid to
set aright what fate ordained." Cassandra, scorned, reiterates
the prophecy, "What does it matter now if men believe or no?
What is to come will come." And when at the end of the
Agamemnon the Chorus in bitter anger at Aegisthus cries,
"Death you said and death it shall be; we take up the word
of fate," Clytemnestra at once restrains her lover and the
crowd:

No, my dearest, dearest of all men, we have done enough. No more
violence. Here is a monstrous harvest and a bitter reaping time.
There is pain enough already. Let us not be bloody now.
Honored gentlemen of Argos, go to your homes now and give way
to the stress of fate and season. We could not do otherwise
than we did. If this is the end of suffering, we can be content
broken as we are by the brute heel of angry destiny. . . .

In *The Libation Bearers* Electra, sorrowing, says to her at-
tendant women: "The day of destiny waits for the free man
as well as for the man enslaved beneath an alien hand." The
Chorus, stiffening Orestes toward revenge, cries out:[13]

Almighty Destinies, by the will
of Zeus let these things
be done, in the turning of Justice.

and as it waits:

> Right's anvil stands staunch on the ground
> and the smith, Destiny, hammers out the sword.

Orestes in his confrontation with his mother attributes her death to the same power which is her excuse:

CLYTEMNESTRA: I raised you when you were little. May I grow old with you?

ORESTES: You killed my father. Would you make your home with me?

CLYTEMNESTRA: Destiny had some part in that, my child.

ORESTES: Why then, destiny has so wrought that this shall be your death.

And at the very end of the play after Orestes' exit driven by the Furies, the Chorus in weariness repeats the doom of the House of Atreus from the curse of Thyestes to the death of Clytemnestra, exclaiming at last:

> ... Where
> is the end? Where shall the fury of fate
> be stilled to sleep, be done with?

What is this "Fate" (*Moira*) which is so pervasive in the *Oresteia*, this "Destiny" (*Eimarmene*) which stands behind the gods as a shadowy reality, a fixed order rather than a power, a divine conscience practically equated with the will of Zeus? If one agrees with Spengler that the Destiny Idea is a mystical notion into which one *feels* one's way through sympathy and intuition, it will be difficult to give a discursive account of it. But if one were to maintain that the Aeschylean conception of fate is an intermediate notion—somewhere between a mystic Destiny and a rationalistic Causality, ever ready to be pushed now one way, now another—then it would not be inappropriate to say that it represents the law which controls the conditions of our birth and death, and that "the wheel of fate" registers "what is written in the stars," the solemnity of necessity, the coercive legality of cosmic power, or, as Plato was so poetically to phrase it in the *Timaeus* (41a), "what is sown into the instruments of time."

For it cannot be denied, I think, that in the development of the Greek concept of Fate, the figure of Aeschylus is an intermediate one, a Janus figure, looking at once backward to its genesis in the mythical imagination of Hesiod and the Homeric poems and forward to its more philosophic development in Plato and Democritus, in Lucretius and the Stoics and in the great Hellenistic dialectic in which not only the voices of Chrysippus and Carneades, but also those of Cicero, Seneca, Alexander of Aphrodesias, and the pseudo-Plutarch are mingled in a vast mélange of metaphysical and moral debate.

In this Janus quality of Aeschylus is to be found again the analogue for the imagination of the distinction which we have already noticed in the realm of the scientific understanding between "causality as production" and "causality as the invariance of law." Destiny too wavers between that cosmic force or demonic agency (always personified by the mythical imagination in its most indigenous forms) and that structural, almost mathematical "necessity" which Stoic mentality reads into the orderliness of the cosmos. When Destiny is recognized as the essential *mode of existence* of all prime phenomena, whether human or natural, then the facts of becoming are assimilated to a teleology indistinguishable from the will of the gods, and *being* unfolds itself immediately to the intuitive vision as congruent with the native anthropomorphism of the mythical consciousness. This congruence is profoundly expressed in the *Theogony* of Hesiod.

Moira, the Greek goddess of Fate, derives from *moira* (a part, portion, or division of a whole, hence "the due portion" or "the share assigned"), and the three Fates (*Moirai*) are thus in the first instance the dividers, the givers of lots, the apportioners. Already in Hesiod the poetic image is fixed and clear. There are in the *Theogony* two accounts of their origin; one the generalized myth, the other a translation mindful of the Olympian gods. The first appears at lines IV, 211-223, the second at XII, 902-908.[14]

Night gave birth to hateful Destruction and the black Specter and Death; she also bore Sleep and the race of Dreams—all these the dark goddess Night bore without sleeping with any male. Next she gave birth to Blame and painful Grief, and also the Fates and the pitiless Specters of Vengeance: Clotho and Lachesis and Atropos, who distribute good and evil among mankind at birth. It is these goddesses who keep account of the transgressions of men and of gods, and they never let their terrible anger end till they have brought punishment down on the head of the transgressor. . . .

Zeus' second consort was Themis (Law), and that radiant lady gave birth to the Hours—Good Order, Justice, and prosperous Peace—who hourly attend the labors of mankind, and to the Fates —Clotho (Spinner), Lachesis (Allotter) and Atropos (Inflexible) —to whom Zeus gave the great privilege of distributing good and evil among mankind.

As one reads these two accounts together, it is impossible not to be struck by the contrast between them, and to sense that the first belongs to some primitive and archaic nightmare of a world full of terror and blood lust, while in the latter all this has been expurgated, leaving the calm Olympian vision of a world dominated by measure and the moral law. In both passages the essential character of Fate is stated: its duality, its power in the distribution of good and evil, but in the first it works as a vengeance, as a punishment for transgression, and its association is with Destruction and Death, while in the second it is generated out of Law and its siblings are Justice, Good Order, and Peace. It is Nietzsche's "Dionysian" and "Apollonian" all over again, but this time combining to form that very conception of Fate in which tragedy has its second birth.

Also, this second version adds that concreteness which comes from our inner world of fantasy, that concern with the immediate apprehension of form which expresses itself in the Apollonian love of images. *Moira* is no longer one, but three: Clotho the spinner, Lachesis the allotter, and Atropos the inflexible. This symbolizes for the mythical imagination the *creative*, the *distributive*, and the *necessary* qualities of Fate. But what is of equal importance with the abstract qualities is the form of the personification, the imagery which is no less poetically interesting than philosophically relevant. Here the Apollonian vision of Hesiod finds its confirmation in the poetic practice of Homer.

Fate runs through the *Iliad* as it does through the *Oresteia*, but if equally mysterious and unfathomable in its ultimate nature, is more articulately characterized in images, and hence more negotiable to imagination. The primary images are three: the life line spun by Destiny, the twin urns of blessings and sorrows, the golden scales of Zeus. Achilles shall be victorious, but afterward "he shall suffer such things as Destiny wove with the strand of his birth that day he was born to his mother" (XX, 127 f.).[15] Hekabe sorrows with her husband: "Let us sit apart in our palace now, and weep for Hektor, and the way at the first strong Destiny spun with his life line when he was born, when I gave birth to him. . . ." (XXIV, 208 ff.). At first (VIII, 68 ff.) the battle goes with the Trojans: "But when the sun god stood bestriding the middle heaven,/then the father balanced his golden scales, and in them/he set two fateful portions of death, which lays men prostrate,/for Trojans, breakers of horses, and bronze-armoured Achaians,/and balanced it by the middle. The Achaians' death-day was heaviest." But later (XXII, 208 ff.), in the crucial encounter in single combat, Fate sides with the Greeks: "But when for the fourth time they had come around to the well springs/then the Father balanced his golden scales, and in them/he set two fateful portions of death, which lays men prostrate,/one for Achilleus, and one for Hektor, breaker of horses,/and balanced it by the middle; and Hektor's death-day was heavier/and dragged downward toward death, and Phoibos Apollo forsook him."

But almost at the very end (XXIV, 525 ff.), when Priam comes to beg his son's body from the victor, Achilles in an unusual moment of clairvoyance—almost of Stoic resignation —restores the old man with such comfort as is possible.

There is not/any advantage to be won from grim lamentation./ Such is the way the gods spun life for unfortunate mortals,/that we live in unhappiness, but the gods themselves have no sorrows./ There are two urns that stand on the doorsill of Zeus. They are unlike/for the gifts they bestow: an urn of evils, an urn of blessings./If Zeus who delights in thunder mingles these and bestows them/on man, he shifts, and moves now in evil, again in good fortune./But when Zeus bestows from the urn of sorrows, he makes a failure/of man, and the evil hunger drives him over the shining/ earth, and he wanders respected neither of gods nor mortals.

4 I HAVE dwelt upon the vision of fate prepared by the mythical imagination of Hesiod and Homer, and of the more lawlike—but hardly less poetic—imagery of Aeschylus' *Oresteia* not because the conception is clearest here, but rather because it is most figuratively immediate—less tinged with the rationalism of the philosophic intellect. But such immediacy is only preparatory of the definitive efforts which are to come, for the concept lies close not only to poetry but to the instinctive convictions of mankind. *Manut* is the Chaldean goddess of destiny; the *Moirai* are the divine daughters of Zeus; and *Fortuna* is a Roman divinity. And from these ritual personifications it is but a step to the *Eimarmene* of Plutarch and the Stoics, the *Fatum* of Cicero, the *Providentia* of Seneca and the Christian Fathers.

Throughout the entire range of religious, poetic, and philosophic expressions of fate there runs a common thread: that of a cosmic plan, a moral finality, a generalized directive greater than the mere will of individual beings. That there is indeed Destiny, says Alexander of Aphrodesias,[16] "the innate conviction of mankind sufficiently establishes." He is perhaps the first to use the phrase "the drama of destiny" (*to tes eimarmenes drama*), and he further expands the notion according to the principle of totality: "Destiny is . . . a goddess . . . who employs the proper nature of everything existing for the administration of the whole." This emphasis upon totality runs through the treatment of Destiny by Stoics and Platonists alike. The pseudo-Plutarch remarks,[17] "Fate as a substance appears to be the entire soul of the universe," and when he explicates its "active quality" he asserts: "Although events are infinite, extending infinitely into the past and future, fate, which encloses them all in a cycle, is nevertheless not infinite but finite, as neither a law, nor a formula, nor anything divine can be infinite. . . ." Fate, whether law, formula, or divinity means the "enclosure" of events, their encapsulation into a single comprehensive process, and this reference to organic unity, to a "wholeness" in the concept of time, again displays that nisus toward organicity which we have found to be the peculiar quality of the teleological imagination.

But we may go even further. For the concept of fate is itself intrinsically "dramatic," and its essence may be defined as the acknowledgment of a cosmic teleology. Therefore in its dramatic and teleological character it repeats those qualities which are distinctive of the humanistic complex and the imagination which is its generating source. At the prephilosophic level it is difficult to distinguish between "destiny" and "chance." For here both are charged with imaginative content and hence are close to their anthropomorphic origins. This makes them affectively significant but epistemologically uncertain. But reflection reveals their profound difference. "Chance" belongs to the scientific chain of meaning, to the effort toward a naturalistic explanation of the world. It refers to causal relations, to objective events, to nature as it is opposed to man, or, at least, as it is indifferent to his concerns.

"Destiny," on the contrary, is relative to man, who proves its formulas and submits to its decrees. Chance appears as an essential notion in probability theory, as a part of the physico-mathematical perspective. Destiny is the properly *human* and *individual* specification of chance, its reference being to a small segment of the infinite course of events, or to the career line of the particular man. And here teleology is of its essence.

Bergson has seen this clearly. Mere chance, he says in *The Two Sources of Morality and Religion,* is understood to be operative only when some human interest is not at stake. In the objective operations of nature we see nothing but mechanism, and the element of destiny vanishes. For destiny to intervene, it is indispensable that the "effect should have a human significance, which reacts upon its "cause" and colors it, so to speak, with humanity. Fate is, then, "a mechanism behaving as though possessing an intention."[18] The implication of this recognition (although M. Bergson does not specifically say so) is to discover a logic for tragedy which is the precise inverse of that which Bergson finds to hold in the case of comedy. As the comic arises out of our seeing living human behavior as mechanical, so the tragic arises out of that fate which comes from seeing mechanical causation as "living"— as instinct with vital significance and human purpose.

When Spengler says that words like "destiny" and "fate" are those into whose meaning "we must let ourselves sink," and which we can therefore never completely grasp from the outside, he is reproducing an experience which is closer to autobiography than to descriptive science. For the deepening of the notion of objective chance into *destiny* (which, however sharply felt, remains an ontological mystery) is an activity which can give a sense to any narrative chain by invoking the principle of organic unity. And from the point of view of the individual experience, however suddenly and surprisingly the concept appears, it systematically and significantly organizes the felt incoherence of our life. Destiny creates anew my personal history almost existentially—in that it gives a sense to my past by virtue of the future action I have decided to accomplish. Any attempt to contemplate the self merely in its atomistic present is (as Proust and Bergson have both shown) to automatically reduce the past to the fragmentary and the contingent. But a consciousness of destiny restores this multiplicity to parts which fall into place as the segments of a direct thrust of action, and by this qualitative modification causes a biography (either our own or that of another) to pass from contingency to necessity. It was not by accident that the third of the Fates was named Atropos, "the inflexible."

It is true, of course, that to find "necessity" in one's own life is unusual. Rather, this is the externalized perspective from which we view the lives of others or the events of a history in which we are not ourselves directly engaged— when, in short, we are spectators rather than participants. But even viewed "internally," destiny functions as the obscure certitude which comes mysteriously out of the future into the present to authorize our acts. As Hegel saw, it appears in the lives of world historical figures as a kind of categorical imperative, and to others as a fundamental mode of the moral consciousness justifying choice and precipitating action. Thus in the concept of "fate" or "destiny" lies the connectedness and the totality both of history and of the personal biography.

My appeal to Hegel is by no means accidental. For he (in that curious and interesting section on "Religion in General" which appears toward the end of *The Phenomenology of Mind*),[19] distinguishes between a "Fate without self" (*Verhaengnis*) which "remains the darkness of night devoid of consciousness, which never comes to draw distinctions within itself and never attains the clearness of self-knowledge" and that "final Destiny" (*Schicksal*) which absorbs the contradictory processes of nature and morality and is, in fact, "the self conscious of itself as the controlling necessity of what is essential and actual" in our life. The Hegelian language is, as usual, obscure, but its meaning is not. For what Hegel wishes to emphasize is simply that the mysterious power which we call "Destiny" is merely the sense that all our acts form a whole, an organic unity which the historical future will reveal to consciousness as an objective reality. Here is how in Hegelian terms the imagination invokes its latent teleology. Under the guise of destiny the world itself becomes a totality sympathetic to our acts. And, as against the neutral mechanism of the understanding, the external world of causal connections becomes emotionally relevant to those decisions which originate within the self. Kant was right. The concepts of "fortune" and "fate" are neither empirical nor contingent sentiments. They are the universal and necessary products of an imagination which interprets historical action and personal behavior alike according to the model of a universal totality.

5 WE HAVE now, I think, answered that plaintive question which Cicero asks in the first pages of his famous, but now little known, *De Fato*: "*Quid ergo attinet inculcare fatum, cum sine fato ratio omnium rerum ad naturam fortunamve referatur?*"—Why then destiny, if without it all things can be explained by nature or by chance?[20] Because to utilize either "nature" or "chance" as explanation means to appeal to the contingent and the empirical, to utilize a mode of explanation which is intrinsically inappropriate to the needs of the imagination for drama, for teleology, and for organic unity.

It is therefore inevitable that a doctrine of Fate should run through the course of Western civilization, should infuse its religious origins, its philosophic musings, its literary representations of reality. This thread, or process, or dialectic of the imagination has, perhaps, three "moments" in the history of Western culture: that of *Fate* in the antique world, *Provi-*

dence in early Christian thought, and *Destiny* as it appears in the Romantic movement. To a brief consideration of each of these I should now like to turn.[21]

The concept of fate forms an important segment of the horizon of ancient knowledge. We have already seen the form which it takes in Homer and Hesiod and in Aeschylus' *Oresteia*. Whether as *eimarmene* (the allotting), *anagke* (necessity), or *pronoia* (foreknowledge), it haunts the pages of the dramatists and the philosophers as it animates the religious rituals and the common consciousness. As the universal *logos* which directs the universe, the terrible and crushing weight of necessity, or the divine character endowed with foreknowledge, it sets a problem for ancient thought which relentlessly tends to recur throughout the entire course of Western civilization—that of the problematic status of free will and voluntary human action in a universe dominated by cosmic necessity and divine foreknowledge. In its earliest form the concept of fate is primarily cosmological, embedded in Hesiodic myth and Platonic "likely stories." But as Greek thought grows less cosmological and more ethical, the locus of its relevance shifts, and the built-in features of the universe become a problem for the happiness of man. This is at the center of the prolonged Hellenistic discussions upon the question of reconciling the freedom of men with the givens of destiny. And the great residue of Graeco-Roman thought on this point is, of course, the Stoic analysis.

It is Cicero again who in his appeal to Greek thought states the issue: "It seems to me that between the two opinions that divide the ancient philosophers, one side believes that all that happens falls under destiny in such fashion that destiny gives it the force of necessity . . . the other believing that there are voluntary movements of the soul excluding fatality. . . ."[22] And he develops the position of Chrysippus, which mediates between the two. Chrysippus wishes to avoid "necessity" while maintaining "destiny"; his method for doing this is to distinguish "primary and perfect" causes from "proximate and auxiliary" ones. But the argument loses itself in the usual Stoic mixture of logic and physics, where the principle of universal causality is discussed à propos of the logic of our knowledge concerning the future.

The Stoic discussion centers about the necessity of finding man's true place in the cosmos, and is, thus, intrinsically humanistic in intent, but the rationalism by means of which it develops is a far cry from the mythical insights of Hesiod and Homer. It thus tends to flatten the imaginative problem into a format where it is resolvable according to the logic of the understanding. From time to time some image from the mythic past reenters the discussion. Alexander of Aphrodesias centers one part of his treatise upon the profound fatality of Oedipus. Cicero cites the poetic image of Chrysippus in which the manifestations of destiny are compared to the unwinding of a cable. The Stoics in general (for whom the image of time governs that of destiny) reconstitute the doctrine of eternal recurrence, adopt with modifications the principle found in Plato's *Timaeus* of a "world-soul," and (since they, instead of isolating destiny in a part of the universe, identify it with the universe as a whole) return to a pantheism almost indistinguishable from the cosmological affirmations of Hesiod.

It is perhaps unnecessary to reassert that the Stoic doctrine of fate finds its natural continuation in the Christian idea of predestination, which depends upon a Providence uniting the necessity for salvation with the natural goodness of God. How closely the two concepts merge into one another is evident if we compare the Stoic Seneca (4 B.C.–65 A.D.) with the Christian Boethius (480–524 A.D.). Almost five hundred years separate their meditations and yet their conceptual framework—the preoccupation with the problem of evil—is almost identical.

"You have asked me, Lucilius," Seneca begins his *De Providentia*, "why if a Providence rules the world, it still happens that many evils befall good men," and he answers not only that *we must* believe that there exists a divine guardian of

the great world order, but also that the things which seem to
be evils are not really so. This means that the moral life of
man, the natural world, and the course of the gods are congruent, since they partake of a single destiny. *"Quid est boni
viri? Praebere se fato."*²³ "What then is the part of a good
man? To offer himself to Fate. It is a great consolation that
it is together with the universe we are swept along; whatever
it is that has ordained us so to live, so to die, by the same
necessity it binds also the gods. One unchangeable course
bears along the affairs of men and gods alike. Although the
great creator and ruler of the universe himself wrote the decrees of Fate, yet he follows them."

The *De Providentia* of Seneca and the *Philosophiae Con-
solationis* of Boethius have a common theme—how the good
man may reconcile himself to the accidents of fortune—and
if Boethius avoids Seneca's underwriting of suicide in favor
of a more passive acquiescence in the Divine Will, his identification of Providence and Fate is expressed with equal certi-
tude.²⁴

The generation of all things, and all the proceedings of mutable
natures . . . take their causes, order, and forms from the stability
of the Divine mind. This . . . hath determined manifold ways for
doing things; which ways being considered in the purity of God's
understanding, are named Providence, but being referred to those
things which He moveth and disposeth, they are by the ancients
called Fate. . . . For Providence is the very Divine reason itself,
seated in the highest Prince, which disposeth all things. But Fate
is a disposition inherent in changeable things, by which Providence
connecteth all things in their due order. For Providence embraceth
all things together . . . but Fate putteth every particular thing into
motion . . . so that this unfolding of temporal order being united
into the foresight of God's mind is Providence, and the same uniting, being digested and unfolded in time, is called Fate.

As Oedipus is at the center of late Greek thought about
Fate, so Judas is at the center of Christian reflection upon
predestination. Was Judas' betrayal a matter of God's fore-

knowledge? If so, it could have been prevented. If not, is not the Divine power and omniscience seriously compromised? But the moral in the two cases is not dissimilar. Stoic *ataraxia* (calmness) is merely Greek contentment before the inexorability of nature as the Christian "resignation" is an achieved peace before the infinite will of God. Thus the "problem" of Oedipus reflects a temper akin to the "problem" of Judas, as the concept of Fate is akin to the doctrine of Providence, and as the Hymn of Cleanthes is akin to the twenty-third Psalm.

For one type of European "Romantic," *destiny* is entirely an imaginative *experience*, a kind of "lived poetry." For another it is the response of imaginative wholeness *in the mind* to the polarity of nature and human selfhood. The first is the romanticism of Hoelderlin; the second is the romanticism of Hegel. It would not be going too far to say that in both the romantic rhythm has its source in the same dialectical contradiction felt by the Stoics. Cut off from an organic society, it expresses the anguish of modern man in the face of isolation, the passion for completeness in an experience of solitude and fragmentation. Beginning in its modern form not long after the French Revolution, it has continued into the present day in the great stream of poets and thinkers which includes Wordsworth and Novalis, Hoelderlin and Hegel, Tolstoy and Leopardi, Nietzsche and Rilke.

In Hoelderlin the romantic "destiny" is closest to its Greek original, a fate which is encompassing, compelling, almost objective. It is the environment within which one lives and by which one is relentlessly pushed. Such is the conclusion of "Hyperion's Song of Fate" (*Hyperions Schiksaalslied*):

> *Doch uns ist gegeben,*
> *Auf keiner Staette zu ruhn,*
> *Es schwinden, es fallen*
> *Die leidenden Menschen*
> *Blindlings von einer*
> *Stunde zur andern,*
> *Wie Wasser von Klippe*

Zu Klippe geworfen
Jahr lang ins Ungewisse hinab.

Yet it is given us
To have no place to rest
But rather—suffering men—
To waste away and fall
Blindly from hour to hour
Like water
Endlessly downwards
From crag to crag
Hurled to uncertainty.

"The Rhine," one of Hoelderlin's most characteristic poems, is saturated with it. The poet says that "he unsuspectingly entered a destiny" ("... *so/Vernahn ich ohne Vermuthen/ein Schiksaal* . . ."). The river Rhine had longed to flow toward Asia:

Doch unverstaendig ist
Das Wuenschen vor dem Schiksaal.
Die Blindesten aber
Sind Goettersoehne. . . .

Quite without understanding is
The Will before its destiny.
But blindest of all are
The gods' own sons.

Well it is for him who has found "A destiny well-designed" ("*Ein wohl-beschiedenes Schiksaal*") for generally it is the reverse, and only in glorious moments when God rests from his creative labors and day bends down to earth,

Dann feiern das Brautfest Menschen und Goetter
Es feiern die Lebenden all,
Und ausgeglichen
Ist ein Weile das Schiksaal.

Then men and gods alike will celebrate
The wedding feast. All life will celebrate
And for a while
The scales of Fate are balanced.

The Greeks too see in fate the mark of a force which, even in those cases where it is hostile, is not *strange*, since it is the order of reality and the atmosphere of our life. The romanticism of Hoelderlin (and of Wordsworth) comprehends "a living nature" and a humanity whose history unrolls within its ambience. But whereas destiny in Hoelderlin is essentially the expression of an aesthetic attitude, a "feeling" uniting humanity, nature, and the gods, in Hegel it is a dialectical necessity, the opposite of ethical experience, yet needed by it for the achievement of self-consciousness. Hegel's romanticism implies a new logic: to think dialectically, and by this act to resolve the tension between the individual and universal spirit. As he says in the *Phenomenology*:[25] ". . . the powers and forms of the ethical world sink in the bare necessity of mere Destiny. This power of the ethical world is the substance turning itself back into its ultimate and simple nature. But that absolute being turning into itself, that very necessity of characterless Destiny, is nothing else than the Ego of self-consciousness."

World history, said Hegel, is the development of Spirit in Time, just as nature is the development of the Idea in Space. And after the battle of Jena he added: "I have seen the world-spirit pass on horseback." The remark is typical for its time, since just as Oedipus is the embodiment of fate for the Stoics and Judas for the Church Fathers, so the great personage of Napoleon is the central focus of the romantic imagination. Here, as Hegel and the whole of romanticism is to see, is Destiny conscious of itself, making its fateful decisions through the multiple events of Napoleon's career. And even Tolstoy, anything but an admirer of this giant of history, yet is deeply drawn under the spell of the romantic fatalism. Prince Andrey in *War and Peace*, lying wounded upon the plain of Austerlitz, sees Napoleon engrossed in his paltry vanity, and muses on "the nothingness of greatness and the nothingness of life." And yet when Tolstoy ponders upon the day of June 12, 1811, when Napoleon's army crosses the frontier to begin the fateful march against Russia, all the detailed causal ex-

planations of the historians seem to him insufficient before
the vastness of the accomplished fact, and he decides that the
acts of Napoleon and Czar Alexander were as little voluntary
as the acts of each common soldier. "We are forced," he
says,[26]

to fall back upon fatalism in history to explain irrational events
(that is those of which we cannot comprehend the reason). The
more we try to explain those events in history rationally, the more
irrational and incomprehensible they seem to us. Every man lives
for himself, making use of his free-will for attainment of his own
objects, and feels in his whole being that he can do or not do any
action. But as soon as he does anything, that act, committed at a
certain moment in time, becomes irrevocable and is the property
of history, in which it has a significance, predestined and not subject to free choice. . . . Consciously a man lives on his own account
in freedom of will, but he serves as an unconscious instrument in
bringing about the historical ends of humanity. . . . The higher a
man's place in the social scale, the more connections he has with
others, and the more power he has over them, the more conspicuous
is the inevitability and predestination of every act he commits.
"The hearts of kings are in the hand of God." The king is the slave
of history. . . . In historical events great men—so called—are but
the labels that serve to give a name to an event, and like labels,
they have the least possible connection with the event itself. Every
action of theirs, that seems to them an act of their own free-will, is
in an historical sense not free at all, but in bondage to the whole
course of previous history, and predestined from all eternity.

Romanticism is one of the great expressions of the teleological imagination, for it (and Tolstoy with it) comes to see
that fatalism is the seal of history on all the great historic
personalities. In Napoleon Fate *becomes* History! For to romanticism all life and all history must be *symbolic*; must
establish for the imagination a symbolism which the understanding cannot acknowledge. Destiny itself is now the universal symbol, and plays the part in a theory of meaning
which was for the ancients played by fate in the theory of
nature. All those "symbolic coincidences" which haunt the

pages of Spengler are but the legacy from Nietzsche and from romanticism to which he has fallen heir.

6 WE HAVE now examined the concepts of destiny, fortune, and fate, both as products of the imagination in its opposition to the scientific understanding and as dramatic ideas occurring in ancient literature, in historiography, and in the development of Western culture from the Stoics to Hegel. In all this we have paid attention to these ideas as organizing concepts rather than as literary constructs, as modes of perception rather than as counters in the literary representation of reality. Even in calling attention to the uses of fate in Aeschylus and Homer we have been more concerned to explicate the mythic message than to show how it functions in the epic narrative and in the dramatic construction. But it is clear that the idea of destiny has a certain *intrinsic* relevance to the tragic drama. Tragedy is a martyrdom of pity and fear—pity for the powerlessness of man, and fear before the inexorable force of his destiny. To a more detailed development of these and similar notions our next chapter will be devoted. But here I want to turn specifically from fate as a merely philosophic concept to fate as a literary presupposition, and I want to treat the problem in a very particular context—that of the idea of *suicide* as it projects itself in the modern novel. Even from this restricted area we may derive insights indicating that "fate" is not an accidental product of Western culture in its historic past, but a permanent part of the furniture of the imagination, conditioning modern literary perception no less than that of Racine, Sophocles, and Shakespeare.

The crucial thing here is the concept of *necessity*, the inexorable functioning of social and symbolic action. Emma Bovary retching miserably from the cyanide, Anna Karenina crushed under the wheels in the Nizhigorod station, present a *quod erat demonstrandum* within the ambience of the bourgeois conventions. And if Stavrogin hanging in his attic, Kirillov and Svidrigailov putting the revolver to their temples, and Smerdyakov dead by his own hand seem to lie within another realm of discourse, that is only because the genius of Dostoyevsky has interiorized what in Tolstoy and Flaubert follows from personal frustration as a product of social environment.

In comparing the methods which Racine, Flaubert, and Dostoyevsky use in the portrayal of suicide, we have further evidence for the truth of Erich Auerbach's thesis that in the form of a story lies a peculiar representation of reality. We can understand Sartre's insistence that divergent philosophies lie concealed in the majestic flow of fictional time (*"le cours majestueux de la durée romanesque"*). A novel, as Sartre says in "M. Francois Mauriac et la Liberté,"[27] is a thing made with time and free minds, as a picture is painted with oil and pigments (*"un roman est une* chose, *comme un tableau, comme un édifice d'architecture . . . on fait un roman avec des consciences libres et de la durée, comme on peint un tableau avec couleurs et de l'huile"*). The structure of the materials is an implicit moral argument, masquerading sometimes as a form of perception or as a sense of life. Thus the portrayal of self-destruction in fiction, its modalities and its rationale, expresses at once a demonstration of free will and of the limits of free will as it responds to the pressures of inexorable social necessity. It is a documentation of, and a commentary upon, fate.

In *La Machine infernale* Cocteau has put the idea clearly: *"Regarde, spectateur, remontée à bloc, de telle sorte que le ressort se déroule avec lenteur tout le long d'une vie humaine,* une des plus parfaites machines, construites par les dieux infernaux pour l'anéantissement mathématique d'un mortel."[28] Cocteau speaks here in his own version of the Oedipus story, but he (as is also the case with Gide, Anouilh, Giraudoux, and all the other modern French dramatists who have been so Gallicly driven in their adaptations of the stories of ancient Greek tragedy) obviously owes more to Descartes than to Sophocles. The "slow unwinding throughout the entire course of a human life" emphasizes that continuity and totality of circumstance which is "fate" in novelistic terms (less suitable, perhaps, to the truncated time perspective of the stage), while the "perfect machine" constructed by the gods for "the mathematical annihilation of an individual" perfectly expresses the *necessity* of the mechanistic causal chain. I say "mechanistic causal chain" purposely, because Cocteau's mode of speech suggests here much more the language of the understanding than the language of the imagination. But this is simply the confusion of two modes of discourse by a Frenchman still under the rationalistic influence of Descartes. In Cocteau's "modern" Greek tragedy—as in that of Gide, Anouilh, and Giraudoux—the obscurity, the overarching mystery of the original mythical sense has been completely lost. Everything is clear—in fact, too clear.

Just what is novelistic fate? How (in terms which are equally applicable to an ancient religious or a modern secular culture) could we define Cocteau's "infernal machine"? Whitehead has told us that the pilgrim fathers of the scientific imagination are Aeschylus, Sophocles, and Euripides, and that "their vision of fate, remorseless and indifferent, urging a tragic incident to its inevitable issue, is the vision possessed by science."[29] We can accept the insight. We can see that in some analogical sense the laws of physics are the decrees of fate. But we have already clearly established that natural laws represent fate divorced from all that makes it relevant to literature and the imagination: its dramatic structure, and its connection with human purpose. So we must amend Whitehead slightly and say that the same remorseless working of things which science calls laws of nature or general causal series is what the novelist treats as *destiny*. But to say that Cocteau's "infernal machine" is the literary counterpart of natural law is not to freeze it into a single mold or restrict it to a single possibility. And here we are back again to the idea that the mode of literary expression itself constitutes a representation of reality. Fate (as we shall see in the next chapter) functions differently in Aeschylus and in Shakespeare. Spengler (long before Sartre) distinguished the classical drama of *situation* from the Faustian drama of *character*. What happens to Macbeth is the consequence of a character formed and solidified in its controlling ambition. What happens to Oedipus has been prepared at a level beyond his control, and worked out in a situation "presented" but hardly "chosen." "Character is fate" is good English but it is bad Greek. "Fate is circumstance," on the other hand, is excellent Greek. The distinction suggests that there are varieties of literary perspective through which the mechanism of necessity may be presented, and that if we attend to this variety, we may again learn something of the way in which implicit philosophic presuppositions condition the literary enterprise.

It is an axiom of literary criticism to expect homogeneity within cultural periods and heterogeneity between them. Francis Fergusson finds in Racine's "dramaturgy of reason" the portrait of an age and in Richard Wagner's "theater of passion" the portrait of another.[30] Erich Auerbach can contrast the acceptance of the prevailing structure of society in Molière with the implicit political and social criticism of Schiller's "middle-class tragedy."[31] But on the contrary, when we come to modern culture, the expectation of homogeneity breaks down. Auerbach can find little in the nineteenth century to justify such an axiom. Hardly a rubric exists which can at once accommodate the multifariousness of the Goncourts, Zola, Baudelaire, Balzac, Hauptmann, and Dostoyevsky. And Fergusson can do little with Chekhov and Pirandello, Cocteau and Eliot, Obey and Shaw except to speak of "the partial perspectives of the modern theater."

The phrase "partial perspectives" is important, for it indicates a fact which Fergusson and Auerbach both know; the fragmentation of modern culture. And it suggests that the weakness of our general intellectual life may mean not so much literal weakness as diversification—the lack of a central tendency or dominant moral concern, and a plurality of philosophical perspectives which conditions our approach to literary and artistic experience because it conditions contemporary life. This is also responsible for a pluralism in our contemporary conceptions of "fate," and it is this which I wish to explore in what follows.

My examples will not come from the greatest of contemporary novelists, from the list which includes Joyce and Proust, Mann and Gide, Hemingway and Faulkner. But the novels I have chosen have this in common; each is perhaps its author's most successful novel and each is a skillful example of the novelistic art; well written, artful in construction, stylistically suited to the expression of its dominant theme. Aldous Huxley's *Point Counterpoint*, John O'Hara's *Appointment in Samarra*, and Graham Greene's *The Heart of the Matter* are workmanlike and professional jobs, produced during the two decades 1928-1948, and if (with the partial exception of *Point Counterpoint*) they lack that multipersonal representation of consciousness, disintegration of the continuity of exterior events, and constant shifting of narrative viewpoint which is the distinctive feature of the modern novel, still each in its own way is modern. The stories which they tell (at least *Appointment in Samarra* and *The Heart of the Matter*) make a constant, moving chronology, passing from stasis to partial crisis, and from partial crisis to final catastrophe. If there is nothing here which is alien to the novel of the nineteenth century, twentieth-century ideology appears in the "form" of the stories. Each novel is a disquisition upon contemporary "fate," and it is the concept of "final catastrophe" which must solicit our concern. It is the problematic issue of the use of the power of free will for its own destruction which is preeminently here in question. What I wish to briefly consider is therefore a comparison of three suicides: the fictions of Maurice Spandrell, who died in London in 1924; of Julian

English, who died in Gibbsville, Pa., during the Christmas holidays of 1930; and of Henry Scobie, who died in British West Africa during the early days of the second World War.

7   IN THE complication of intersecting stories which Huxley has constructed in *Point Counterpoint*, that of Maurice Spandrell is one of the more important. In the first scene in which he appears, he is presented physically, a young man of thirty-three (already ravaged so that he might be fifty), unwholesome and gargoyle-like, with a gaunt face more sinister than tragic, deep-set grey eyes, the wide fleshy mouth set in a cadaverous mask. The symbolism is obvious; the physical description suggests the moral decay. Later, as Spandrell boasts theatrically to the assembled company of his carefully planned and cynically accomplished seduction of poor little Harriet Watkins (in which her innocence is calculatingly transformed into depravity for his amusement) something else has become clearly apparent: Spandrell's self-hatred, and above all the hatred of sex (of which Rampion accuses him) which comes out in his utilization of seduction as vengeance. The motivation is here hinted at, but its true nature not yet revealed.

Nor can it be until considerably later, when Maurice's mother, the wife of General Knoyle (Spandrell's stepfather) comes to his flat to see him in the late afternoon. Tearfully she reproaches him for making her unhappy with his present way of life, and the following exchange occurs:[32]

"When you married that man," he went on, "did you think of my happiness?"

"You know I thought it would be for the best," she answered brokenly. She had explained it so often; she couldn't begin again. "You know it," she repeated.

"I only know what I felt and said at the time," he answered. "You didn't listen to me, and now you tell me you wanted to make me happy."

"But you were so unreasonable," she protested. "If you had given me any reasons. . . ."

"Reasons," he repeated slowly. "Did you honestly expect a boy of fifteen to tell his mother the reasons why he didn't want her to share her bed with a stranger?"

The clue to the understanding of Spandrell, Huxley intimates, lies here: he is the victim of an unresolved Oedipal situation. The clinical details are spread out in *Point Counterpoint* according to the classical Freudian pattern. Ever since his mother's second marriage, Spandrell has always perversely made the worst of things, chosen the worst course, deliberately followed his own worst tendencies. It was an infallible way to grieve his mother and so take upon her a calculated and unsubtle revenge. And in it was the unconscious and compulsive path to his own self-destruction. Living in a miserable flat on such money as he can wring from his guilty and despairing mother, he gives himself Baudelaire-like to a histrionic and dedicated satanism. He absolutely refuses to work. Habitually lazy and chronically bored, even debauchery, he finds, is subject to a law of diminishing returns. Spandrell's corruption of young girls is now his only pleasure, but it is a titillation of the mind and not the senses, mired in sadism and destruction.

But even these pleasures finally fail. When his sense of essential evil begins to undergo the same deadening sclerosis as his sensuality, out of pure cynicism (and hope) he undertakes with the Communist Illidge the murder of Everard Webley the Fascist leader. It is not for political reasons. Spandrell is no Communist. When Webley lies dead on the floor, Maurice eyes him without horror. With one foot he touches the dead cheek. The imprint remains dust grey on the white skin. He raises his foot again and grinds his heel into the socket of the dead eye. But even this delicate experiment with outrage yields no twinge of sense or laceration of moral fiber. Spandrell is as dead as Webley. And having demonstrated this, Huxley then prepares the histrionic climax in which Spandrell takes his own life.

Spandrell insists that Mark Rampion come to his flat to hear the A Minor Quartet. Infantile and melodramatic to the end, Spandrell believes that if there are any values whatsoever, they are certified in the music of Beethoven. Granted that while the violins are playing one can forget the monstrous garbage of the world, is the *heilige Dankgesang* a final proof of the existence of God? The childishly delicate Dostoyevskian murderer hangs upon Rampion's judgment, but Rampion refuses to be convinced. The music proves nothing. All at once Spandrell is deflated. Depressed, tired to death, he walks out while the music is still playing. Suddenly a shot. Rampion jumps up and runs to the door. In the passage lies Spandrell's body with a hole in his head and a patch of blood upon his shirt. The method of self-destruction has been complex, but we must not be deceived by the rationalization implicit in the unsuccessful appeal to Beethoven. The boy who did not want his mother to share her bed with a stranger has exacted his final price.

The story of Maurice Spandrell, if it may be called a tragedy, is independent of place. It works itself out in London as Baudelaire's did in Paris, but *The Brothers Karamazov* and *The Possessed* have already demonstrated that diabolism can flourish as successfully in the provinces as in the Empire City. For both Spandrell and Baudelaire the metropolitan locale is a backdrop for the fate which originates in an abstract relationship: mother, son, stepfather. The family structure is the core, and the urgencies of locale are irrelevant.

The story of Julian English is the exact opposite. Here place is agency, and the tragedy depends upon the disguised impetus of the sociological forces. As the oppression of a social milieu dooms Emma Bovary, so the narrow constraint of the Pennsylvania small town snowballs into the suicide of Julian English. "Snowballs" is not quite the right metaphor. "Avalanche" is better, for the time span here is collapsed: not the weeks or months of *Point Counterpoint,* but the mere forty-eight hours between the Christmas eve party and the

night of the day after Christmas when he drunkenly goes
into his garage, climbs into the car, closes the windows, and
turns on the motor.

Julian's unhappy destiny is shown in a series of interlocked
and socially significant episodes. The first occurs in the Lan-
tenengo Country Club on Christmas, when, in the presence
of everybody who really counts, Julian drunkenly throws a
drink (ice cubes and all) in Harry Reilly's face. The second
occurs at the "Stage Coach"—a road house just out of town
where the following night Julian, drunk again, goes out alone
into a car with a cheap blond singer in front of his wife and
their best friends. The third is the fist fight he provokes at the
Gibbsville city club the next noon with one of his good
friends in the dining room in full sight of the professional
men lunching at the surrounding tables. These three occasions manage to alienate the community generally, Julian's
wife Caroline, and his best friends, and thereby cause the feeling of loneliness, ostracism and "what the hell" which lead to
his suicide. But this sense of "the end of the line" is not felt
by him alone. His wife Caroline, loving him with whatever
depth is possible to her, numb and grief-stricken after his
death, yet says: ". . . but he was right. It was *time* for him to
die,"[33] thereby expressing what is essentially not a personal,
but a community judgment. The fate here is entirely sociological.

The occasions of Julian's downfall are all similar, for while
they display his immaturity and essential defensiveness (expressed in excessive irritability and complete carelessness in
human relations), they are lethal not in their internal, but in
their external effects. It is the shame before the community of
spectators which mobilizes whatever of personal guilt appears.
The drink throwing occurs at three in the morning. By that
noon the telephones are buzzing. The night club indiscretion
appears only before a rather small number, but the humiliation of Julian's wife is witnessed by her best friends. The fight
in the Gibbsville club is shameful not because it is a fight, but

because it is a public spectacle. The stakes which have been lost are the intangibles of status and reputation, but given the iron encompassment of a society based on status and reputation, the conclusion makes a kind of pathetic sense. That it is a judgment upon the community as well as the individual contributes whatever of tragedy there may be.

But there is also one thing more. When Julian English throws the highball in Harry Reilly's face, he is drunk. And when he turns on the motor in the closed garage, he is so drunk that he can hardly stand. With the semi-lucidity of the intervals, it can be said that Julian English drinks almost without interruption for the entire two days in which the action of *Appointment in Samarra* takes place. This adds just the proper mechanistic agency for the sociological fate to be effective. That Julian acts while drunk or almost drunk removes, or at least seriously qualifies, the burden of rational choice. It highlights the Greek "inevitability" by eliminating the agency of the conscious free will. And again the structure of the story is congruent with the theory from which it springs.

The Heart of the Matter contains all of the exotic trappings for which Graham Greene is famous: a tropical settlement in British West Africa, Henry Scobie, a middle-aged deputy commissioner of police, his pathetic wife, atabrine and mosquito netting, two powerful and corrupt Syrians, Yusef and Tallit (both diamond smugglers), foreign ships to be searched, ships torpedoed by the enemy, spies sent down from the home office, a native boy Ali, a sweating Portuguese captain, and a kindly Roman Catholic priest, Father Rank.

Against this exotic background unrolls a plot which is the perfect illustration of Cocteau's metaphor—the causal chain producing the mathematical annihilation of an individual. Scobie's superior, the Commissioner, is resigning, but Scobie is passed over, and another is being brought in from outside to succeed him. Scobie's wife Louise finds the shame and humiliation more than she can bear, and Scobie promises to send her on a long-desired trip to South Africa. He needs three hundred pounds for the passage money and, refused a loan at the bank and driven by his wife's despair, he finally borrows it at the legal interest rate from the only man who will lend it to him, the corrupt Syrian, Yusef. While Scobie's wife is away, a British passenger ship is torpedoed, and among the pitiful survivors is Helen Rolt, a young widow of nineteen. Out of pity Scobie befriends her and they become lovers. He writes her a compromising love note which falls into the hands of Yusef, who then uses the note to blackmail Scobie into assisting him in his diamond smuggling. Scobie's wife Louise returns, and he is forced to pretend that all is as before she left. Meanwhile the Commissioner now informs Scobie that he is to be appointed police Commissioner after all, but Scobie says it is now too late. Yusef arranges the murder of Scobie's native boy Ali, and Scobie, feeling guilty complicity in the murder, disgusted at what he must do to assist Yusef, and torn between his genuine love for Louise and his guilty passion for Helen, deliberately takes a lethal dose of sleeping pills. The original accident of his non-promotion has produced as by an iron necessity the conclusion of his suicide.

This is the setting and the plot, but in the end, neither is central. For the real meaning of *The Heart of the Matter* lies in something which makes these mere externals, lies in fact in the inner facets of Scobie's character, and ultimately in his relationship with God. For, exotic background and mechanistic plot aside, *The Heart of the Matter* is an examination of the nature of pity and a Roman Catholic drama of sin, repentance, and salvation.

The contradiction in Scobie's character is the contrast between an absolute personal integrity and the weakness of being infinitely moved by the plight of others. He looks at his wife, the victim of fifteen years in the tropics, as she lies asleep under the netting, her face the yellow tinge of atabrine and her hair dark and stringy with sweat, and Greene says: "These were the times of ugliness when he loved her, when pity and responsibility reached the intensity of a passion." It is the fatal combination of moral responsibility and creature-pity which really works Scobie's downfall, for they are the twin sources of his vulnerability and of his guilt. It is impossible for him to feel superior to his sordid environment of venality and petty crime, for he recognizes that as the others are corrupted by money, so he is corrupted by sentiment. It is responsibility which moves him toward Helen Rolt in the temporary hospital to which she has been moved, friendship and pity for her youth and aloneness which make them finally lovers, pity and responsibility for his returned wife which leads to the act of his damnation.

The dilemma which *The Heart of the Matter* presents is that of mortal claims and divine commands. The love and pity which are Scobie's undoing seem (at least to his limited vision) in conflict with the morality of his church. When Helen Rolt needs him, he comes to her. "God can wait, he thought; how can one love God at the expense of one of his creatures?"[34] This, perhaps Greene wants us to understand, is "the heart of the matter," and Father Rank's mildness after Scobie's suicide is Greene's insistence that perhaps no human being is authoritative in the matter of God's mercy.

Scobie's suicide is, then, a tragedy neither of Freudian deformation nor of sociological pressure, but of free will in all its painful consciousness. When Scobie acts, he is aware of the circumstances and of the stakes: the happiness of his wife, the need of Helen Rolt, his responsibility for Yusef's crimes and Ali's death, his betrayal of his professional duties and of his church. And when he chooses to take his own life in the face of God's decree, he is following a premeditated plan which is the product neither of a momentary despair nor of an alcoholic befuddlement. It is a choice made in full awareness of the consequences. The concept of God and the moral virtues of pity and responsibility are the presuppositions of Scobie's story. That their intrusion into the human drama produces bitterness and death is a quaint commentary upon the relation between theology and fate.

8 *Point Counter Point, Appointment in Samarra*, and *The Heart of the Matter* are all treatises upon the necessity which determines man, and they show the quality of action to be less what one chooses than what one is mixed up in. Chaplin's movies expressed it perfectly: *caught in the works*. It is Cocteau's conception of *the world as machinery* with the actions of the participants confused, stubborn, endangered. Each of these stories explores the formal patterns of destiny. Each is the portrayal of a failure where failure means the incongruity of a pattern of value and a structure of experience. Each story, therefore, uses the imaginative mechanism of "fate" to dramatize the way in which morality and experience conflict.

The novels themselves have the rationality of the pattern of events, almost the mechanical logic of the understanding through which the chain of physical causation recommends itself to the natural scientist. What might have happened if Spandrell's mother had not married Major Knoyle? If Julian English had not thrown that drink in Harry Reilly's face? If Scobie had not been first passed over, but promoted to the Commissionership at once? The questions are pointless and unanswerable, but they show the way in which the events flow as hemorrhages from a wound. It is only the inner meaning of the flow which varies from case to case.

Some clue toward these inner meanings is provided by the passages which the authors have chosen as epigraphs for their novels. For *Point Counter Point* Huxley has chosen six lines from Fulke Greville:

> Oh, wearisome conditions of humanity!
> Born under one law, to another bound
> Vainly begot and yet forbidden vanity:
> Created sick, commanded to be sound.
> What meaneth Nature by these diverse laws—
> Passion and reason, self-division's cause?

"Created sick, commanded to be sound"; "passion and reason, self-division's cause"; these are the Elizabethan equivalents of the Freudian message, and they foretell Spandrell's destiny.

For *Appointment in Samarra* O'Hara has chosen a paragraph from W. Somerset Maugham:

DEATH SPEAKS: There was a merchant in Bagdad who sent his servant to market to buy provisions and in a little while the servant came back, white and trembling, and said, Master, just now when I was in the market-place I was jostled by a woman in the crowd and when I turned I saw it was Death that jostled me. She looked at me and made a threatening gesture; now lend me your horse, and I will ride away from this city and avoid my fate. I will go to Samarra and there Death will not find me. The merchant lent him his horse, and the servant mounted it, and he dug his spurs in its flanks and as fast as the horse could gallop he went. Then the merchant went down to the market-place and he saw me standing in the crowd and he came to me and said, Why did you make a threatening gesture to my servant when you saw him this morning? That was not a threatening gesture, I said, it was only a start of surprise. I was astonished to see him in Bagdad, for I had an appointment with him tonight in Samarra.

The illustration is more superficial, less pointed here. The inevitability of death for Julian English is foretold, an almost Oriental fatalism is set forth, but no hint of the social agency through which the inevitability is expressed comes through.

For *The Heart of the Matter* Graham Greene has chosen a sentence from Péguy:

Le pécheur est au coeur même de chrétienté. . . . Nul n'est aussi compétent que le pécheur en matière de chrétienté. Nul, si ce n'est le saint.

The sinner Scobie expresses the meaning of Christianity, and his dilemma is the Christian dilemma writ large. Between sin and saintliness the chasm looms immeasurable, but obscured by a mist which does not distinguish clearly between the two rims. The meaning of free will is clear, but its ultimate consequence is known only to the mercies of God.

Point Counter Point, Appointment in Samarra, and *The Heart of the Matter* all appeared within the two decades 1928-1948, and it is possible to read within their conceptions of fate something of the intellectual history of the modern world. The story of Maurice Spandrell is not only the projection of the mind of Aldous Huxley; it is also the expression of the spirit of the twenties, and a tribute to the way in which Freudian modes of explanation had ravished the literary mind. The story of Julian English is not only the child of the fictional imagination of John O'Hara; it is also the expression of the decade of the thirties, and the way in which the Marxian mode of perception (not directly so much as through the willing mediation of literary naturalism and the American sociologists) had influenced the direction of the social novel in England and America. The story of Henry Scobie is not only the mind of Graham Greene at work in its religious explorations; it is also the intellectual history of the forties and the expression of how the revival of religious interest had established its repercussions in the literary experience.

But the intellectual history is less interesting than its philosophical significance. And if we find in these three novels modes of perception which have their sources in Freud, Marx, and St. Augustine, this is important less for its sociological implications than for its expansion of our understanding of the mechanisms of fate. Destiny for Greek tragedy is inscrutable but simple, for although its purposes are problematic, its agencies appear in a universe which is both finite and manageable. But the fragmentation of modern culture and the "partial perspectives" which are its consequence requires even for fate a pluralistic interpretation.

Maurice Spandrell's is a "psychological" destiny, experienced in the individual self as the feeling of *guilt.* Julian English's is a "sociological" destiny, expressed in the individual as a feeling of *shame.* Henry Scobie's is a "moral" and "religious" destiny, experienced within the individual as a sense of *sin.* In each of these climates of feeling—guilt, shame, sin—is implicit a moral theory and a cosmology. Guilt is the

emotional climate of an ethics geared to a psychological causality. Shame is the emotional climate of an ethics viewed as
social demand. Sin is the emotional climate of an ethics inseparable from theology. Our age has not committed itself
exclusively to any of the three, and this is why neither *Point
Counter Point* nor *Appointment in Samarra* nor *The Heart
of the Matter* considered separately, but only the three suicides which they present taken in conjunction, illuminate the
continuum of contemporary fate. They exemplify the range
of possibility and the plural perspectives inseparable from the
literary representation of reality in the modern world. And
they show that the concept of destiny is not tied to a particular
moment of Western culture, but that it is a permanent fixture
of the literary mind, dwelling where imagination dwells, and
expressing itself where the categories of imagination are
expressed.

*Eight / The Problem of Tragedy & the Nature
of Peace*

1 THE CONCEPTS of destiny, fortune, and fate
are intermediate constructs of the imagina-
tion. They derive their peculiar quality from their purposiveness, from the way in which they infuse a persistent teleology
into the literary and historical accounts of human experience.
But they also point to the culminating ideas of the humanistic
complex: to the problem of tragedy and the nature of peace.

Here once again the contrast between the language of the
understanding and the language of the imagination is pressing and obvious. As the logical division between true and
false propositions find its analogue in the metaphysical distinction between reality and appearance, as the scientific
assumption of the principle of causality is countered by the
historical principle of destiny, and as the scientific chain of
meaning opposes its objective concepts of chance and prediction to the subjective and mysterious notions of fortune and
fate, so there is an analogue between a neutral scientific
examination of conflict and stasis and the implicit meditations of Aeschylus and Shakespeare and Racine upon the
tragic destiny of human life and the final reconciliation of the
storm-tossed spirit to which it may ultimately lead. Science
must concern itself with fact and with "matter of fact"; the
imagination sees all experience as inherently dramatic, and
in the construction of tragedy (perhaps the culminating
artistic experience of the entire Western tradition) confines

the loose untidiness of crude human experience within the orderly perfection of the dramatic event, and thereby presents an implicit argument for the existence of human value.

It may not perhaps be obvious at first sight why I have chosen to associate the concept of tragedy with that of peace, but that the functioning of the dramatic imagination does imply them both, I hope to make clear. And to indicate one of the possibilities of this "tragic rhythm of action"—how conflict, suffering, and reconciliation form a seamless web—I should like briefly to compare two famous examples of what I wish to call *tragedies of purgation: Hamlet* and the *Oedipus Rex*. In speaking of these dramas as "tragedies of purgation," I am not re-raising the Aristotelian riddle of *catharsis*. I am not referring to the purgation through pity and fear of the emotions of the spectators of the tragic drama, but rather to *the structure of the situation given within its plot*.

Since Aristotle no ancient drama has so persistently represented the Greek approach to the problem of destiny as the *Oedipus Rex*. Since Goethe and Coleridge no Renaissance tragedy has so consistently occupied the Western consciousness as *Hamlet*. But although they have so deeply stirred the imagination of the West, it has seldom, if ever, been noted how identically each participates in the tragic rhythm of action, how in each case a pollution of the natural order or a violation of the traditional ethos presents its consequences in sickness or blight or the uncanny intervention of supernatural powers, and how the ultimate "solution" is a "ritual cleansing" which accomplishes itself through mutilation, banishment, or a stage yielding a rich harvest of corpses in the final act. In each play we begin with a natural and moral universe wrenched out of its normal order, dimly pointing to the source of its dislocation in some person or act (as of the presence of some malignant foreign body), then slowly focusing the attention upon the tumor, and finally with a terrible surgery purging the afflicted body of its gross offense.

It is in this sense that both *Hamlet* and *Oedipus Rex* are tragedies of purgation. Each exploits the concept of *the un-natural,* describing a crisis wherein "nature" and "convention" are alike affronted and where, in fact, the symbolism of a diseased and rebellious Nature provides a metaphor both for "some strange eruption" in the state and for the moral corruption which is finally revealed as its generating source. Each likewise curiously mingles the "natural" and the "moral" order, the private lives and the public responsibilities. They are at once family tragedies and tragedies of state. It is not accidental that Hamlet is the royal prince of Denmark and Oedipus the reigning king of Thebes, and that in each play when the interior and vicious "mole of nature" is discovered, it is found to be relevant to the royal succession and to an illegitimate and usurpatory exercise of political power.

The entire first act of *Hamlet* is saturated with the mood of corruption. The appearance of the ghost of Hamlet's father leads Horatio to reflect upon a similar dread appearance of unnatural events before the assassination of Caesar, when

> The graves stood tenantless and the sheeted dead
> Did squeak and gibber in the Roman streets;
>   . . . and the moist star
> Upon whose influence Neptune's empire stands
> Was sick almost to doomsday with eclipse.
>
> (I, i, 115)[1]

Claudius himself reports the state of mind of Fortinbras. He does it scoffingly, but in language which we know to be the truth:

> . . . thinking by our late dear brother's death
> Our state to be disjoint and out of frame.
>
> (I, ii, 19)

Hamlet's meditation upon the Danish world—

> Fie on't, ah, fie, 'tis an unweeded garden
> That grows to seed. Things rank and gross in nature
> Possess it merely. . . .
>
> (I, ii, 135)

is reiterated in Marcellus' "Something is rotten in the state of Denmark." And finally the ghost, urging Hamlet to revenge, speaks of his own murder as "foul, strange, and unnatural" (I, v, 28), and in a single lengthy diatribe reveals the joining of murder, incest, and usurpation into one syndrome of corruption.

What Shakespeare needs an entire act to reveal, Sophocles states in three straightforward speeches.[2] The Theban priest reports the situation:

> A blight is on the fruitful plants of the earth,
> a blight is on the cattle in the fields,
> a blight is on our women that no children
> are born to them; a God that carries fire,
> a deadly pestilence, is on our town,
> strikes us and spares not, and the house of
> Cadmus is emptied of its people while black
> Death grows rich in groaning and in lamentation.

Oedipus responds with conspicuous Sophoclean irony:

I pity you, children. You have come full of longing, but I have known the story before you told it only too well. I know you are all sick, yet there is not one of you, sick though you are, that is as sick as I myself.

And Creon, returning from Delphi, announces the oracle's decision:

CREON: King Phoebus in plain words commanded us to drive out a pollution from our land, pollution grown ingrained within the land; drive it out, said the God, not cherish it, till it's past cure.

OEDIPUS: What is the rite of purification? How shall it be done?

CREON: By banishing a man, or expiation of blood by blood, since it is murder guilt which holds our city in this destroying storm.

The development of the *Oedipus Rex* follows this same deft pattern. The sudden manifestations of "the unnatural" hide a mystery. Thus the dialectic of "being and seeming" haunts the early moments of this play as it does the second act of *Hamlet*. But in a miracle of swiftness, by a series of breath-taking confrontations (Oedipus with Tiresias, Oedipus with Creon and Jocasta, Oedipus with the Messenger from Corinth, Oedipus with the Old Herdsman) appearances are penetrated and the dreadful reality revealed. The plague becomes meaningful as the indication of a supreme unnaturalness; of a man who has usurped at once his father's throne, his mother's bed, and the potent prerogatives of the gods. And the horrible retribution of the climax leaves a denouement of pity and pathos, but also of lowered tension and of resignation.

In *Hamlet* the essence of the movement is the same, although a greater complexity makes for a greater retardation in the achievement of the climax. The mood of corruption of Act I turns into the comedy of masks, the play of appearance and reality, the mutual probings of Hamlet and Claudius in Act II, followed by the preclimactic revelation of reality through "the play within a play" of Act III. Act IV is a causal interlude (almost a mistake)[3] consequent upon the "accident" of Polonius' murder in Act III. Act V brings the inevitable climax and the final purgation of the sea of corpses.

If we now compare the strategy of *Hamlet* and *Oedipus Rex*, we shall find Shakespeare and Sophocles employing a common structure of dramatic action. Both (1) begin with a trouble in the state. This is indicated (2) by the eruption of the unnatural (in *Oedipus* the plague, in *Hamlet* the ghost), whereupon (3) a movement of destruction begins (in *Oedipus*: to seek the culprit, in *Hamlet*: to seek revenge). And when (4) the culprit has been revealed, and the revenge (with all its secondary consequences) has been secured, then (with Oedipus exiled to Cithaeron and the sovereignty of Thebes in Creon's hands, and Gertrude, Claudius, and Hamlet dead and the power of Denmark passed at last to Norway's Fortinbras) (5) we have the restoration of order. Purgation has been accomplished. The slate has been wiped clean. Life (natural and political) can begin again.

In one of his shorter critical essays "On the Knocking at the Gate in Macbeth" Thomas DeQuincy has attempted (brilliantly, I think) to account for the profound and mysterious effect which the offstage knocking at the gate in Act II of *Macbeth* (just after the murder of Duncan) has upon the spectators of the play, and what it suggests for the psychology of the tragic drama. The murderers and the murder, he says,[4]

must be insulated—cut off by an immeasurable gulf from the ordinary tide and succession of human affairs—locked up and sequestered in some deep recess; we must be made sensible that the world of ordinary life is suddenly arrested, laid asleep, tranced, racked into a dread armistice; time must be annihilated, relation to things without abolished; and all must pass self-withdrawn into a deep syncope and suspension of earthly passion. Hence it is that, when the deed is done, when the work of darkness is perfect, then the world of darkness passes away like a pageantry in the clouds: the knocking at the gate is heard, and it makes known audibly that the reaction has commenced; the human has made its reflux upon the fiendish; the pulses of life are beginning to beat again; and the re-establishment of the goings-on of the world in which we live first makes us profoundly sensible of the awful parenthesis that had suspended them.

DeQuincy has been speaking of a particular effect in the play *Macbeth,* but in doing so he has managed to give a remarkable formulation of the tragedy of purgation as it is exemplified in *Hamlet* and in *Oedipus Rex.* Here too at the conclusion "the human has made its reflux upon the fiendish," "the pulses of life are beginning to beat again," and the entire interlude of the tragic action can from the standpoint of the laws of the natural and the moral order be recognized as "the awful parenthesis that had suspended them."

2 *Hamlet* and the *Oedipus Rex* are both tragedies of purgation, and as such they share a common structure of dramatic action. But if they are similar in this respect, they are very dissimilar in others, and

these dissimilarities are equally instructive in helping us to understand the paradox of the dramatic imagination.

Their profound differences we feel at once. *Hamlet* is a secular drama; it contains perhaps an epistemology, but hardly a metaphysics. *Oedipus Rex,* on the other hand, like Dante's *Divina Commedia,* presupposes a *cosmos.* Its universe is total, with a sustaining Nature below the level of human action and an actively interested Olympian hierarchy above, not quite actively intervening (as in the *Hippolytus* of Euripides) but *hovering* in the felt presence of the Delphic oracle, in the prophetic "sight" of Teiresias, and in the spectator-chorus. And the latter in particular has one eye upon the tragic action within the *polis* and the other focused upon the divine order and the immortal gods, so that its privileged commentary is equally balanced by doubt of the human action, modulating reference to the decrees of Fate, and intermittent invocation to Apollo the golden healer, Athena, daughter of Zeus, and Artemis the Huntress, her sister. Between the mortal storm of Oedipus' obsessive search and awareness of the decree of Zeus and Fate, the chorus stands bewildered, without firm purchase in the debate, and its intense unrest feeds the Sophoclean tension through the uneasy mingling of two intersecting worlds.

In Shakespeare there is none of this. There is only the world of human society magnified to the proportions of Elizabethan pride. It is as if the notion of the total cosmos eludes him, as if he feels no metaphysical need to frame and explore this cosmological idea. As Santayana puts it: "He depicts human life in all its richness and variety, but leaves that life without a setting, and consequently without a meaning."[5] And Karl Jaspers agrees: "Shakespeare moves across a purely secular stage. In him a proud society recognizes its own heightened image."[6]

Now there is one interesting consequence of this "absence of religion" in Shakespeare compared to its presence in Sophocles. The pervasive sense of an eternal order which is implicit in the *Oedipus Rex* is almost entirely lacking in

Hamlet. Both Santayana and Spengler have commented upon this in the diverse vocabularies for which they are famous. Shakespeare, Santayana reminds us, is unique among the major poets in being without a philosophy and without a religion. In his drama there is no fixed conception of any forces, natural or supernatural, dominating and transcending our mortal energies. And he adds: "Those who think it wise or possible to refrain from searching for general principles, and are satisfied with the successive empirical appearance of things without any faith in their rational continuity or completeness, may well see in Shakespeare their natural prophet. For he, too, has been satisfied with the successive description of various passions and events. His world, like the earth before Columbus, extends in an infinite plane which he is not tempted to explore."[7] But this is to interpret Shakespeare in terms of naturalism or empiricism or positivism, as some David Hume of the poetic life, writing in *Hamlet* and *Othello, Lear, Coriolanus,* and *Macbeth* his "Treatise of Human Nature," but content to detail empirical succession without recourse to cosmological principle, and it suggests the contrast with the world of Sophocles, where the imposition of order comes Kantian-wise in the constancy of a mode of perception—in the ever-present assertion of that cosmic order attested by the presence and the active intervention of the gods.

But just this distinction between dramatic action dependent upon human accident and that consequent upon cosmic forces and their fated evolution is the meaning of Spengler's contrast between "Destiny" and "Incident." It is this insight, he says,[8]

that constitutes the singularity and the power of Shakespeare. Hitherto, neither our research nor our speculation has hit upon this in him—that he is *the Dramatist of the Incidental*. And yet this Incidental is the very heart of Western tragedy, which is a true copy of the Western history idea. . . .It is incidental that the political situation of "Hamlet," the murder of the King and the succession question impinge upon just that character that Hamlet is. Or, take Othello—it is incidental that the man at whom Iago, the commonplace rogue that one could pick up in any street, aims his blow is one whose person possesses just this wholly special physiognomy. And Lear! Could anything be more incidental (and therefore more "natural") than the conjunction of this commanding dignity with these fateful passions and the inheritance of them by the daughters? . . . Further, this Western species of the Incidental is entirely alien to the Classical world-feeling and therefore to its drama. . . . What happened to Oedipus—unlike the fate of Lear—might just as well have happened to anyone else. This is the Classical "Destiny," the *Fatum* which is common to all mankind, which affects the "body" and in no wise depends upon incidents of personality. . . . Consider Oedipus once more: that which happened to him was wholly extrinsic, was neither brought about nor conditioned by anything subjective to himself, and could just as well have happened to anyone else. This is the very *form of the Classical myth.* Compare with it the necessity—inherent in and governed by the man's whole existence and the relation of that existence to Time—that resides in the destiny of Othello, of Don Quixote, of Werther. It is, as we have said before, the difference of situation-tragedy and character-tragedy. And this opposition repeats itself in history proper—every epoch of the West has character, while each epoch of the Classical only presents a situation.

The passage is of the greatest interest, for it shows how the metaphysical distinction between "Destiny" and "Incident" embodies itself historically in the situation-drama of the Greeks and the character-drama of the Faustian West. And it throws considerable light upon the vague feeling which we have that the *Oedipus Rex* (like the works of Homer and Tolstoy which we have examined in our treatment of the novelistic imagination) is a work of objectivity, while (in the spirit of St. Augustine and Dostoyevsky) *Hamlet* is a work of subjectivity. For objectivity means the exploitation of "object," "quality," and "situation," as subjectivity means a particular emphasis upon "meaning," "inwardness," and "character."

It would be foolish to raise again the dead issue of the quar-

rel between character and plot. It is obvious that the Aristotelian distinction cannot be made into an absolute separation. *Character in a pattern of action* is the primary datum of
the tragic drama. But dramatic practice may well vary in its
relative emphasis, and this variation seen from one perspective is surely related to intellectual and sociological factors
which exhibit themselves as a part of cultural history. Aristotle's assertions that "Plot is the principle and the soul of
tragedy" and that "the tragedies of most of our modern poets
fail in the rendering of character" fit perfectly with the practice of the situation-drama of the Greeks. A. C. Bradley's
statement that in *Hamlet* "the whole story turns upon the
peculiar character of the hero," and that "Hamlet deserves
the title 'tragedy of moral idealism' quite as much as the title
'tragedy of reflection' "[9] is a perfect instance of the practice of
the character-drama which has followed from the inward,
subjective, morally oriented conception of man which the
Christian community has inherited from *The Confessions* of
St. Augustine.

The character of Oedipus is, from the modern point of
view, underdeveloped. He has little inwardness, little tendency toward reflective elaboration. Even his long speeches are
speeches of action: he calls down curses upon Laios' murderer
and maledictions on Creon; objectively relates the story of
his life; finally begs for banishment. Hamlet, on the contrary,
ponders and doubts, meditates, hesitates, deliberates. He expresses moral indignation, thinks on man's nature and his
death, considers the problem of appearance and reality, indulges in self-interrogation, ponders suicide. And this too is
the consequence of a changed cosmology and a changed philosophic conception of human life.

As we have seen, there is an enormous difference between
the Greek and the Elizabethan drama, and if we wish to characterize it finally, we shall come to a distinguishing characteristic which has been implicit in all that has been said before.
We shall see it ultimately not merely as the distinction be-

tween the sacred and the secular, subjectivity and objectivity, character and situation, but as the distinction of "destiny versus justice" or "free will versus fate." *Hamlet, Julius Caesar, Othello* and *Macbeth* are *tragedies of free will. Oedipus* and *Agamemnon, Electra* and *The Trojan Women* are *tragedies of fate.*

Psychology and ethics have little to do with Oedipus. For the interest of Greek tragedy lies in the progressive revelation of the separate strands which are unalterably interwoven in the web of Fate. In this complex net Oedipus is fixed like a struggling creature. His efforts to escape fail. His undoubted virtue and sense of responsibility as King of Thebes do not affect the situation. Any attempt to establish a relation between his guilt and his misfortune (which is a common error of those under the spell of Christian moralism) is irrelevant and beside the point. For the Greeks see Fate as a structure of the world, singularly like that of the system of their Euclidean geometry. Like the deduction of the theorems from the axioms, postulates, and definitions, Fate embodies a geometric necessity. No human endeavors can change the pattern. And therefore the plot of the *Oedipus Rex* unrolls (as Cocteau has intimated) with the swift and dreadful movement of a *logical* entailment.

However we should like to assimilate a Creon *(Antigone)* to a Claudius, a Clytemnestra to a Lady Macbeth, a Medea to a Goneril or Regan, we shall fail. Greek tragedy has no villians like Claudius, Richard III, or Iago. And the Christian presupposition of "temptation," "free will," "moral decision," and "retribution" simply will not work for the *Oedipus Rex,* the *Oresteia,* or *The Seven Against Thebes.* That post-Augustinian moral drama which came to its finest flower in Racine and the Elizabethans, that superb conception of "making trial of human character and human powers" which works so well for Hamlet, Othello, and Macbeth, for Phèdre, Britannicus, and Andromache, is powerless to explain the Greek tragic protagonist, and is warped out of its original context when applied to the Aeschylean myth of destiny or to the Sophoclean story of Fate. It is just such an incongruous mixture of cultural incompatibles which constitutes the irony of Sartre's performance in the creation of *The Flies,* where a classical format originating in the dramatic requirements of ancient Greek sensibility becomes the vehicle of a treatise on free will and the decisive act, and where a complete inversion of the philosophical presuppositions of the Greek mind put into the mouths of characters called Orestes, Electra, and Aegisthus produces an existentialist manifesto.

3   IN DISTINGUISHING between the essential spirit of Greek and Elizabethan tragedy, in making a separation between that view of the world which enthrones fate or destiny, and that view which finds man free to act, and seeks justice in its examination of his interpersonal relations, we have come at last to a paradox of philosophical interpretation which dogs the history of Western civilization. Whitehead has expressed it amusingly and cogently:[10]

We quickly find that the Western peoples exhibit on a colossal scale a peculiarity which is popularly supposed to be more especially characteristic of the Chinese. Surprise is often expressed that a Chinaman can be of two religions, a Confucian for some occasions and a Buddhist for other occasions. Whether this is true of China I do not know; nor do I know whether, if true, these two attitudes are really inconsistent. But there can be no doubt that an analogous fact is true of the West, and that the two attitudes involved are inconsistent. A scientific realism, based on mechanism, is conjoined with an unwavering belief in the world of men and of the higher animals as being composed of self-determining organisms. This radical inconsistency at the basis of modern thought accounts for much that is half-hearted and wavering in our civilization. It would be going too far to say that it distracts thought. It enfeebles it, by reason of the inconsistency lurking in the background.

This "radical inconsistency" is a "problem" for ethics and the social sciences, but it is the very climate of poetry and dramatic literature. It springs from an inherent tension of the creative mind, and it is for this reason that I should like to call it *the ultimate antinomy of the dramatic imagination*. It is implicit in mind's mythic origins, and it haunts the progress of mind's most sophisticated endeavors. We have seen it in the two accounts of the origin of the Fates in Hesiod: on the one hand their description as daughters of Night who "distribute good and evil among mankind at birth," on the other as the children of Themis (Law) "who hourly attend the labors of mankind." It is equally implicit in the Sophists' early distinction between *nomos* ("law" or "convention") and *phusis* (nature), that is to say, the "natural" and the "moral," which is ultimately to flower in the diverse worlds of Kant's first and his second Critique. For to contrast *Hamlet, Richard III*, and *Macbeth* as "tragedies of free will" with *Oedipus, Agamemnon*, and *The Trojan Woman* as "tragedies of fate" is to use the dichotomies of character and situation, subjectivity and objectivity, natural necessity and moral contingency as instances of an impulse which varies between two poles of thought and feeling because it is the product of an imagination which encompasses them both.

Already the antinomy is suggested in the *Poetics*. Speaking in Chapter XIII about the requisites of the tragic plot, Aristotle asks that the action shall excite pity and fear, and draws the corollary that the change of fortune presented shall not be the spectacle of a virtuous man brought from prosperity to adversity (since this is morally shocking) nor of a bad man passing from adversity to prosperity, since this neither *satisfies the moral sense*[11] nor calls forth pity or fear. It is true that a moment later in describing the tragic flaw *(hamartia)*, Aristotle refuses to reduce it to moral terms. It is "error" or "frailty," not "vice" or "depravity," and yet the prior reference to "the moral sense" ("human feeling") shows an unmistakable mixing of the levels of requirement—the logic of plot construction with the psychology of the moral emotions. And when Hamlet in his famous denigration of Claudius (I, iv) translates the Aristotelian doctrine into Shakespearean imagery, the antinomy has finally been made both plausible and explicit.

> So oft it chances in particular men
> That (for some vicious mole of nature in them,
> As in their birth, wherein they are not guilty,
> Since nature cannot choose his origin)
> By the o'ergrowth of some complexion,
> Oft breaking down the pales and forts of reason,
> Or by some habit that too much o'erleavens
> The form of plausive manners—that (these men
> Carrying, I say, the stamp of one defect,
> Being nature's livery, or fortune's star)
> Their virtues else, be they as pure as grace,
> As infinite as man may undergo
> Shall in the general censure take corruption
> From that particular fault.

If the defect is "nature's livery," her "vicious mole," something present "in their birth," then, indeed, particular men "are not guilty," and we are in the ambience of unavoidability which permeates an *Oedipus Rex* or an *Agamemnon*. But if the defect is a complex of traits which end by a successful assault upon the citadel of reason or a cumulative effect of wrong habit, then we are truly in the realm of human character, of the voluntary and purposive choices of a Macbeth, an Iago, or a Richard III, and the nemesis which overtakes them belongs not to the impersonal mechanism of fate, but to the conventional workings of justice.

Thus it becomes clear that the antinomic character of the dramatic imagination not only allows for, but actually demands, alternative interpretations of Aristotle's *hamartia* (the tragic flaw), and that the ambiguity of the dramatic event hides two conflicting dimensions of the problem of evil: one metaphysical, the other moral. Tragedy as an artistic form.

as an aesthetic convention, is a perfect expression of an imagination anchored at one extreme in cosmology, and at the other in ethics, and this duality (raising problems akin to those of philosophy and theology) expresses itself perfectly in questions concerning the primacy of "justice" or of "fate." And even if the tragic drama always carries with it the pleasures of overflowing life and intense vitality, even if by showing man morally triumphant (while physically defeated), it satisfies some craving close to the human heart, yet the mind can be left curiously uneasy, its ultimate questions insistent and unanswered.

If there is a determining force in the universe to the explication of which the tragic poet sets his talents, is this in the end a factor of natural necessity or of moral retribution? To this persistent question neither the Greeks nor the Elizabethans (despite their opposite emphases) could give absolutely unambiguous answers. Aeschylus performs at once as cosmic moralist and metaphysician; in the *Oresteia*, as we have seen, fate and justice seem inordinately close. Shakespeare is primarily a humanist, expressing explicitly that men are the masters of their fate, yet from time to time noting uneasily the claims upon behavior of a necessity from outside, and treating the dislocations of character (as in the speech of Hamlet just above) as alternatively fated and humanly self-produced. And the youthful Goethe of 1771, even then possessed of the reconciling passion, sees the very essence of the Shakespearean tragedies in Promethean terms, requiring not a choice *between* free will and necessity, but constituted by the very rhythm of action which involves them both. "His plays," says Goethe,[12] "all hinge upon that mysterious point (which no philosopher has as yet noted and fixed) in which the peculiar property of our ego, the assumed freedom of our will, comes into conflict with the necessary course of events."

The modern consciousness finds this conception tantalizing if not hopelessly confused. Profoundly Christian in inspiration even when atheistically existential in fact, it prefers to see the tragic flaw expressed in the freedom of moral choice. But this would require that destiny and character work to the same inscrutable end. From this point of view Oedipus' impatient anger and Creon's obstinacy become the vehicles through which the primal curse hanging over the house of Laius expresses its bitter consequences. It is precisely this mixture of modes which Sartre will not permit. Writing on "M. François Mauriac et la Liberté," he says:[13] "If I suspect that the hero's future actions are determined in advance by heredity, social influence or some other mechanism, my own time ebbs back into me; there remains only myself, reading and persisting, confronted by a static book. Do you want your characters to live? See to it that they are free."

Sartre is, of course, speaking about the modern novel, not the tragic drama, but the conclusion is relevant to both. The protagonist here, whether conceived in dramatic or in novelistic terms, is a center of indeterminacy, and if he has, as Aristotle asserted, some fixity of character, it is a fixity from which he may, paradoxically, from time to time escape. Men are free above and beyond their natures, and if, as Cocteau would have us believe, they get caught up in a psychological machinery, they themselves are never mechanical. For Sartre this follows from an express denial of that very cosmological assumption which a Homer or an Aeschylus makes willingly, and perhaps altogether unconsciously. For it is built into the *Iliad,* the *Odyssey,* and the *Oresteia* that although we struggle against our destiny, a part of our character is itself an element of Nature. But Sartre's obsessive voluntarism denies this absolutely. *If freedom accepts Nature, the reign of fatality begins.* And this fatality cannot be assimilated to the determinism of our inclinations. Let us not, says Sartre, confuse destiny and character.

Precisely because he wishes *to avoid* the dialectic of free will and fate, Sartre complains about Mauriac's novelistic method, which at one moment presents his heroine Thérèse Desqueyroux from inside, as she is to herself, and at another from outside as she appears to others. Sartre shrewdly comments that to assume the first perspective is to assert through novelistic technique a doctrine of freedom, while to assume the second is to place oneself on the side of determinism. But just this technique of dual presentation which Sartre criticizes in Mauriac *was* the device of protagonist *and* chorus by which the Greek dramatists retained the interest of an audience *which knew in advance* the fate of a Creon, an Ajax, or an Agamemnon. By knowing in advance, the Greek audience could suspend the sense of inevitability in such a way as to intensify it, could concentrate upon the present moment the entire *weight* of the future. And thus the alternating appearance of protagonist and chorus, the one acting with an unwitting "freedom," the other pondering and commenting upon the causality of inevitable decree, superbly presents the antinomy of the dramatic imagination, the mutual implication of participant and spectator, free will and fate, without at the same time exploding the dramatic arena into a thousand fragments of skepticism and improbability.

4 THE TOTAL freedom of the self upon which Sartre insists is a source of human dignity, but it carries with it a paradoxical consequence. The very "radical contingency" which makes it possible ends inevitably with the emotion of existentialist "absurdity." And whereas the profound belief in destiny is in a certain sense antihumanist and opposed to the Apollonian "individuation" of which Nietzsche spoke, it does at the same time serve to reconcile the individual with the imperatives of a cosmic law. The dialectic of the tragic response is in some sense geared to these two extremes.

A recognition of the omnipotence of fate at once recalls to man (whether in the person of Oedipus, or the Chorus which chants his downfall) the *fragility* of his existence, the peculiar sense of his *mortality*, but it at the same time (as in the *Oresteia*) provides an *order* which lies above and beyond the compass of individuality. At the very moment when the real Greek city falls into decay, Stoic "fate" gives meaning to the idea of a universal City not of this world. At the very moment when the barbarians are destroying the hegemony of the Roman *imperium*, Augustinian "predestination" invokes a City of God and a community of the elect. And in an age when old faiths seem to be crumbling into dust, Romantic "destiny" suggests a temporal State in which all the fragmentations of the nineteenth-century world are to find their wholeness in the manifestation of an absolute spirit. The forces which are at work in these activities of the historical imagination also permeate the tragic drama.

In one sense Sartre is right. One cannot really reduce destiny to the fatality of character. There is a double quality, a double exigence about the self which exemplifies the antinomy of the dramatic imagination. The profound belief in the spontaneity of his decisions which seems to rule the emotions of Oedipus is presented by Sophocles in such a way as to dissociate it from the necessary causal chain of his acts which unwinds before the ritual astonishment of the horrified Chorus. But the sense in which Sartre is right more nearly relates to the youthful insight of Goethe. Tragedy is the play between destiny and character, the mysterious region where the freedom of the will comes into conflict with a cosmic necessity. At the same time nothing is more complex than the dramatic logic followed by the tragic impulse. At the hands of the Greek gods (say, the struggle of Artemis and Aphrodite which lies behind the action of Euripides' *Hippolytus*) destiny takes on a curiously anthropomorphic character —that of caprice, or jealousy, or vengeance. As in Homer, each god protects the hero whom he favors, and the human intelligence accommodates itself to this irrationality as to a law of nature. But the accommodation even in Homer is never complete. For human consciousness is torn between a submissive bow to the inevitable, and a defiant affirmation of the dignity of human thought and feeling. The *Oedipus at Colonus* represents one pole of this continuum; the *Prometheus Bound* or the *Medea* represents the other.

The conventions of Attic tragedy have, as we have seen, built into the dramatic structure that interplay between destiny and character which on the one hand constitutes the essence of tragedy, and on the other poses its most perplexing philosophic problem. For it provides the double experience of destiny of the hero and of the chorus. One *lives* it, the other *witnesses* it, and in this dual experience of spectator and participant is provided a clue to the assumed incompatibility of determinism and freedom. Freedom is destiny lived. Determinism is destiny described from the outside. But this candidly dual presentation remains an accident of cultural history—a gift of the miraculous naïveté of a Greek theater still close to its ritual origins.

After the Greeks the antinomy becomes more subtle, more dependent upon the nuances of character and plot, more determinable by mood and feeling. For purposes of emphasis I have distinguished between the Greek and the Elizabethan modes of tragedy, the one emphasizing an encompassing fate, the other the force of free will and character, but the distinction represents tendencies only. After Shakespeare an even greater mixture of modes is inevitable. And in Racine, Goethe, and Schiller this will express itself largely as a character-drama, haunted now and again by vestiges of the destiny-drama which was its traditional source and upon which it from time to time drew for inspiration and refreshment.

Of the three, it is perhaps Racine who has hit upon the most ingenious solution: to find in reason the voice of a limited free will, in passion the representative of a cosmic force, demonic and fateful, and seriously compromising an ethics of total responsibility. Thus a conflict expressed originally at the intersection of inner self-determination and outer cosmic pressure has become internalized (and formalized) as a Platonic (or Freudian) schism within the self. At the beginning of *Andromaque,* Orestes speaks with the self-conscious accents of a modern who has been reading the Greeks:[14]

> *Hélas! qui peut savoir le destin qui m'amène?*
> *L'amour me fait ici chercher une inhumaine;*
> *Mais qui sait ce qu'il doit ordonner de mon sort,*
> *Et si je viens chercher ou la vie ou la mort?*

> Alas! who knows the destiny which draws me on?
> Since love compels me here to seek a cruel fair one;
> Who knows which wind of fate will blow its fickle breath,
> And if I shall find now my life or my death?

But the destiny to which he refers is, nevertheless, real, and he no less than Phèdre possesses "the motive and the cue for passion" which accomplishes the death of Pyrrhus and his own ultimate madness. As for the former, Racine in his original preface of 1677 declares:[15] "In fact, Phèdre is neither wholly guilty nor wholly innocent: she is entangled by her destiny and by the anger of the gods in an illegitimate passion of which she is horrified from the very beginning: she makes every effort to overcome it, she would prefer to die rather than reveal it to anyone; and when she is forced to declare it, she speaks with a confusion which indicates that her crime is more a punishment of the gods than a consequence of her free will." Racine has read his Euripides well. In our passions lies our fate. But the specter of Christian responsibility haunts the classic origins. And the result is a compromise of illogic which only a Cartesian and a Jansenist age could manage. "Neither wholly guilty nor wholly innocent"—how better to express the intersection of Christianity and classicism which states (since it cannot solve) the permanent dilemma of the dramatic imagination.

In Racine the Christian legacy almost overpowers the Greek apparatus which gives it form and body. But a century later the German classical age finds itself closer to Shakespeare. As with him their exploitation of character in its immediacy and power reduces the pressure of situation to its subordinate dimension. And yet here too the presupposition of the classic destiny from time to time creeps through the potent profile of will. In Schiller's *Maria Stuart,* Elizabeth the Queen of England is a tower of triumphant resourcefulness, a woman whose dedication to statecraft exhibits the cold operations of a monumental intellect as it sacrifices some fineness of feminine feeling to the claims of political necessity. Yet self-reliant as she is, she speaks to Leicester, Talbot, and Burleigh like some fugitive from a chorus of Sophocles:[16]

> *Verzeiht, Mylords, es schneidet mir ins Herz,*
> *Wehmut ergreift mich, und die Seele blutet,*
> *Dass Irdisches nicht fester steht, das Schicksal*
> *Der Menschheit, das entsetzliche, so nahe*
> *An meinem eignen Haupt vorueberzieht.*

> Pardon, my Lords, but I am cut to the heart,
> Melancholy seizes me and the spirit bleeds,
> That earthly things are so unstable, that Fate,
> The dreadful ruler of mankind, approaches now
> So near to my own head.

And the noble Egmont, who strides through Goethe's play cheerfully, magnanimously, and above all, wilfully, struck down at last by malevolent men, and awaiting his end in a prison cell, can only meditate upon the poverty of human self-determination:[17] "... *Es glaubt der Mensch, sein Leben zu leiten, sich selbst zu fuehren; und sein Innerstes wird unwiderstehlich nach seinem Schicksale gezogen. Lass uns darueber nicht sinnen. . . ."* (Man thinks that he directs himself, that he is in control of his life; while actually his inmost self is irresistibly forced toward his destiny. Let us not think on't. . . .)

But perhaps the most interesting case of all is that of Schiller's *Wallenstein.* In a letter dated Jena, November 28, 1797, Schiller writes to Goethe as follows:[18] "In these last days I have been reading the plays of Shakespeare which treat of the War of the Roses, and now after finishing Richard III, I am filled with real astonishment. This latter play is one of the most sublime tragedies that I know. . . . [In it] the great destinies spun out are accomplished in a truly marvelous fashion. . . . A lofty nemesis moves through the work. . . . No Shakespearean play has so much reminded me of Greek tragedy. . . ." He concludes: "My Wallenstein gains more form from day to day, and I am pleased with its progress."

The juxtaposition is curious. For if the letter suggests some relation of influence between the two plays, it would be paradoxical indeed. No two postclassic works are more divergent in spirit than *Richard III* and *Wallenstein*. In fact the striking contrast between them is precisely that of the two poles of the antinomy of the dramatic imagination to which we have called attention. *Richard III* is a tragedy of moral retribution in which villainy, self-conscious and self-confessed, in a final nemesis earns its just deserts. *Wallenstein* is the tragedy of a strong man whose freedom of choice always seems but the expression of an exterior fate, whose decisiveness is inseparable from necessity, and whose ambition turns to astrology for its guidance and confirmation.

Richard III deals with the coming of justice. It is written out of a faith that history embodies an *ethos*, that blood cruelly and wantonly spilt cries out for its vindication, and that there is a slow power of righteousness to draw God's hand upon the guilty. The play is full of the power of conscience: existent, though purposefully inefficacious in Gloucester; superstitiously present in the two murderers; avengingly present in Richmond and in the ghosts that haunt Gloucester's tent on the eve of Bosworth Field. It is, of course, easy to see why the play reminded Schiller of Greek tragedy. For the fate of self-confident intellect is terrible and tragic, and when that intellect is clothed in deformity, it turns to its villainy with a peculiar fury. As in the *Oedipus Rex*, throughout the play there are warnings against human certainty, against the obsession of self-confidence, and curses called down at moments of passion come home to roost with true Sophoclean irony. But unlike the *Oedipus Rex*, the protagonist is a moral monster; his end is a *moral nemesis,* and the action, like the landscape of Dante's *Inferno,* symbolizes the consequences of an ethics of total responsibility.

Wallenstein is completely different. Hegel said of it: "The immediate impression after reading *Wallenstein* is a shocked silence over the example of a powerful individual at the mercy of a muted and unfeeling Destiny."[19] We know from Schiller's correspondence that it was his intention to write a fate-tragedy in the tradition of *Oedipus Rex,* and that he felt that he had failed. He believed that in *Wallenstein* fate contributed too little and the hero's own *hamartia* too much, and he consoled himself that the same was true of Shakespeare's *Macbeth*. But Schiller failed far less than he thought. For the mood and effect of *Wallenstein* is, indeed, far closer to Sophocles than to *Macbeth* or *Richard III.*

The pervasive dependence on astrology (it is known that in fact the renowned Kepler actually drew up Wallenstein's horoscope) is more than a dramatic device. It sets the mood of the entire trilogy within a constant ambience of fatalism as sharp as that of the Stoics or the ancient Babylonians. Wallenstein declares:[20]

> *Die himmlischen Gestirne machen nicht*
> *Bloss Tag und Nacht, Fruehling und Sommer—nicht*
> *Dem Saemann bloss bezeichnen sie die Zeiten*
> *Der Aussaat und der Ernte. Auch des Menschen Tun*
> *Ist eine Aussaat von Verhaengnissen,*
> *Gestreuet in der Zukunft dunkles Land,*
> *Den Schicksalsmaechten hoffend uebergeben.*
> *Da tut es not, die Saatzeit zu erkunden,*
> *Die rechte Sternenstunde auszulesen. . . .*

The heavenly constellations make not merely
The day and nights, summer and spring, not merely
Signify to the husbandman the seasons

Of sowing and of harvest. Human action,
That is the seed, too, of contingencies,
Strewed on the dark land of futurity
In hopes to reconcile the powers of fate
Whence it behooves us to seek out the seed-time,
To watch the stars, select their proper hours. . . .

And his daughter Theckla, in a swift sentence which might
have been literally lifted from the *Oresteia,* asserts:

Es geht ein finster Geist durch unser Haus,
Und schleunig will das Schicksal mit uns enden.

There's a dark spirit walking in our house,
And swiftly will the destiny close on us.

In these plays, fatalism, a destiny written in the stars, the
inescapable power of necessity, dominates the action as it does
the mentality of the hero. Wallenstein denies the possibility
of free choice. He holds that every outcome of human behavior is determinable in advance, governed by a universal
necessity which is the supreme law of the cosmos, and it is
this theme that he meditates in the early pages of *Wallensteins Tod* in a soliloquy as noble and as moving as any in
Hamlet.

Wie anders, da des Mutes freier Trieb
Zur kuehnen Tat mich zog, die rauh gebietend
Die Not jetzt, die Erhaltung von mir heischt!
Ernst ist der Anblick der Notwendigkeit.
Nicht ohne Schauder greift des Menschen Hand
In des Geschicks geheimnisvolle Urne.
In meiner Brust war meine Tat noch mein;
Einmal entlassen aus dem sichern Winkel
Des Herzen, ihrem muetterlichen Boden,
Hinausgegeben in des Lebens Fremde,
Gehoert sie jenen tueck' schen Maechten an,
Die keines Menschen Kunst vertraulich macht.

How else! since that the heart's unbiased instinct
Impelled me to the daring deed, which now

Necessity, self-preservation, *orders*.
Stern is the on-look of necessity,
Not without shudder may a human hand
Grasp the mysterious urn of destiny.
My deed was mine, remaining in my bosom;
Once suffered to escape from its safe corner
Within the heart, its nursery and birthplace,
Sent forth into the foreign, it belongs
For ever to those sly malicious powers
Whom never art of man conciliated.

To "grasp the mysterious urn of destiny"—that is the shud-
dering fate of Wallenstein, and the poetic image, deriving, as
we have seen, from the archaic language of the *Iliad*, indicates
how even the classic German drama remains partly under the
spell of an antique world which Christianity has never been
able to completley subdue because it represents a permanent
element of the dramatic imagination—built into the human
mind, and persisting under countless layers of "enlightened"
and "progressive" thought.

5 WHEN HEGEL in his brief remarks *"Ueber
Wallenstein"* spoke of the play as "an ex-
ample of a powerful individual at the mercy of a muted and
unfeeling Destiny," he did not elaborate his own theory of
tragedy: he presupposed it. And when he went on to point out
the double character of Wallenstein's destiny—the making of
a certain resolution followed by the future course of this
resolution and its adverse consequence upon him—his vocabulary unconsciously took on the flavor of the dialectical oppositions to which his mind was attuned: the opposition of
freedom and determinism in Wallenstein's conduct; the
play between character and fate, the destiny "within" and the
destiny "without"; the ironic contrast between Wallenstein's
ambiguous personal ambition and his idealistic dream of a
peaceful and united German nation.

As always, it pays to give the most careful attention to Hegel's remarks, whether concerning *Wallenstein* or the general Hegelian theory of the tragic, to which I now wish to turn, for the latter is one of the authentic insights into tragedy since Aristotle, and if it is, as I believe, one-sided and in this respect mistaken, yet the general framework of development into which Hegel puts the dramatic experience cannot be ignored, and his treatment of this framework in his *Aesthetik* (like that in Aristotle's *Poetics*) provides a crucial clue to the working of the dramatic imagination. Kenneth Burke and Francis Fergusson have had much to say about "the tragic rhythm of action," but its original formulation is not theirs —it is Hegel's.

When Fergusson in *The Idea of a Theater* outlines the "three moments" of this rhythm as "purpose," "passion" (or "pathos"), and "perception," even the framework of his insight is Hegelian, although he has obviously derived it not from Hegel, but from the reconstruction of the ancient Greek Dionysiac ritual as performed by Jane Harrison and Gilbert Murray and containing (1) an Agon or Contest, (2) a Pathos or Disaster, and (3) a Discovery or Recognition or Resurrection or Epiphany.[21] There is surely some value in drawing one's dramatic archetype from the empirical materials of ritual and tradition; but if, as Fergusson does, one then generalizes these materials into a universal paradigm of dramatic perception, the suspicion arises that the original ritual material expresses not a cultural accident, but a propensity of the human mind. This is my conclusion, and I believe it is also Hegel's. For when he puts forward his own "tragic rhythm of action" as that of "conflict," "pathos," and "reconciliation," it not only accounts for the existence of the ritual material, but gives it epistemological grounding—in the natural operations of the mind as it expresses the world, or, as I should say, in the native functioning of the dramatic imagination.

Hegel's theory of tragedy is but the generalization for the field of action of that dialectic which projects its oppositions into the customary workings of the philosophic spirit as into the secret operations of all natural processes. Therefore it must begin with *conflict.* The circumstances best adapted for dramatic action are those in which the purposes of the strong individual meet with obstruction at the hands of other personal agents whose contradictory ends stand in his path and so produce a reciprocal relation of conflict. Therefore says Hegel:[22] "Dramatic action . . . rests essentially upon an action that is involved with *resistance;* and the genuine unity can only find its *rationale* in the entire movement which consists in the assertion of this collision relatively to the definition of the particular circumstances, characters, and ends proposed . . . but in such a way as *to resolve the opposition implied."* Such a resolution obviously has two aspects: that of an adjustment in the opposed moral *ends,* and some ultimate disposition of the *characters* who have committed their total volitional energy to the undertakings they strive to accomplish. But what is important here is the nature of the *dramatic progression* which begins with the outbreak of conflict and makes a continuous onward movement toward final catastrophe, which may itself contain the seeds of reconciliation. The tension of discord in the contradiction of views, ends, and activities works toward some higher synthesis in which each is reconciled. But it was not so originally.

It is a condition of what Hegel calls "the ethical substance" that mere difference in individual personalities must inevitably produce contradiction and collision, and that, once the unmediated contradiction is posited, a countermovement begins to annul the contradiction in a tragic resolution. Tragedy lies in the one-sidedness of an ethical demand: Creon's legitimate assertion of civic power against Antigone's legitimate assertion of familial piety, Orestes' paternal revenge against Clytemnestra's original mother love, Socrates' steadfast critical individualism against the conservative organicity of the Athenian state. And the tragic issue is simply the pathos and the suffering following from the one-sided partic-

ularity of the subject, in the intensity of his passion unable
to disengage himself from the inevitable movement of destruction, frustration, or loss. When therefore the tragic resolution occurs, it is, says Hegel, with this result: that "Eternal
Justice restores the ethical substance by bringing about the
downfall of the individuality which disturbs its repose."[23]

For Hegel tragedy arises out of the collision of two incompatible ethical demands. This results either in the violent
catastrophe where both are destroyed (as in the *Antigone*), or
in a final reconciliation (as in *The Eumenides*). Hegel had a
particular predilection for the *Antigone* (in one place he says:
"Among all the fine creations of the ancient and the modern
world, the *Antigone* of Sophocles is in my judgment the most
excellent and satisfying work of art"), but, of the two types of
conclusion, it is the latter which is obviously required by his
theory. Therefore throughout *The Philosophy of Fine Art*
there is a constant admiring reference to *The Eumenides*, the
Oedipus at Colonus, and (among the modern works) to
Goethe's *Iphigenie.*

There are obviously two senses in which the term "reconciliation" is applicable to the tragic experience. One refers
to what happens *within* the play. In this sense in *Oedipus at
Colonus* Sophocles has made of the aged Oedipus a ritual
figure, weary but acquiescent, and reconciled to the meaning
of his destiny. The other refers to the effect upon the spectators; to their understanding and to their passions. This is
the problem which Aristotle first raised in his treatment of
catharsis. Hegel does not truly distinguish these two meanings
of reconciliation, and the reason, I think, is that he finds a
natural correspondence between them. For the vision of
eternal justice works cathartically, both upon those who experience it (however traumatically) as characters, and upon
those who merely witness its symbolic presence as audience
to the tragic drama. "The true course of dramatic development," says Hegel,[24]

consists in the annulment of *contradictions* viewed as such, in the reconciliation of the forces of human action, which alternately strive to negate each other in their conflict. Only so far is suffering and misfortune not the final issue, but rather the satisfaction of spirit, as for the first time, in virtue of such a conclusion, the necessity of all that particular individuals experience, is able to appear in complete accord with reason, and our emotional attitude is tranquillized on a true ethical basis, rudely shaken by the calamitous result to the heroes, but reconciled in the substantial facts. And it is only in so far as we retain such a view securely that we shall be in a position to understand ancient tragedy. . . .

In ancient tragedy it is the eternal justice which, as the absolute might of destiny, delivers and restores the harmony of substantive being in its ethical character by its opposition to the particular forces which, in their strain to assert an independent subsistence, come into collision, and which, in virtue of the rational ideality implied in its operations, satisfies us even where we see the downfall of particular men.

The additional insight which this gives us into the tragic *catharsis* is, I think, significant and important. Above and beyond the mere fear and tragic sympathy which are celebrated in the *Poetics,* there is the feeling of reconciliation produced by the vision of eternal justice. And therefore tragedy, while in no sense a theodicy (as Hegel remarked about *Wallenstein*), is, nevertheless, an argument for the absolute power of a cosmic justice which satisfies the demands of rationality at the very moment in which it arouses our horror at the contingency of merely individual passions. It is a demonstration, full of suffering and blackness, that reason will not tolerate the continuance of division, and that conflict is inevitably defeated in an objective world where ethical powers are fundamentally and essentially concordant.

In saying that Hegel's theory of "reconciliation" is significant and important, I do not mean to be underwriting his cognate doctrine of a cosmic justice which satisfies the demands of rationality. For here once again Hegel has gone too far. His identification of "the real" with "the rational" has always been suspect, and his moral optimism is no more justified than his logical faith that the structure of thought and the structure of the world are identical. The passion for unity can be taken to extremes, and it is clear that Hegelian rationalism has not faced with candor what I have previously called "the ultimate antinomy of the dramatic imagination"—the opposition of the moralized and the naturalistic conceptions of fate. Hegel does not wish to recognize the validity of the darker version (sometimes haunting the pages of Homer, and faced by the earlier Stoics with resignation and courage) that destiny is both *necessary* and *blind,* and that the unintelligibility and irrationality of the universe is a fact of ultimate evil, permitting the innocence of our suffering as it solicits the fortitude of our virtue. For Hegel, "eternal justice" and "the absolute might of destiny" are one and the same, and just such an easy solution dries up the sources of our moral indignation as it provides us with the rewards of ethical tranquillity.

But the solution will not finally work. Hegel's theory is like a motet of Bach or a suite of Couperin. It recognizes the fact of tragedy and examines it in the light of an intuitive certainty that the universe will ultimately be found to be reasonable. His theory of reconciliation must be taken with the greatest seriousness, but its ultimate virtues do not lie here.

6 THE HEGELIAN pattern of the tragic action—conflict, pathos, reconciliation—is grounded in the natural operation of the mind as he discerned it, and is, therefore, but a translation for the world of art of a "dialectic *ueberhaupt*" which begins with opposition and inevitably concludes with synthesis. And it almost seems as if the moments of this pattern of tragic action could be taken out of their unified context and emphasized according

to a more narrow metaphysical bias. In Hegel himself the chief emphasis seems to be upon the conflict of one-sided but mutually justified powers, as in Schopenhauer it is upon the second stage—the pathos or suffering inseparable from existence and pointing to the necessity for a denial of the will to live. And the difference in metaphysical bias leads to a difference in interpretation of the final stage of reconciliation. Hegel's rationalism never deserts him; his reconciliation therefore is almost Christian and providential—the vision, as he says, of an eternal justice. But for Schopenhauer there is no escape from the ineradicable evil at the heart of things except in the Stoic (or Buddhistic) mobilization of human defense.

There are then at least two different versions of "reconciliation," and of the two the Hegelian is the more optimistic, the more cosmologically naïve; it seems closer to the Olympian world of classic Greece, where beauty exists as a reality uncompromised by the darker forces, and where the illusion of a universe of Appollonian images stands clear, untainted by metaphysical evil. Since Nietzche we have been unable to believe that the Apollonian illusion is the sole reality, and this is why, when Karl Jaspers describes not tragic, but *pretragic* modes of perception, we are forced irresistibly to think of Hegel. Pretragic knowledge arises in a harmonious universe where, as Jaspers says,[25] "There is no horror, rejection, or justification of the ways of this world—no indictment, only lament. Man is not torn in desperation: he suffers and even dies with composure. There are no hopeless entanglements, no dark frustrations; all is basically clear, beautiful, and true."

It is obvious that there *are* other forms of tragic reconciliation where man *is* torn in desperation, where there *are* hopeless entanglements, dark frustrations, a morally ambiguous universe. Even a Schopenhauerean version which emphasizes the fact of suffering can give important quality to tragic knowledge. For it cannot deny that tragic experiences touch the inmost being of man, make him deeply receptive to reality, cleanse him *(catharsis)* of everything in ordinary experience which is trivial and petty, of everything that narrows him and makes him blind. Suffering, as Nicolai Hartmann has said,[26] is the energy-test of a moral being, the load-test of his elasticity.

Within the limit—and indeed the nearer to it, so much the more— suffering means the awakening of his inner-most moral nature, the unlocking of the depths of his being, the liberation of his noblest energies. Whoever has been tested in suffering is tempered steel. . . . The gaze of the unburdened man falls only upon the sparkling surface; the man matured in suffering sees the same situations and conflicts, the same aspirations and struggles, but he sees below the surface; in another way he shares the life of others, his outlook is broadened and sharpened. Suffering has lent to him the capacity to see values which before were hidden from him. Perhaps it is not too much to say that *suffering is the teacher of the consciousness of values.*

Suffering as "the special teacher of the consciousness of values" is a clue to the tragic reconciliation both within and without the tragic drama: as it lies implicit in the final denouement, and as it characterizes the moved and silent spectators. For the relationship between "reconciliation" and "knowledge" is intimate, and "the power of meaning" is an intrinsic property of "the power of healing." The *Oedipus at Colonus* and *The Eumenides* both teach this lesson in their divergent ways: for the individual, and for the society. The Schopenhauerean sentiment which Sophocles has put into the Choral Poem at the end of the *Oedipus at Colonus* is terrible, but it carries with it the hint of peace.[27]

> The last attendant is the same for all,
> Old men and young alike, as in its season
> Man's heritage of underworld appears:
> There being then no epithalamion,
> No music and no dance. Death is the finish.
> Not to be born surpasses thought and speech.

> The second best is to have seen the light
> And then go back quickly whence we came.

For now the blind and ruined man, whose grave even at the end is destined to remain undisclosed (thus retaining forever his mythical, monumental, and mysterious character), may go to his rest. "Eternal sleep," says the Chorus in invocation, "let Oedipus sleep well!" And it concludes:

> Now let the weeping cease;
> Let no one mourn again.
> These things are in the hands of God.

The conclusion of the *Oresteia* provides a more cosmic, a more Hegelian lesson, for it culminates in the reconciliation of Zeus and Destiny, of the matriarchal, archaic, and barbarous Furies with the patriarchal, civilized, and enlightened Apollo, and its agent is Athena, goddess of divine Reason *persuading* the daughters of Necessity (the Furies) to acquiesce in her peaceful purpose. Orestes, hounded to the foot of the Areopagus, is tried for murder, the Furies crying for his blood, but the Greek powers of order, of measure, and of justice have seen too much. One bloody deed has called forth another. From the days when Thyestes seduced his brother's wife and attempted to usurp his throne, to the final matricide of Orestes, the story of the House of Atreus is a fateful chain of murder and outrage. Public justice has been continually sacrificed to private vengeance, and *The Eumenides* is a demonstration that cosmic Reason will tolerate no more. Violence must yield to persuasion, for only so can the conflict of cosmic powers (mother-principle and father-principle, new deities and objects of ancient worship, rationality and the irrational) find reconciliation. The opposition of powers is a permanent disaster, and at the end of *The Eumenides* Aeschylus personifies the Hegelian message in the Chorus' dream of the Athenian future:[28] "This is my prayer: Civil War fattening on men's ruin shall not thunder in our city. Let not the dry dust that drinks the black blood of citizens through pas-

sion for revenge and bloodshed for bloodshed be given our
state to prey upon. Let them render grace for grace. Let love
be their common will; let them hate with single heart. Much
wrong in the world thereby is healed."

But there are other conclusions to the tragic drama than
the guarantees of peace which end the *Oedipus at Colonus*
and *The Eumenides,* and convulsive though these others be,
they do not leave us rebellious, desperate, or dissatisfied with
the portrayal of tragic suffering, but rather acquiescent in the
presence of a catastrophe to which for some strange reason the
mind assents. So it is with *Macbeth* and *Lear,* with *Julius
Caesar* and *Othello.* And it is even more true of those other
Shakespearean tragedies which, equally tragedies of passion,
are yet not so deeply touched by the grosser forms of evil.
A. C. Bradley has called particular attention to "the feeling
of reconciliation" which we experience at the end of *Coriolanus* and at the death of the Queen which concludes *Antony
and Cleopatra.*[29] In these plays it is impossible to detect the
moralized universe upon which Hegel insisted, and this too
implies that the tragic reconciliation is independent of the
moral premises upon which the Hegelian rhythm of tragic
action depends.

The clearest evidence here is the dramatic theory of I. A.
Richards. Like Hegel, Richards finds the experience of
tragedy harmonious and coherent. "Tragedy," he says, "is
perhaps the most general, all-accepting, all-ordering experience known."[30] But whereas the Hegelian "reconciliation"
refers in the first instance to the composition of powers in the
universe (and is, therefore, objective), Richards' universe of
discourse is not metaphysical, but psychological, and the reconciliation is for him subjective—confined in its effect to the
spectators of the tragic drama. "What clearer instance," Richards asks,[31] "of the 'balance or reconciliation of opposite and
discordant qualities' can be found than Tragedy?"

Pity, the impulse to approach, and Terror, the impulse to retreat,
are brought in Tragedy to a reconciliation which they find no-

where else, and with them who knows what other allied groups of equally discordant impulses. Their union in an ordered single response is the *catharsis* by which Tragedy is recognized, whether Aristotle meant anything of this kind or not. This is the explanation of that sense of release, of repose in the midst of stress, of balance and composure, given by Tragedy, for there is no other way in which such impulses, once awakend, can be set at rest without suppression.

It is essential to recognize that in the full tragic experience there is no suppression. The mind does not shy away from anything, it does not protect itself with any illusion, it stands uncomforted, unintimidated, alone and self-reliant. The test of its success is whether it can face what is before it and respond to it without any of the innumerable subterfuges by which it ordinarily dodges the full development of experience. . . .

The moral implications of this doctrine of reconciliation are the very opposite of those of Hegel's. For the comfort and content, the serenity, even perhaps the "joy" which is so strangely at the heart of the tragic experience, is not the implicit reinforcement of the faith in justice, but, on the contrary, a satisfaction with a world whose moral content is ambiguous. And thus Richards concludes: "Tragedy is only possible to a mind which is for the moment agnostic or Manichean."

The psychological theory of Richards is, still, not wholly divorced from objective content. For the courage of the mind which views the tragic spectacle "unintimidated, alone and self-reliant" may draw upon the resources of courage revealed in the tragic protagonist—in the greatness of spirit which shows through his suffering, and in the nobility and grandeur with which he may react to his inevitable fate. No tragic destiny need efface the sense of human dignity. And this is why there is a kind of reconciliation which is quite un-Hegelian, quite apart from the consciousness of a universe ultimately just. For it is possible that tragedy finds its peace and repose not in a dogma of Christian providence or ultimate ethical righteousness, but through the very brilliance of the images

of suffering and evil which the tragic hero projects, respond-
ing to them sublimely, at a level prior to the conceptualiza-
tion of reason. Tragedy can therefore present an argument
for human nobility which is reconciling and peace-bringing
even in the face of dramatic circumstances themselves inaccessible to reason and to moral sense, which imply a universe
neither intellectually explicable nor morally justifiable.

In the diverse qualities of tragic "reconciliation" illustrated respectively by Hegel and I. A. Richards, we see the
inevitable consequence of the antinomy of the dramatic imagination. The two versions of fate and of free will, of natural
occurrence and of moral sense, end with two versions of tragic
reconciliation: a vision of eternal justice, and a vision of
human courage in a universe dreadful in its appearances and
finally unknown.

7 WRITING IN his *Journal* for November 23,
1949, André Gide exclaims:[32] "The sole
art that suits me is that which, rising from unrest, tends toward serenity." *(Seul l'art me'agrée, parti de l'inquiétude, qui
tende a la sérénité.)* Years before, his compatriot Camille Corot
had said much the same thing. "One should," he insisted,
"love the art that procures calm." In their preference for an
art of peace and reconciliation, Corot and Gide are expressing
an attitude which is close to the classic French spirit, but the
bias which they assert is far from being a French monopoly.
The same literary spirit is beautifully illustrated in the work
of Hoelderlin and Goethe. Goethe's avoidance of the wilder
disharmonies of existence is legendary, and even in his experiment with Greek tragedy, his *Iphigenie auf Tauris,* he elects
to write upon a theme of Euripides, but in the steadfast nobility of Iphigenie and the large-hearted maturity of Thoas man-

ages to purge Euripides' play of bitterness and deception. Its last line is Thoas' parting words: "Lebt wohl!"

Hoelderlin is even closer to the classic spirit, expressing in his deeper meditations as in his wayward lyrics an ultimate serenity, which rivals the sentiments of Hegel as it surpasses Hegel's heaviness in its airy imagery. His brilliant *Hyperion* ends with cosmic reassurance: "Like lover's quarrels are all the dissonances of the world. Reconciliation shines through in the midst of strife, and all that is divided comes together again." (*Wie der Zwist der Liebenden, sind die Dissonanzen der Welt. Versoehnung ist mitten im Streit, und alles Getrennte findet sich wieder.*)[33] It is worth a hundred pages of *The Phenomenology of Mind!*

One lyric after another breathes the atmosphere of peace; the earlier "Then and Now":

> *In juengern Tagen war ich des Morgens froh,*
> *Des Abends weint' ich; jezt, da ich aelter bin,*
> *Beginn' ich zweifelnd meinen Tag, doch*
> *Heilig und heiter ist mir sein Ende.*

> (In younger days the mornings brought me joy,
> At eventide I wept; now that I've grown in years,
> Though doubtfully I begin my day,
> Serene and holy for me is its end.)

and even the fragment written during his madness:

> *Die Linien des Lebens sind verschieden,*
> *Wie Wege sind, und wie der Berge Graenzen,*
> *Was hier wir sind, kann dort ein Gott ergaenzen,*
> *Mit Harmonien und ewigem Lohn und Frieden.*

> (The lines of life are separate,
> Like highways, like the mountains' furthest ends
> What here we are, can there a god repair,
> With harmonies, eternal recompense and peace.)

I have appealed to the preferences of Corot and Gide, and to the poetic practice of Hoelderlin and Goethe, not because of their "classicism," but because I believe that the bias which they express is intimately related to the dramatic imagination and is implicit in the tragic rhythm of action to which I have previously referred. Thus the emphasis upon the intrinsic connection between "the problem of tragedy" and "the nature of peace." Also, it should now be clear why I began with a comparison of *Hamlet* and the *Oedipus Rex,* plays the very structure of whose plot permits them to be called "tragedies of purgation." Hegel himself, although not referring to dramatic art as such but to types of world-situation, yet speaks in a fashion which covers them perfectly: "These situations of tragic significance introduce a peculiar difficulty in dealing with them which is inherent in their very conception. For inasmuch as they obviously arise from violations of the world-condition they offer to our consideration circumstances which are unable to continue as they are, which render necessary something of a remedial nature to reclothe them."[34] *Hamlet* and *Oedipus Rex* arise in the atmosphere of "violations of the world-condition," the tension which gives them momentum arises out of "circumstances unable to continue as they are," and their climax produces exactly that "something of a remedial nature to reclothe them." These plays are paradigms of the tragic drama, perfect examples of that art which, as Gide says, "rising from unrest, tends toward serenity."

In the very progression of the tragic rhythm of action—conflict, suffering, reconciliation—lies the connection of peace with the tragic drama, and therefore Aristotle, however mistaken in detail, was right in including *catharsis* as a part of the definition of tragedy. The entire conception of the tragic drama is inseparable from that of the "purgation" or "purification" of the emotions. For this there are two different reasons, which have been suggested in Chapter 4, but I shall recall them here in order to indicate the two qualities of *catharsis* and therefore two aspects of peace implicit in tragedy: that which derives from *the release of tension,* and that which arises through *formalization.*

The very fact remarked by Aristotle—that every drama has a beginning, a middle, and an end; a complication, a turning point, and a denouement—suggests not merely "parts" of an organic whole, but also the "moments" of a serial progression of experience in time. And this fits in very well with our elementary perception of the qualitative rhythm of life; its ebb and flow, stability and instability, concentration and thinning out, maxima and minima of feeling, tension and release. The dramatic art-work imposes a form upon this shifting flux of experience, but always with a particular and inescapable order. For a tragedy to begin with a denouement and end with a complication or begin with a reconciliation and end with a conflict would violate our entire "sense" of the dramatic experience. It would, in Aristotle's terms, be to end with the beginning and to begin with the end. And this makes it eminently clear, I think, that the dramatic experience is inevitably associated with the rhythm of tension and release.

That there is such a rhythm of experience is, perhaps, the crowning insight of the entire Pragmatic movement in philosophy. William James found the whole of the religious impulse to consist in "an uneasiness and its solution" and the whole of philosophy as the transition from "a state of puzzle and perplexity" to one of "ease, peace, and rest." Charles Sanders Peirce defined "Inquiry" as the process or struggle by which we attempt "to pass from the irritation of doubt to a state of calm belief." And John Dewey has generalized all justified search (moral, religious, philosophic, or scientific) into *the Problematic Situation* in which we pass from the troubled, the confused, the ambiguous, and the questionable in experience to the settled, the clear, the unquestionable, the "warranted assertability" of things. The pragmatic language repeats over and over the same basic dichotomy: "problem," "conflict," "difficulty" on one side, "solution," "resolution," "reconciliation" on the other. This suggests not merely how much Pragmatism owes to its Hegelian sources, but also how close in this one respect is the implicit "logic" of the dramatic imagination to the more generalized logic of the mind as it cognitively responds to the pressure of environmental demand.

The second aspect of dramatic *catharsis* is the reconciling and healing effect implicit in formalization. We touch nothing new here, only the nature of the aesthetic experience, the fact that it is contemplative, self-justifying, self-contained, and that the intellectual pleasure it produces is derived from a recognition of form, and a delight in it *independent of content*. Still, as it applies to tragedy, the case appears to be singular. Why does tragedy please? Why does one receive satisfaction from seeing a representation of human misery? This question has been much debated, even called "the paradox of tragedy."[35] And I suppose it is true, as George Steiner has said, both that the representation of personal suffering and heroism which we call tragic drama is distinctive of the Western tradition and that "it has become so much a part of our sense of the possibilities of human conduct . . . that we forget what a strange and complex idea it is to re-enact private anguish on a public stage."[36]

But it is not really so strange and complex after all when we pay attention to the crucial words *representation* of suffering and *reenactment* of private anguish, for in these (as we have seen in Chapter III) lies the whole secret of the dramatic imagination. There is *tragedy in life* and there is tragedy as *a form of drama,* and the two are singularly different. One must distinguish between literature and experience, for the latter is uneven, disorderly, untidy, upsetting, maddening, anguished, while the former, no matter how it imitates the latter, in the very logic and structure of its imitations, produces neatness, order, equilibrium, equivalence, and peace. The Plot of the tragic drama, as Aristotle saw, is quite different from the formless story of the actual biography, and if, in this sense, art is a lie in the realm of fact, it may still remain the supreme truth in the realm of value.

Tragedy is written into the structure of the world, for the very reason that metaphysical evil is inescapable. Things fade, alternatives exclude, potentialities remain unrealized. And the consequence is that there is an unalterable bias toward suffering, inhumanity, and destruction implicit in the nature of things. Karl Jaspers has dealt brilliantly with this phenomenology of the human condition, with the *Grenzsituationen*, the extreme and inescapable situations within whose absolute limits the necessities of human life are set.[37] Guilt, suffering, conflict, and finally death are the ultimate conditions which qualify the appearance of human existence. And just these qualities of existence are the basic data, the givens of the tragic drama.

But the tragic drama is a work of art, shaped by the creative imagination, manifestly both "artificial" and "ideal;" it gives, therefore, not an "immediate" but a "distanced" view of life. Such distancing has usually been accomplished by the trappings of "remoteness"—remoteness of time, place, and rank. Precisely because the prosenium arch must perform its work of absolute separation, the distanciation of stage and audience is essential, and therefore the minimizing of this distance either in the "pathos" of Euripides' psychologized drama, or in a technical device like "theater in the round" or "intimate theater" seriously compromises the tragic experience upon the stage. Actor and spectator exist across a gulf of imagination, and if the genius of a Pirandello can, in a rare case, seem to abridge this convention, it is a miracle and not a possibility implicit in the tragic medium.

The tragic empathy is peculiarly fixed and circumscribed within its rational limits—a magnitude and intensity of feeling artificially concentrated as hardly even in real life, and yet suspended over a void of incipient action—"vivid enough to interest intensely," but "not acute enough to wound."[38] This is why verse is so admirably the vehicle of the tragic formalization. There are poignancies almost too wounding for prose to bear, tragic sufferings too intense to take the risks of mimetic vision or unadorned description. *Therefore* Macbeth pours out his final anguish in iambic pentameters, the horror of Hippolytus' death is cradled in Racine's Alexandrines, and

Othello dies with a rhymed couplet upon his lips. One aspect of the purgation of the emotions inseparable from tragedy as a literary form is the healing worked through the objectivity of aesthetic contemplation. For to present the sufferings of the world *"sub specie aeternitatis"* is to formalize the terrors of existence.

8 "ONE NIGHT," says Ortega,[39] "Bouvard and Pecuchet buried poetry in the Cemetary of Père Lachaise—in honor of verisimilitude and determinism." But from this burial there will always be a resurrection, accomplished by the imagination and in the name of literary transformation and free will.

The burial to which Ortega referred (fifteen years before Joseph Wood Krutch was saying the same thing in *The Modern Temper)* was carried out in an atmosphere which had denigrated the self as it had exalted the environment, denied the will at the moment that it asserted those principles of causality characteristic of a Darwinian and deterministic epoch. For in a certain sense Ortega is right; the tragic character is not tragic (and therefore poetic) in so far as he is the unconscious product of "forces" or "pressures" or "conditions," but only in so far as he wills, and the will—whether operating alone in the solitary but brilliant space which it allots to itself, or (as Goethe said) when it is at that mysterious point where it comes into conflict with the necessary course of events—is the true theme of tragedy.

We have here, in the diminution of the tragic sense, in the eclipse of the concept of "nobility," in the atrophy of the illusions of human amplitude and importance, one of the consequences of that triumph of the understanding as an instrument of knowledge which is revealed equally in the literary theory of Robbe-Grillet and in Kant's *Critique of Pure Reason* —in that phenomenalism where the appearances are the reality, and where the structure of these appearances is revealed by an impersonal science seeking uniformities of causal sequence, mechanical determinism, and mathematical necessity.

The imagination, as I have tried to show, operates differently. For the knowledge which it produces suggests the superiority of value to fact, and the supreme importance of organicity, purposiveness, and drama in the ambience of human life. We may turn to science with confidence that its descriptions illumine the physical world, and we can turn to the imagination which culminates in the tragic drama with an equal confidence that its categories (or forms of experience) —"purpose," "conflict," "suffering," "reconciliation," "reversal," "irony," and "freedom"—are the clue to whatever is peculiarly human in experience, the subsoil not of Nature but of our *Lebenswelt*.

It follows from this that our distinction between "tragedy in life" and "tragedy as a form of drama," valuable though it is in the solution of certain problems in the arts, cannot be taken too far, for the validity of the art form is dependent upon the modalities of human experience. It is far from paradoxical that Hegel should have treated Tragedy in this dual context —as a qualification of the world-condition and as an expressive form mirroring this world-condition in the media of the arts —and that I. A. Richards, his adversary in much else, should yet urge that "the central experience of Tragedy and its chief value is an attitude indispensable for a fully developed life."[40] Opposed as they are, each emphatically presupposes what I have taken as central in this book—that between metaphysics and the philosophy of literature there is an undeniable and necessary relation.

If, as Jaspers suggests, "the poet delivers us from tragedy when he shows us tragedy conquered by the awareness of a larger context of fundamental reality,"[41] this is because the presupposition of poetry is the entanglement of human life with the uncharted expanse of its shadowy background. And it is with a Platonic reading of this "shadowy background" that Whitehead demonstrates the intrinsic relationship between the problem of tragedy and the nature of peace with which this chapter has been centrally concerned.

Peace is the final moment consequent upon the tragic conflict and the tragic suffering. It is, as Whitehead said,[42] "a broadening of feeling due to the emergence of some deep metaphysical insight, unverbalized and yet momentous in its coordination of values," and for Sophocles, Shakespeare, Hegel, and Jaspers alike, this metaphysical insight is most clearly elicited by the tragic issues inseparable from the nature of things. Peace, then, is *the understanding of tragedy*.

Amid the passing of so much beauty, so much heroism, so much daring, Peace is then the intuition of permanence. It keeps vivid the sensitiveness to the tragedy; and it sees the tragedy as a living agent persuading the world to aim at fineness beyond the faded level of surrounding fact. Each tragedy is the disclosure of an ideal: —What might have been, and was not: What can be. The tragedy was not in vain. The survival power in motive force, by reason of appeal to reserves of Beauty, marks the difference between the tragic evil and the gross evil. The inner feeling belonging to this grasp of the service of tragedy is Peace—the purification of the emotions.

Whitehead has caught it exactly; the intuition of an order, the disclosure of an ideal, the vividness of feeling, the sense of meaning amid the loss. That vocabulary of values which I have called "the humanistic complex," founded upon purposiveness and drama, and following the winding road of appearance and reality, illusion, fortune, and destiny, free will and fate, comes at last to the fact of tragedy and its resolution in peace. *Catharsis* is the natural conclusion of humanistic thought. The purification of the emotions is the last gift of the imagination.

Notes

CHAPTER TWO. FROM KANT TO CASSIRER: THE SCIENTIFIC CHAIN OF
MEANING AND THE HUMANISTIC COMPLEX

1. Immanuel Kant, *Critique of Pure Reason,* trans. Norman Kemp Smith
(London: Macmillan, 1953), p. 120.

2. *Ibid.,* p. 7.

3. *Ibid.,* p. 30.

4. *Ibid.,* p. 300.

5. I have in mind here Richard Kroner's *Kant's Weltanschauung* (University of Chicago Press, 1956) and particularly Chap. V, "Primacy of the
Practical."

6. Immanuel Kant, *Critique of Judgment,* trans. J. H. Bernard (London:
Macmillan, 1914), p. 260.

7. *Ibid.,* p. 261.

8. Kant, *Critique of Pure Reason,* p. 549.

9. Hans Vaihinger, *The Philosophy of 'As if'* (New York: Harcourt, Brace,
1925), Preface to the English edition.

10. *Ibid.,* p. xlvii. Reprinted by permission of the publisher.

11. Friederich Nietzsche, *Werke in Drei Baenden* (Munich: Carl Hanser
Verlag, 1954), III, 309-322. I have used the partial translation from Walter
Kaufmann's *The Viking Portable Nietzsche* (1954) and it is reprinted by per-
mission of the publisher.

12. F. A. Lange, *The History of Materialism,* trans. E. C. Thomas, 3d ed.
(New York: Harcourt, Brace, 1925). The quotations are all taken from the
final chapter, Part III, pp. 335-362. Reprinted by permission of Humanities
Press, Inc.

13. Rudolph Carnap, *The Logical Syntax of Language* (London: Routledge
and Kegan Paul, 1949), p. 278.

14. Philip Wheelwright, *The Burning Fountain: A Study in the Language
of Symbolism* (Indiana University Press, 1954), p. 4.

15. *Ibid.,* p. 49.

16. Oswald Spengler, *The Decline of the West,* trans. C. F. Atkinson (New
York: Alfred A. Knopf, 1939), I, 6. All quotations from this work reprinted
by permission of Alfred A. Knopf, Inc.

17. *Ibid.,* I, 118.

18. *Ibid.,* I, 120.

19. George Santayana, *Interpretations of Poetry and Religion* (New York: Harper Torchbook edition, 1957), pp. 2-3. Reprinted by permission of the original publisher, Charles Scribner's sons.

20. *Ibid.*, p. 5.

21. Wallace Stevens, *The Necessary Angel: Essays on Reality and the Imagination* (New York: Alfred A. Knopf, 1951), p. 136. Reprinted by permission of the publisher.

22. Santayana, *Interpretations*, p. 8. Reprinted by permission of Charles Scribner's Sons.

23. Ludwig Wittgenstein, *Philosophical Investigations* (New York: Macmillan, 1953), 32e.

24. Gilbert Ryle, *Dilemmas* (Cambridge University Press, 1954), p. 1. This and the following reprinted by permission of the publisher.

25. *Ibid.*, pp. 31-32. Italics mine.

CHAPTER THREE. THE TELEOLOGICAL IMAGINATION

1. *Hobbes's Leviathan*, reprinted from the edition of 1651 (Oxford: Clarendon Press, 1929), pp. 13-18.

2. David Hume, *A Treatise of Human Nature*, ed. L. A. Selby-Bigge (Oxford: Clarendon Press, 1928), p. 10.

3. *Ibid.*, p. 86.

4. Gilbert Ryle, *The Concept of Mind* (London: Hutchinson, 1958), p. 8.

5. *Ibid.*, p. 265.

6. S. T. Coleridge, *Biographia Literaria* (New York: E. P. Dutton, 1921), pp. 159-160.

7. *Ibid.*, p. 166.

8. Brand Blanshard, *The Nature of Thought* (New York: Macmillan, 1940), II, 129.

9. From T. S. Eliot's famous essay of 1921, "The Metaphysical Poets" in *Selected Essays, 1917-1932* by T. S. Eliot, copyright, 1932, Harcourt, Brace & World, Inc.; renewed, 1960 by T. S. Eliot.

10. I. A. Richards, *Coleridge on Imagination* (New York: W. W. Norton, 1950; Indiana University Press, 1960), p. 33.

11. Ernst Cassirer, *An Essay on Man* (New York: Doubleday Anchor Books, 1953), p. 43. This and the following quotations reprinted by permission of Yale University Press, the original publisher.

12. *Ibid.*, p. 44.

13. *Ibid.*, p. 93. Italics mine.

14. Ernst Cassirer, *The Philosophy of Symbolic Forms*, Volume Two: *Mythical Thought* (Yale University Press, 1955), p. 4.

15. *Ibid.*, pp. 48-49. Reprinted by permission of the publisher.

16. *Ibid.*, p. 60.

17. *Ibid.*, p. 63.

18. From T. S. Eliot, "Burnt Norton," in *The Complete Poems and Plays* (New York: Harcourt, Brace, 1952), p. 117. Copyright, 1952, by Harcourt, Brace and World, Inc. and reprinted by their permission.

19. Cassirer, *Mythical Thought*, p. 64.

20. These matters are treated in Cassirer's *Philosophy of Symbolic Forms*, II, 83-140 and in *An Essay on Man*, pp. 62-79.

21. See for example Victor Bérard, *Les Navigations d'Ulysse*, 4 vols. (Paris: Armand Colin, 1927-29).

22. Cassirer, *Mythical Thought*, p. 239. Reprinted by permission of Yale University Press.

23. *Ibid.*, p. 252.

24. Cassirer, *Essay on Man*, pp. 111-112. Reprinted by permission of Yale University Press.

25. Ernst Cassirer, *The Myth of the State* (New York: Doubleday Anchor Books, 1955), p. 58. Reprinted by permission of Yale University Press.

26. *Ibid.*, p. 60.

27. *Das mythische Denken* was published in 1925, *Les Deux sources de la morale et de la religion* in 1932. Cassirer's *The Myth of the State* (1946), from which the quotations are taken, does not mention Bergson, but *An Essay On Man* (1944) makes explicit reference to *Les Deux sources* and to its theories of religion. In 1933 Cassirer published in *Der Morgen* "Henri Bergson's Ethik und Religions-philosophie."

28. Henri Bergson, *The Two Sources of Morality and Religion* (New York: Henry Holt, 1935), pp. 98-99. Reprinted by permission of Holt, Rinehart and Winston, Inc.

29. *Ibid.*, p. 121.

30. *Ibid.*, p. 130.

31. Wallace Stevens, *The Necessary Angel* (New York: Alfred A. Knopf, 1951). This and the quotation which follows are from "The Noble Rider and the Sound of Words." Reprinted by permission of the publisher.

32. Immanuel Kant, *Critique of Judgment*, trans. J. H. Bernard (London: Macmillan, 1914), p. 260.

33. *Ibid.*, p. 278.

34. *Ibid.*, p. 297-298.

35. The quotations which follow are all from *The Aeneid of Virgil*, a verse translation by Rolfe Humphries (New York: Charles Scribner's Sons, 1953). No translation, of course, does full justice to the original, but Humphries' attention to Virgil's careful composition and his ear for the cadence of the Latin line make this translation memorable. The Virgilian simile here advertises itself with delicacy *and* strength. Reprinted by permission of the publisher.

36. Charner Perry, "The Semantics of Political Science," *The American Political Science Review*, Vol. XLIV, No. 2, June 1950, p. 397.

37. D. G. James, *Scepticism and Poetry: An Essay on the Poetic Imagination* (London: George Allen and Unwin, 1937), p. 42.

38. Stevens, *The Necessary Angel*, pp. 77, 118.

39. James, *Scepticism*, p. 47. Reprinted by permission of the publisher.

40. *Ibid.*, p. 9.

41. Stevens, *The Necessary Angel*, p. 33.

CHAPTER FOUR. THE DRAMATIC IMAGINATION

1. Jane Ellen Harrison, *Prolegomena to the Study of Greek Religion* (Cambridge University Press, 1903), p. vii.

2. John Dewey, *Experience and Nature* (New York: W. W. Norton, 1929), p. 62. All quotations from this work reprinted by permission of the publisher.

3. *Ibid.*, p. 89.

4. *Ibid.*, p. 220.

5. T. S. Eliot, *Four Quartets*, "Burnt Norton" II, in *Collected Poems: 1909-1935* (New York: Harcourt, Brace, 1936).

6. John Dewey, *Art as Experience* (New York: Minton, Balch, 1934), p. 267. Copyright 1934 by John Dewey and reprinted by permission of G. P. Putnam's Sons.

7. Dewey, *Experience and Nature*, p. 291.

8. Gilbert Ryle, *The Concept of Mind* (London: Hutchinson, 1958), p. 256. Reprinted by permission of the publisher.

9. John Dewey, *Human Nature and Conduct* (New York: Modern Library, 1930), p. 190.

10. *Ibid.*, p. 192.

11. Ryle, *Concept of Mind*, p. 264.

12. Chapters by J. L. Austin and G. E. M. Anscombe in the symposium "Pretending," *The Aristotelian Society:* Supplementary Volume XXXII (1958), pp. 261-294.

13. Dewey, *Human Nature and Conduct*, p. 160.

14. *Ibid.*, p. 162.

15. *Hugo von Hofmannsthal*, by H. A. Hammelmann (Yale University Press, 1957), p. 35.

16. Bertolt Brecht, *Schriften zum Theater: Ueber eine nichtaristotelische Dramatik* (Berlin and Frankfurt: Suhrkamp Verlag, 1957), p. 127. The translation is my own and is by permission of Hill and Wang, Inc. A complete translation of the work is expected from this publisher during 1962-1963.

17. Aristotle, *Poetics*, ed. and trans. S. H. Butcher (London: Macmillan, 1907), p. 13. All subsequent quotations from the *Poetics* are in this translation and from this edition.

18. Paul Goodman, *The Structure of Literature* (University of Chicago Press, 1954), p. 153.

19. Aristotle, *Poetics*, Chap. VI.

20. Wilhelm Dilthey, *Gesammelte Schriften* (Stuttgart: Teubner, 1958), VI, 100-115. Also referred to in Richard McKeon, *Thought, Action, Passion* (University of Chicago Press, 1954), pp. 200-208. McKeon's whole essay "Imitation and Poetry" (Chapter IV of his book) is a valuable contribution, and I have learned much from it.

21. Aristotle, *Poetics*, IV.

22. *Ibid.*, XVII.

23. *Ibid.*

24. The concept of nemesis in Shakespeare has been interestingly treated in Richard G. Moulton, *Shakespeare as a Dramatic Artist* (Oxford: Clarendon Press, 1906), Chaps. I, IV-VI. Moulton's book on Shakespeare, practically contemporary with A. C. Bradley's *Shakespearean Tragedy,* has been neglected in favor of the latter. In some ways this has been unfortunate. Bradley's overemphasis upon character needs correction by Moulton's equally careful (if less gracefully expressed) treatment of plot.

25. Frederick J. D. Woodbridge, *The Son of Apollo* (New York: Houghton Mifflin, 1929), p. 55. Reprinted by permission of the publisher.

26. *Ibid.*, p. 49.

27. For a useful account see Richard Robinson, *Plato's Earlier Dialectic* (Oxford: Clarendon Press, 1953), pp. 69 ff.

28. These and similar observations are to be found in Mortimer J. Adler, *Dialectic* (New York: Harcourt, Brace, 1927), pp. 75, 76.

29. From André Gide's lecture "The Evolution of the Theater" delivered in Brussels in March, 1904. Reprinted, in *Pretexts: Reflections on Literature and Morality* by André Gide, ed. Justin O'Brien (New York: Meridian Books, 1959), p. 66.

30. Thaddeus Zielinski, *The Religion of Ancient Greece* (Oxford University Press, 1926), p. 10.

31. Alfred North Whitehead, *Science and the Modern World* (New York: Macmillan, 1925), pp. 10, 11. Reprinted by permission of the publisher.

32. George Santayana, *Three Philosophical Poets* (Harvard University Press, 1910), p. 73. Reprinted by permission of the publisher.

33. *Ibid.*, pp. 79, 80. My italics.

34. George Santayana, *Interpretations of Poetry and Religion* (Harper Torchbooks, 1957), p. 6.

35. Francis Fergusson, *The Idea of a Theater* (Doubleday Anchor Books, 1953), pp. 250-255.

36. Dewey, *Experience and Nature*, p. 96.

CHAPTER FIVE. FORMS OF LITERARY IMAGINATION: POETRY AND THE NOVEL

1. John Dewey, *Art as Experience* (New York: Minton, Balch, 1934), pp. 16, 17.

2. *Collected Papers of Charles Sanders Peirce,* ed. Charles Hartshorne and Paul Weiss (Harvard University Press, 1931), I, 141-181. The brief passages quoted all appear within these pages. Copyright 1931, 1959 by the President and Fellows of Harvard College and reprinted by permission of the publisher.

3. "East Coker," II; "Little Gidding," I.

4. A. N. Whitehead, *Symbolism: Its Meaning and Effect* (New York: Macmillan, 1927), p. 44.

5. The poems quoted in this section are all from *The Collected Poems of Wallace Stevens* (New York: Alfred A. Knopf, 1954) and are reprinted by permission of the publisher.

6. Ernest Fenollosa, *The Chinese Written Character as a Medium for Poetry*, ed. Ezra Pound (New York: John Kasper, Publisher, n.d.).

7. *Artists on Art*, ed. R. Goldwater and M. Treves (New York: Pantheon Books, 1949), p. 421.

8. Wallace Stevens, *The Necessary Angel* (New York: Alfred A. Knopf, 1951), p. 76. Reprinted by permission of the publisher.

9. *Ibid.*

10. *Ibid.*, p. 58.

11. *The Cantos of Ezra Pound* (New York: New Directions, 1951). Copyright 1934, 1937, 1940, 1948 by Ezra Pound. Reprinted by permission of New Directions, Publishers.

12. *Literary Essays of Ezra Pound*, ed. T. S. Eliot (New York: New Directions, 1954), p. 9.

13. *Ibid.*, p. 384.

14. This appears in Eliot's unpublished lecture "English Letter Writers" (1933). Quoted in F. O. Matthiessen, *The Achievement of T. S. Eliot* (New York: Oxford University Press, 1935), p. 90.

15. T. S. Eliot, *Collected Poems: 1909-1935* (New York: Harcourt, Brace, 1936). All quotations from Eliot's verse are from *The Complete Poems and Plays*, copyright, 1952, by Harcourt, Brace and World, Inc. and are reprinted by permission of the publisher.

16. Eliot has described Dante's visual imagination and commented upon its quality in a fashion which is at the same time descriptive of his own: "What we should consider is not so much the meaning of the images, but the reverse process, that which led a man having an idea to express it in images. We have to consider the type of mind which by nature and practice tended to express itself in allegory: and for a competent poet, allegory means *clear visual images*. And clear visual images are given much more intensity by having a meaning— we do not need to know what that meaning is, but in our awareness of the image we must be aware that the meaning is there too. Allegory is only one poetic method, but it is a method which has very great advantages." T. S. Eliot, *Dante* (London: Faber and Faber, 1929), p. 22.

17. Eliot, *Collected Poems: 1909-1935*.

18. T. S. Eliot, *Four Quartets* (New York: Harcourt, Brace, 1943).

19. Jean-Paul Sartre, *Literary Essays* (New York: Philosophical Library, 1957), p. 79 ("Time in the Work of Faulkner"). Reprinted by permission of the publisher.

20. Leo Tolstoy, *Anna Karenina* (New York: Modern Library, 1950), p. 43.

21. Fyodor Dostoyevsky, *The Possessed* (New York: Modern Library, 1936), pp. 563-564.

22. Tolstoy, *Anna Karenina*, p. 93.

23. *Ibid.*, p. 98.

24. Dostoyevsky, *The Possessed*, p. 529.

25. Tolstoy, *Anna Karenina*, p. 110.

26. Erich Auerbach, *Mimesis: The Representation of Reality in Western Literature* (New York: Doubleday Anchor Books, 1957), pp. 1-20.

27. *Ibid.,* p. 4.

28. Sartre, *Literary Essays,* p. 96. Reprinted by permission of the publisher.

29. *Ibid.,* p. 484.

30. James Joyce, *Ulysses* (New York: Modern Library, 1946), p. 766. Reprinted by permission of the publisher, Random House, Inc.

31. Alain Robbe-Grillet, "Three Reflected Visions," in *Evergreen Review,* Vol. I, No. 3, p. 105. Reprinted by permission of The Grove Press, Inc.

32. Alain Robbe-Grillet, "A Fresh Start for Fiction," *ibid.,* p. 100.

33. *Ibid.,* p. 104.

34. Alain Robbe-Grillet, "Old Values and the New Novel," *Evergreen Review,* III, 9 (Summer, 1959), pp. 109-110. Reprinted by permission of The Grove Press, Inc.

35. *Ibid.,* pp. 114-115.

CHAPTER SIX. APPEARANCE AND REALITY, ILLUSION—THE META-PHYSICAL IMAGINATION

1. Alain Robbe-Grillet, *Evergreen Review,* I, 3, p. 103. Reprinted by permission of The Grove Press, Inc.

2. Samuel Beckett, *Proust* (American ed., Grove Press), p. 64.

3. André Gide, *If It Die (Si le Grain ne meurt)* (Penguin Books, 1957), p. 24.

4. The first chapter of Russell's early *The Problems of Philosophy* (Home University Library, 1912) was entitled "Appearance and Reality," and dealt with the relation of sense data to physical existences. But Russell's statement of the "causal theory of perception" does not reach classic formulation until *The Analysis of Matter* of 1927.

5. C. D. Broad, *Scientific Thought* (New York: Humanities Press, 1952), p. 268. Reprinted by permission of the publisher.

6. Plato's *Timaeus,* trans. R. G. Bury, Loeb Edition (New York: G. P. Putnam's Sons, 1929), p. 33.

7. F. M. Cornford, *Plato's Theory of Knowledge: The Theatetus* and the *Sophist* of Plato translated with a running commentary. (New York: Humanities Press, Inc., 1951), p. 230. Reprinted by permission of the publisher.

8. *Timaeus,* p. 49. Reprinted by permission of Harvard University Press.

9. Cornford, *Plato's Theory of Knowledge,* p. 32. In a footnote on the same page Cornford says "*Phantasia* is simply the substantive corresponding to the verb *phainesthai,* as at *Sophist* 264 a. We can substitute Thaetetus' word *aisthanetai* for Protagoras' word *phainetai* without change of meaning."

10. Speaking in another connection (with reference to what Hegel inherited from the Greeks), Mure says: "The term 'real' in this context must be understood as translating either *to alethes* or *to (ontos) on.* It means in Plato and Aristotle—and this, indeed, is in the last resort its only possible meaning—the opposite of the sham. It is that which actually does possess the nature which it claims, or which is claimed on behalf of it." G. R. G. Mure, *An Introduction to Hegel* (Oxford: Clarendon Press, 1940), p. 3.

11. Immanuel Kant *Critique of Pure Reason*, trans. Norman Kemp Smith (London: Macmillan, 1953), p. 257. The passage quoted introduces a chapter on the distinction between "noumena" and "phenomena"–roughly equivalent to Plato's *to on* and *eidolon*. Kant often uses *Erscheinungen* as equivalent to "phenomena," but not, I think (as Plato might), *"Wirklichkeit"* for "noumena." Instead he uses the substantive of his own coinage *Dinge an sich selbst* ("things-in-themselves"). This at once distinguishes noumena as *objects outside the knowledge process* and implicitly refuses to dignify them with the metaphysically commendatory term "reality."

12. *Ibid.*, p. 272.

13. *Ibid.*, p. 614.

14. Schopenhauer's *The World as Will and Idea* contains as its first appendix a long and interesting "Criticism of the Kantian Philosophy." And in the first few paragraphs of this Criticism Schopenhauer states the situation admirably: "What I have in view in this Appendix to my work is really only a defense of the doctrine I have set forth in it, inasmuch as in many points that doctrine does not agree with the Kantian Philosophy, but indeed contradicts it. A discussion of this philosophy is, however, necessary, for it is clear that my train of thought, different as its content is from that of Kant, is yet throughout under its influence, necessarily presupposes it, starts from it. And I confess that, next to the impression of the world of perception, I owe what is best in my own system to the impression made upon me by the works of Kant, by the sacred writings of the Hindus, and by Plato." (Haldane and Kemp Edition, London: Kegan, Paul, Trench, Trubner, 1896, Vol. II, p. 5). Exactly! The similarity of Hindu thought and that of Parmenides has been often pointed out. But the crux is the contradiction in Schopenhauer of the ideas of Kant and Plato. It is as if one could characterize the intrinsic problem of his philosophizing thus: How, starting from Kant, to get to Plato?

15. "Dennoch ist im Grunde das Ziel und das Ideal aller Naturwissenschaft ein voellig durchgefuehrter Materialismus." *The World as Will and Idea*, I, 7.

16. *Ibid.*, II, 28.

17. How disingenuously Schopenhauer engages in this task will appear from the following (*ibid.*, III, 31), where the whole matter of the relation of Kant to Plato is "explained." "In order to bring Kant's mode of expression nearer the Platonic, we might say: Time, space, and causality are that arrangement of our intellect by virtue of which the *one* being of each kind which alone really is, manifests itself to us as a multiplicity of similar beings, constantly appearing and disappearing in endless succession. The apprehension of things by means of and in accordance with this arrangement is *immanent* knowledge; that, on the other hand, which is conscious of the true state of the case, is *transcendental* knowledge. The latter is obtained *in abstracto* through the criticism of pure reason, but in exceptional cases it may also appear intuitively. *This last is an addition of my own.* . . ." (Last italics mine.)

18. *Ibid.*, III, 35.

19. F. H. Bradley, *Appearance and Reality* (Oxford: Clarendon Press, 1951), p. 1.

20. *Ibid.*, p. 3.

21. *Ibid.*, p. 5. Reprinted by permission of the publisher.

21a. Schopenhauer, *The World as Will and Idea*, I, p. 3.

22. C. M. Bowra, *The Romantic Imagination* (Harvard University Press, 1949), p. 271.

23. Lionel Trilling, *The Liberal Imagination* (New York: Doubleday Anchor Books, 1953), pp. 202-203. Reprinted by permission of The Viking Press, Inc., Publishers.

24. *The Portable Cervantes*, trans. Samuel Putnam (New York: Viking Press, 1958), pp. 100-101. Reprinted by permission of the publisher.

25. Miguel de Unamuno, *The Tragic Sense of Life* (New York: Dover Publications, 1954), p. 325.

26. *The Portable Cervantes*, pp. 695 ff.

27. *Naked Masks: Five Plays by Luigi Pirandello*, ed. Eric Bentley (New York: E. P. Dutton, 1957) pp. 366-367. This and the following quotations reprinted by permission of the publisher.

28. *Ibid.*, pp. 70-71.

29. *Ibid.*, pp. 97-98.

30. These matters are treated in the brief section "Transcendental Illusion." Kant, *Critique of Pure Reason*, pp. 297 ff.

31. This is an entry in Mill's Diary for January 11, 1854. The Diary itself was kept only between January 8 and April 15 of this year, at a time when Mill was separated from his wife by illness and facing the prospect of an early death. *The Letters of John Stuart Mill*, ed. Hugh S. R. Elliot (London: Longmans, Green, 1910), II, 358.

32. Wallace Stevens, *Transport to Summer* (New York: Alfred A. Knopf, 1947), p. 31.

33. *The Collected Poems of W. B. Yeats* (London: Macmillan, 1955), p. 333.

34. *The New Science of Giambattista Vico*, trans. T. G. Bergin and M. H. Fisch (Cornell University Press, 1948), pp. 67-68. Reprinted by permission of the publisher.

35. *Ibid.*, p. 64.

36. Otto Rank, *Will Therapy* and *Truth and Reality* (New York: Alfred A. Knopf, 1950), p. 250. Reprinted by permission of the publisher.

37. Friedrich Nietzsche, *Die Geburt der Tragoedie*, Dritte Auflage (Leipzig: C. G. Naumann, 1894), p. 9. " . . . denn alles Leben ruht auf Schein, Kunst, Tauuschung, Optik, Nothwendigkeit des Perspectivischen und des Irrthums."

38. George Santayana, *Dialogues in Limbo* (New York: Charles Scribner's Sons, 1925), pp. 74-75. Reprinted by permission of the publisher.

CHAPTER SEVEN. DESTINY, FORTUNE, AND FATE

1. Oswald Spengler, *The Decline of the West* (New York: Alfred A. Knopf, 1939), I, 117.

2. *Ibid.*, I, 118.

3. Immanuel Kant, *Critique of Pure Reason*, trans. Norman Kemp Smith (London: Macmillan, 1953), p. 248.

4. The scientific controversy—philosophically inspired to be sure—over causality has provided an enormous bibliography. That side of the imagination/understanding distinction is not here really our concern, but two classic sources may be mentioned. The chief questions are raised by Bertrand Russell in his early paper "On the Notion of Cause" in *Mysticism and Logic* (New York: W. W. Norton, 1929) and they are interestingly answered by R. B. Braithwaite in his *Scientific Explanation: A Study of the Function of Theory, Probability and Law in Science* (New York: Cambridge University Press, 1953), especially Chaps. IX, X, XI. The most recent treatise in this field is Ernest Nagel, *The Structure of Science: Problems in the Logic of Scientific Explanation* (New York: Harcourt, Brace, 1961).

5. Useful in this matter of first approximation or general definition is Vincenzo Cioffari, *Fortune and Fate: From Democritus to St. Thomas Aquinas* (New York: privately printed, 1935), Chaps. I, II.

6. *Plutarch's Moralia*, Loeb Edition, trans. Frank Cole Babbitt (Harvard University Press, 1957), IV, 323-377, 383-487.

7. *Plutarch's Lives*, Loeb Edition, trans. Bernadotte Perrin (New York: G. P. Putnam's Sons, 1918), VI, 261-355.

8. *Ibid.*, p. 267. Reprinted by permission of Harvard University Press.

9. Jacob Burckhardt, *Force and Freedom*, ed. J. H. Nichols (New York: Pantheon Books, 1943), Chap. VI.

10. Nicolo Machiavelli, *The Prince*, trans. W. K. Marriott (Everyman Edition, 1925), pp. 203, 204. This and the following quotations reprinted by permission of E. P. Dutton and Co., Inc., Publishers.

11. *Ibid.*, p. 207.

12. Aeschylus, *Oresteia*, trans. with an Introduction by Richmond Lattimore (University of Chicago Press, 1953). The three immediately following quotations are from pp. 37, 171, 89. Copyright 1953 by The University of Chicago. Reprinted by permission of the publisher.

13. *Ibid.* The following quotations are from pp. 104, 116, 125, 131. Reprinted by permission of the publisher.

14. *Hesiod's Theogony*, trans. with an Introduction by Norman O. Brown (New York: Liberal Arts Press, 1953), pp. 59, 78. ("The Library of Liberal Arts" No. 36) Reprinted by permission of the publisher, The Bobbs-Merrill Company, Inc.

15. *The Iliad of Homer*, trans. with an Introduction by Richmond Lattimore (University of Chicago Press, 1952). The three longer quotations which follow are from pp. 184, 440, 489. Copyright 1951 by the University of Chicago and reprinted by permission of the publisher.

16. *Alexander of Aphrodesias "On Destiny" (Peri Eimarmenes)*, text and translation by Augustine Fitzgerald (London: Scholartis Press, 1931), p. 13. The phrase "the drama of destiny" appears on p. 130, the reference to Destiny as a goddess on p. 99.

17. *Plutarch's Moralia*, Vol. VII, with an English translation by Phillip H. De Lacy and Benedict Einarson. Loeb Classical Library (Harvard University Press, 1959), p. 313. The quotation following is from p. 317.

18. Henri Bergson, *Les Deux sources de la morale et de la religion* (Paris: Libraire Félix Alcan, 1939), p. 155ff. ". . . vous ne voyez plus que du mécanisme, le hasard sèvanoait. Pour qu'il intervienne, il faut que, l'effet ayant une signification humaine, cette signification rejaillisse sur la cause et la colore, pour ainsi dire, d'humanité. Le hasard est donc le mécanisme se comportant comme s'il avait une intention."

19. G. W. F. Hegel, *The Phenomenology of Mind,* trans. J. B. Baillie (London: George Allen and Unwin, 1949), pp. 686-687.

20. Cicero, *De Fato (Traité du Destin),* Budé Edition, Texte établi et traduit par Albert Yon (Paris: Edition "Les Belles Lettres," 1944), p. 4.

21. The literature on this subject is extensive. For the historical treatment I have found the following useful: Dom David Armand, *Fatalisme et liberté dans l'antiquité grecque* (Louvain: Bibliothèque de l'Université, 1945); William Chase Greene, *Moira: Fate, Good and Evil in Greek Thought* (Harvard University Press, 1944); L. Guilermit and J. Vuillemin, *Le Sens du destin* (Neuchâtel: Editions de la Baconnière, 1948); Elisabeth Klemann, *Die Entwicklung des Schicksalsbegriffs in der deutschen Klassik und Romantik* (Wurzburg, 1936); Vincenzo Cioffari, *Fortune and Fate: From Democritus to St. Thomas Aquinas* (New York, 1935).

22. Cicero, *De Fato,* p. 20: "Ac mihi quidam videtur cum duae sententiae fuissent veterum philosophorum una eorum qui censerent omnia ita fato fieri, ut id fatum vim necessitatis adferret, in quia sententia Democritus, Heracleitus, Empedocles, Aristotelis fuit, altera eorum quibus viderentur sine ullo fato esse animorum motus voluntarii. . . ."

23. Seneca, *Moral Essays I* (Loeb Edition), with an English translation by John W. Basore (Harvard University Press, 1958), p. 39. Reprinted by permission of the publisher.

24. Boethius, *The Consolation of Philosophy* (Loeb Edition), English translation revised by H. F. Stewart (New York: G. P. Putnam's Sons, 1926), p. 341. Reprinted by permission of Harvard University Press.

25. Hegel, *The Phenomenology of Mind,* p. 501.

26. Leo Tolstoy, *War and Peace* (New York: Modern Library), pp. 565, 566.

27. Jean-Paul Sartre, *Situations I* (Paris: Gallimard, 1947), p. 56.

28. Jean Cocteau, *La Machine infernale* (Paris: Bernard Grasset, 1934), p. 15.

29. A. N. Whitehead, *Science and the Modern World* (New York: Macmillan, 1925), p. 14.

30. Francis Fergusson, *The Idea of a Theater* (Doubleday Anchor Books, 1953), pp. 54 ff., 80 ff.

31. Erich Auerbach, *Mimesis* (Doubleday Anchor Books, 1957), Chap. 15, "The Faux Devot," and Chap. 17, "Miller the Musician."

32. Aldous Huxley, *Point Counter Point* (New York: Grosset and Dunlap, 1928), p. 180.

33. John O'Hara, *Appointment in Samarra* (New York: Duell, Sloan and Pearce, 1934), p. 294.

34. Graham Greene, *The Heart of the Matter* (London: William Heinemann, 1948), p. 199.

CHAPTER EIGHT. THE PROBLEM OF TRAGEDY AND THE NATURE OF PEACE

1. William Shakespeare, *The Tragedy of Hamlet Prince of Denmark*, ed. Willard Farnham (Penguin Books, 1957).

2. *The Complete Greek Tragedies*, ed. David Grene and Richmond Lattimore. *Sophocles I*, "Oedipus The King," trans. David Grene (University of Chicago Press, 1959), pp. 12-15. Copyright 1942 by The University of Chicago and reprinted by permission of the publisher.

3. The long controversy which has raged over Hamlet's "hesitation"—his failure to kill Claudius at prayer (III, iii)—has been, despite its intrinsic interest, largely beside the point. Pursuing the psychological method of A. C. Bradley, it has related the question to the matter of Hamlet's character. But obviously, the issue concerns not character, but plot. If complexity is required (and Shakespeare's triple interest in "sons and their revenge"—i.e. in the cases of Hamlet, Laertes, and Fortinbras—shows that it is), then the retardation accomplished by the fourth act is essential. Only in comparison to the simple "swiftness" of *Oedipus Rex* could one say (foolishly) that *Hamlet* should have ended with a climactic third act.

4. *The Collected Writings of Thomas DeQuincy*, by David Masson (London: A. and C. Black, 1897), X, 393.

5. George Santayana, *Interpretations of Poetry and Religion* (New York: Harper Torchbooks, 1957), pp. 154-155. This quotation comes from Essay VI, "The Absence of Religion in Shakespeare." The position represented here may be more familiar to contemporary readers in the version of H. D. F. Kitto in his *Form and Meaning in Drama* (New York: Barnes and Noble, 1960), Chap. 8, "Religious Drama and Its Interpretation." He refers here specifically to an article of F. H. C. Brock, "Oedipus, Macbeth, and the Christian Tradition" (*Contemporary Review*, No. 177, pp. 177 ff.), which is of great interest in this connection. But the original germ of the idea is Santayana's.

It may seem strange to speak of *Hamlet* as a "secular" drama, but that it is, I have no doubt. If Christianity is there as a cultural presupposition, it is as stage setting, not as profound feeling. Hamlet's meditation on suicide (III, i) with its doubts of the after life, is un-Christian. Ophelia's "Christian burial" (V, i) becomes matter for farce. Hamlet's "There's a divinity that shapes our ends/Rough-hew them how we will" (V, ii) is as pagan as religious in intent, and even Claudius' praying (III, iii) is by explicit statement ultimately insincere. His speech "My words fly up, my thoughts remain below" holds both for himself and for Shakespeare. *Hamlet* is a work of Renaissance humanism, not Christian supernaturalism!

6. Karl Jaspers, *Tragedy Is Not Enough* (Boston: Beacon Press, 1952), p. 29.

7. Santayana, *Interpretations*, p. 163.

8. Oswald Spengler, *The Decline of the West* (New York: Alfred A. Knopf, 1939), pp. 142-146.

9. A. C. Bradley, *Shakespearean Tragedy* (New York: Meridian Books, 1955), pp. 79, 97.

10. A. N. Whitehead, *Science and the Modern World* (New York: Macmillan, 1925), p. 106. Reprinted by permission of the publisher.

11. The Greek text reads *philanthropon*. Butcher translates it "moral sense," Bywater "human feeling." The latter is closer to the Greek, but the former is not unjustified.

12. *Goethes Werke* (Insel-Verlag, 1952), VI, 313: " . . . seine Stuecke drehen sich alle um den geheimen Punkt (den noch kein Philosoph gesehen und bestimmt hat) in dem das Eigentuemliche unsres Ichs, die praetendierte Freiheit unsres Willens, mit dem notwendigen Gang des Ganzen zusammenstoesst."

13. Jean-Paul Sartre, *Situations I* (Paris: Gallimard, 1947), p. 37.

14. *Theatre Complet de Racine* par Maurice Rat (Paris: Editions Garnier Frères), p. 119.

15. *Ibid.*, p. 540.

16. Friedrich Schiller, *Dramen* (Munich: Wilhelm Goldmann Verlag, 1958), p. 47.

17. J. W. von Goethe, *Gedichte und Dramen* (Insel-Verlag, 1953), II, 369.

18. Friedrich Schiller, *Briefwechsel zwichen Schiller und Goethe* (Stuttgart, 1881), I, 332.

19. "Der unmittelbare Eindruck nach Lesung Wallensteins ist trauriges Verstummen ueber den Fall eines maechtigen Menschen, unter einem schweigenden und tauben Schicksal. . . ." G. F. W. Hegel, *Werke* 2 Aufl. (Berlin, 1835-1843), XVII, 411.

20. In the three following quotations the German is taken from Friedrich Schiller, *Wallenstein* (Munich: Wilhelm Goldmann Verlag, 1957); the English is from Coleridge's translation, to be found in *The Works of Schiller*, Vol. IV (New York: International Publishing Co., 1902). The German is from pp. 68, 92, 124 of the Goldmann edition: the English from pp. 54, 99, 161 of the International edition.

21. Francis Fergusson, *The Idea of a Theater* (New York: Doubleday Anchor Books, 1953), pp. 45 and 52. The stages of the Dionysiac ritual are outlined by Gilbert Murray in his *Euripides and His Age* (New York: Home University Library, 1913), p. 63.

22. G. W. F. Hegel, *The Philosophy of Fine Art*, trans. with notes by F. P. B. Osmaston in four volumes (London: G. Bell and Sons, 1920), IV, 259. Reprinted by permission of the publisher.

23. *Ibid.*, IV, 298.

24. *Ibid.*, IV, 321, 340. Reprinted by permission of the publisher.

25. Jaspers, *Tragedy Is Not Enough*, p. 33.

26. Nicolai Hartmann, *Ethics*, trans. Stanton Coit (New York: Macmillan, 1932), II, 140-141.

27. *The Complete Greek Tragedies: Sophocles I*, p. 134. Copyright 1942 by the University of Chicago and reprinted by permission of the publisher.

28. Aeschylus, *Oresteia*, trans. with an introduction by Richmond Lattimore (University of Chicago Press, 1953), p. 169. Copyright 1953 by the University of Chicago and reprinted by permission of the publisher.

29. Bradley, *Shakespearean Tragedy*, p. 74.

30. I. A. Richards, *Principles of Literary Criticism* (New York: Harcourt, Brace, 1928), p. 247. Reprinted by permission of the publisher.

31. *Ibid.*, p. 245, 246.

32. André Gide, *Journal 1939-1949* (Paris: Bibliothèque de la Pléiade, 1954), p. 62.

33. Friedrich Hoelderlin, *Gesammelte Werke* (Bertelsmann Verlag, 1954), p. 470.

34. Hegel, *The Philosophy of Fine Art*, I, 273.

35. The most interesting treatment of this question that I know is Chu Kwang-tsien, *The Psychology of Tragedy* (Strasbourg: Libraire Universitaire d'Alsace, 1935). The most recent is D. D. Raphael, *The Paradox of Tragedy* (Indiana University Press, 1960). Chu Kwang-tsien's treatment is the more comprehensive and original, and, in fact, D. D. Raphael draws heavily upon it.

36. George Steiner, *The Death of Tragedy* (New York: Alfred A. Knopf, 1961), p. 3.

37. Karl Jaspers, *Philosophie* (Berlin: Springer Verlag, 1956), II, 201-254.

38. Chu, *Psychology of Tragedy*, p. 249.

39. José Ortega y Gasset, *Meditations on Quixote* (New York: W. W. Norton, 1961), p. 165.

40. Richards, *Principles of Literary Criticism*, p. 282.

41. Jaspers, *Tragedy Is Not Enough*, p. 80.

42. A. N. Whitehead, *Adventures of Ideas* (New York: Macmillan, 1933), p. 367. The longer quotation which follows is from p. 369; and is reprinted by permission of the publisher.

Analytical Table of Contents

6. The distinction between destiny and causality, analogy and mathematical law in Spengler.

7. The summation of this line of argument comes in Santayana. He distinguishes the domains of science and the imagination but takes as central the contributions which the latter makes to human life.

8. An attempt at a semantic solution of the problem following a suggestion of Gilbert Ryle. The understanding and the imagination distinguished by the vocabularies which they respectively produce. Thus there is a "scientific chain of meaning" and a "humanistic complex." The former depends on the ideas of "objectivity" and "factuality," the latter on "purposiveness" and "drama."

CHAPTER THREE. THE TELEOLOGICAL IMAGINATION

1. The empiricist account of imagination: Hobbes, Hume, Gilbert Ryle. It is thin because directed to the prevention of epistemological error. It lacks a positive theory of imagination.

2. But the idealist account errs too. It overemphasizes "Unification" in that it applies this concept also to the understanding. But with Coleridge it stresses the literary image, and so leads toward metaphor, myth, and legend, and thus toward Cassirer.

3. Cassirer does not propose a unified theory of imagination as such, but his philosophy of symbolic forms tries to show the common bond of language, art, myth, and religion. But the crux is his theory of myth.

4. Cassirer's theory of myth. Purposiveness. Emotion. Sacredness. The strategy of mystical unification. Imaginative space and time. How these mythical categories work in Homer and Dante.

5. The difficulty of distinguishing myth and religion. Their common strategy to show the solidarity of life and to deny the fact of death. How this reinforces Bergson's ideas. Religion as the original myth-making faculty, whose purpose is to defend against the dangers of intelligence.

6. Myth is imagination and imagination is a pressure from within. Its intrinsic and extrinsic purposiveness. This intrinsic purposiveness upon which Kant insisted implies a special treatment of experience in terms of connectedness, subjectivity, organic unity.

7. These principles, drawn from Kant's *Critique of Judgment*, illustrated in literature by the purposive functioning of the simile in Virgil's *Aeneid*.

8. Is dramatic imagination grounded in the general character of experience? The preconceptual basis of drama in the qualitative rhythms of life. Appeal to Bergson's duration, Dewey's experience, Heidegger, Merleau-Ponty. In incipience, terminations, enclosures lies the histrionic component of experience.

CHAPTER FIVE. FORMS OF LITERARY IMAGINATION: POETRY AND THE NOVEL

1. The poetic imagination is grounded in metaphysics and epistemology. The categories of Charles Sanders Peirce as analysis of perceptual experience: Firstness, Secondness, Thirdness—qualitative immediacy, dynamic opposition, and symbolic reference. All art as presentation of qualities, delineation of movements, and expression of meanings. The example of contemporary poetry: Wallace Stevens, Ezra Pound, T. S. Eliot.

2. Wallace Stevens and presentational immediacy. His poetry devoted to appearances and the vivid enjoyment of sense data. The man whose center is painting. The exploitation of the imagery of color. The poem of landscape. The importance of light. The poetic morality of the "right sensation."

3. Ezra Pound and dynamic opposition. The key to Pound is his moral intent. Integrity: its positive and negative demonstration. How the technique reinforces the content. The use of the verb. The opposition of juxtaposed fragments. The method of ironic contrast.

4. T. S. Eliot and symbolic reference. The religious metaphor of conversion. The use of tradition as symbolism. The symbolic imagery of natural quality, colors, adjectives. The mystical method of the reconciliation and identification of opposites. Monism as a kind of imagination.

5. The three poets compared. Stevens' logic of analogy. Pound's logic of disjunction. Eliot's logic of identity. Stevens and immediately presented quality. Pound and the tensions and polarities of experience. Eliot and the transcendental symbolism of the Christian mystery. Peirce's categories as phenomenology of poetic experience.

6. The novelistic imagination is dominated by point of view. Objectivity and subjectivity. Novelistic metaphysics and inference from technique. The oysters of Stepan Arkadyevitch. Pyotr Stepanovitch's beefsteak. Tolstoy and things. Dostoyevsky and interior states. Tolstoy as Aristotelian. Dostoyevsky and the subjectivist principle.

8. Summary: The metaphysical imagination and the scientific enterprise. The philosophic confirmations of the preference for illusion in Nietzsche and Santayana. Nietzsche's treatment of the tragic myth and his critique of the scientific spirit. Santáyana as the theorist of "fancy" and as "lover of illusion."

CHAPTER SEVEN.   DESTINY, FORTUNE, AND FATE

1. Spengler's distinction between Destiny Idea and Causality Principle. Its implication for imagination and for scientific understanding. Kant on fortune and fate. Their role in imaginative thought.

2. The concept of fortune, distinguished from chance. Fortune versus the idea of causation in history. The dialectic of fortune. Plutarch, Burckhardt, and Machiavelli.

3. The concept of fate: its occurrence in Aeschylus' *Oresteia*. Fate as intermediate between myth and law. The earlier mythical versions of Hesiod and Homer.

4. Fate as cosmic plan, moral finality, coordination of the whole. Treatment by Stoics and Platonists. Destiny and chance. Destiny as teleological. The concept of destiny applied to biography and history. Fate as necessity and as organic unity. Hegel on fate.

5. The historical moments in the history of the concept of destiny. Stoic fate: Cicero. The doctrine of Providence: Seneca and Boethius. Romantic destiny: Hoelderlin, Hegel, Tolstoy.

6. Destiny as a literary idea. Its relation to the tragic drama. Cocteau and the idea of necessity. Fate and the modern novel. The plural perspectives of modern literature and the plural conceptions of fate.

7. Aldous Huxley's *Point Counter Point* as psychological destiny. John O'Hara's *Appointment in Samarra* as sociological destiny. Graham Greene's *The Heart of the Matter* as moral and religious destiny.

8. Comparison of the three novels. Their ideational sources in Freud, Marx, and St. Augustine. The experience of destiny as guilt, shame, sin. The pluralism of modern destiny and its indication of the relation of destiny and imagination.

CHAPTER EIGHT. THE PROBLEM OF TRAGEDY AND THE NATURE OF PEACE

Index

Abelard, Peter, 128, 144
absurdity, 178, 180, 183, 209, 212, 289
acting, 101
action, 8, 107, 109, 141
Aeschylus, 10, 95, 239, 242, 257, 259, 260, 273; *Agamemnon,* 239, 240, 283, 286; *Eumenides,* 118, 239, 240, 300, 304, 305; *Libation Bearers,* 239, 240; *Oresteia,* 239, 244, 245, 250, 287, 288, 296, 305; *Prometheus Bound,* 291
Alexander of Aphrodesias, 242, 246, 251
allegory, 59, 91, 131, 158, 164, 222
analogy, 35, 38, 91, 93, 162
analysis, 33, 45, 184
Anouilh, Jean, 258, 259
Anscombe, G. E. M., 104
Anselm, St., 128
antinomy, 10, 83, 285, 286, 291; of the dramatic imagination, 10, 285, 286, 289, 290, 294, 302, 308; of pure reason, 14, 17
appearance and reality, 8, 9, 21, 23, 33, 34, 39, 46, 49, 82, 182, 185, 188–90, 195–200, 205, 206, 211, 213, 217, 224, 273, 316
Aquinas, St. Thomas, 129
Aristophanes, 107
Aristotle, 5, 15, 27, 95, 105, 107, 110, 111, 112, 113, 115, 116, 125, 129, 137, 174, 205, 230, 233, 274, 282, 285, 310, 311, 312; *De Anima,* 18; *De Generatione et Corruptione,* 70; *Metaphysics,* 190; *Physics,* 69, 133; *Poetics,* 95, 107, 109, 110, 124, 126, 285, 298; *Politics,* 237
art, 27, 29, 32, 38, 39, 62, 75, 79, 99, 104, 105, 108, 140, 205, 226

Auerbach, Erich, 109, 167, 176, 177, 179, 209, 258, 260
Augustine, St., 84, 176, 177, 178, 271, 281
Austin, John, 100, 104
Avicenna, 6
Ayer, A. J., 28, 44

Bach, J. S., 302
Bacon, Sir Francis, 79, 80, 81, 188
Balzac, Honoré de, 167, 174
Baudelaire, Charles, 264
Beatrice, Dante's, 159
Beauvoir, Simone de, 225
Beckett, Samuel, 186
Beethoven, Ludwig van, 36, 38, 157, 158, 264
Bérard, Victor, 69, 71, 150
Bergson, Henri, 6, 7, 16, 20, 32, 33, 34, 36, 38, 39, 40, 60, 75, 76, 77, 80, 105, 137, 140, 183, 191, 247, 248; on duration, 34, 35, 138; on vital impetus, 77
Berkeley, George, 143, 170, 174, 197
Bernanos, Georges, 94
Blake, William, 85
Blanshard, Brand, 57
Boccaccio, Giovanni, 2
Boethius, 10, 251, 252
Bosanquet, Bernard, 57, 188
Bowra, C. M., 207
Bradley, A. C., 282, 306
Bradley, F. H., 9, 57, 78, 205, 206
Brecht, Bertolt, 1, 107, 176, 217
Broad, C. D., 189 193, 195
Bronowski, J., 4, 5
Brunetière, F., 95
Burckhardt, Jacob, 9, 235, 236, 237, 239
Burke, Kenneth, 109, 298